2155

FINANCIAL AND COST ACCOUNTING
FOR MANAGEMENT

FINANCIAL AND COST ACCOUNTING FOR MANAGEMENT

THE FUNDAMENTALS OF MODERN ACCOUNTING TECHNIQUES

BY

A. H. TAYLOR
M.C., F.A.C.C.A.

AND

H. SHEARING
A.A.C.C.A.
PRINCIPAL LECTURER IN ACCOUNTING AND MANAGEMENT
EALING TECHNICAL COLLEGE

Fifth Edition

MACDONALD AND EVANS LTD.
8 JOHN STREET, LONDON, W.C.1
1969

First published 1956
Second edition 1958
Reprinted 1960
Third edition 1962
Reprinted 1963
Fourth edition 1965
Reprinted October 1966
Fifth edition February 1969
Reprinted September 1970

©

MACDONALD AND EVANS LTD.
1962, 1969

S.B.N. 7121 0613 8

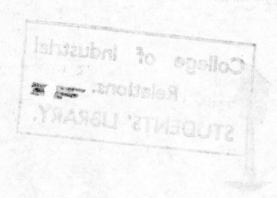

Printed in Great Britain by Richard Clay (The Chaucer Press), Ltd.,
Bungay, Suffolk

PREFACE TO THE FIRST EDITION

A KNOWLEDGE of modern methods of accounting and financial control has become an essential part of the equipment of an efficient manager, and this book has been written with the specific needs of management in mind.

In addition to catering for the business executive the work covers the examination syllabuses of the British Institute of Management and other bodies concerned with management studies. It explains the use of accounting techniques as an essential aid in forward planning and the day-to-day control of business.

It is hoped that students will find it useful to have the subjects of financial accounting, costing and budgetary control dealt with in one volume. Lecturers in management accounting will also find the book suitable as a basis on which their lectures can be planned.

The authors gratefully acknowledge the assistance given by Mr. Herbert Taylor in the preparation of the manuscript and by Mr. J. E. Bostock in the preparation of the diagrams.

A. H. TAYLOR
H. SHEARING

July 1956

PREFACE TO THE FIFTH EDITION

THE passing of the Companies Act, 1967, introduced a number of amendments to the law regarding companies generally. Its provisions and schedules are of importance to the student, and they have to be read in conjunction with the 1948 Act. The principal changes which are relevant to the subject of the book are described in a new Appendix IV. This deals with exempt private companies; directors' emoluments and employees' salaries; The Directors' Report; Directors' interests; notification of changes in voting shares; and disclosure of turnover.

We have also followed the recommendations of the various accountancy bodies and of the examining bodies responsible for National Further Education syllabuses and examinations, and have given decimal currency equivalents where appropriate. These are set out in the form advised by the Decimal Currency Board, as described in *Decimal Currency: Expression of Amounts in printing, writing and in speech,* H.M.S.O., 1968.

A. H. TAYLOR

H. SHEARING

November 1968

CONTENTS

CHAPTER I

ACCOUNTING AND MANAGEMENT

1. The development of management

The evolution and growth of commercial and industrial under-takings has been matched with continual improvements in the techniques of management. It is important that management sciences shall keep pace with the increasing speed of technological development; out-of-date management practices will hinder the true development of industrial undertakings. That all this has been widely appreciated is evident in the growth of management education. Many large companies have their own staff colleges; universities and colleges of further education are finding an increasingly important place for management faculties. Perhaps the most interesting development is the fact that industry and the government are co-operating in the establishment of national business schools. The efforts of the British Institute of Management and the Department of Education and Science are producing a workable framework within which management education can grow.

Increasing specialisation within the organisation structure of the individual business has become essential. Each division is controlled and manned by personnel who by training and experience are experts in their own techniques; and constant developments in each branch of an organisation tend to compel every individual to concentrate more and more on his speciality. But an organisation cannot flourish if it is a collection of individuals immersed in their own jobs; they must work as a team, and it is one of the functions of general management to ensure that this happens.

2. The role of accounting

This book is concerned with one facet of the diverse picture of administration, that of accounting, but it is a facet whose scintillations can illumine all the others. Industrial and commercial activities involve capital, men and machines, and bring into their compass transportation, finance, banking, insurance and all the other features of our complex economic life. Business must exist within the social framework and keep within bounds delineated by legal requirements; if it is to be justified it must exist for the benefit of the community. Within the individual business, management must control production, marketing, research and development, personnel and other departments. A common factor must be used to put all these activities into focus; that common factor is money.

Money may not be the constant measure of value which it was once thought to be, but in the end it is the measure which must be used. The final reconciliation of all the elements of the business is reflected in the accounts, in terms of money, and if the value of money has changed the fact must be recognised and taken into account. For better or for worse the final test of efficient management is profitability. If the business makes a profit and successfully co-ordinates its elements, management is successful; if it does not management will be suspect. One of the tasks of the accounting department is to reduce the multitude of transactions to this vital figure—profit or loss.

3. Managers and accounting

It should not be inferred that managers need only concern themselves with monetary matters, indeed this is far from the truth, but questions of costs and profits will always intrude in the activities of executives far removed from the accounting function. The principle involved is financial control; the modern techniques of accounting, particularly budgetary control, constitute the "long arm of management" which will be described in later chapters.

Since, in his day-to-day activities, the manager must become involved in costs and profits, and since these are the primary concern of the accounting function, it follows that the manager should know something about accounting. One has only to examine the requirements of professional organisations concerned with particular divisions of management to see that accounting has its place among the subjects which the aspiring manager must study. The sales manager, the purchasing officer, the production engineer, the secretary, are all expected to know something about this subject.

How much accounting should a manager know? This is the great problem: the accountant is the expert, and his function to explain and interpret the information which his department makes available is discussed in a later chapter. There is no magic formula which sets out the art of interpretation of accounts. If the manager wishes to appreciate and use the facts disclosed in financial statements he should also appreciate their limitations. If he wishes to use the accounting division to provide him with information, some knowledge of the mechanics of accounting will assist him in assessing the possibilities of such information being produced.

4. The accounting service

The service which the accounting function provides for the assistance of management consists basically in presenting information bearing on the efficiency of past operations and current activities, as well as projections of probable future results. In this context the word "efficiency" has a close relationship with the word "profitability". In an accounting system designed to aid all grades of managers the figures will not only be shown as overall totals for the business but they will also be analysed as far as practicable to demonstrate the contribution of each manager to the final result. The integration of data relating to the efforts of the various managers will help general management to achieve one of its fundamental tasks, that of co-ordination. If the figures are submitted in a form which suggests the corrective action required to overcome inefficiency management will have grounds for the exercise of another of its basic functions, that of control.

The modern use of the accounting service as a management tool demands that figures relating to past operations shall be presented and used primarily as guides to the future. The emphasis has changed from purely "historical" accounting to the submission of purposeful up-to-date information as a means of controlling current operations, and projections of the probable future as a guide to planning. In all these aspects of the art of accounting the figures should be illustrated by apt comparisons and trends. The best form of comparison involves the use of carefully assessed standards of the results which ought to be achieved in the circumstances of the business concerned.

Another area of fundamental importance to the manager in his task of controlling the present and shaping the future is the extent to which available capacity has been and will be used efficiently. In this connection a developing aspect of accounting is the measurement of the capacity of a workshop or even of an administrative function. Not only will an alert accountant, with the necessary technical advice, provide information as to available capacity but he should also demonstrate in figures the profit which is being lost by a failure to employ capacity to the full. Indications as to the probable effect of using available resources in alternative ways also represent a part of the modern business accountant's duties, and he should be capable of analysing the financial implications of future development. Once again it is necessary to emphasise that a manager should have at least a broad knowledge of accounting techniques if he is to make full use of the information provided.

There are certain common elements in the activities of all managers whatever their status, and one of those elements is planning for the future. What has been achieved in the past is history; to-day's activities will soon also be history. The manager must concern himself with what will happen in the future. If an enterprise is to be successful there must be reliable advance planning. It must be planning which will be able to assimilate changes in conditions which may occur and which are at present unforeseen. It is in this field that modern accounting techniques produce their greatest service to industry in general and to managers in particular, and it is on the basis of sound financial accounting that this service is achieved.

5. The plan to be followed

Succeeding chapters describe the principles of accounting and the means by which financial accounts and statements are produced. The methods outlined do not always follow traditional book-keeping methods but seek to organise the accounting procedures to produce the kind of information which will be of most use to management. Then follow chapters which depict the annual accounts as the link between the management and the owners or shareholders. The final sections of the book deal with accounting as the day-to-day control of costs, and the laying-down of reliable lines to guide the organisation in its future progress.

CHAPTER II

THE PRINCIPLES OF ACCOUNTING

A. Definition and Objects

Accounting may be defined as the art and science of recording
business transactions in a methodical manner so as to show: (*a*) the
true state of the affairs of a business at a particular point of time,
and (*b*) the surplus or deficiency which has accrued during a
specified period.

Developments in the application of accounting techniques to
assist all grades of management have, however, expanded this
original view of the accounting function. One of the most important tasks of modern accounting is to assist management in achieving efficiency by the presentation of suitable financial information.
Such information will be designed primarily to assist management in
making its future plans and controlling the execution of those plans.

It is therefore essential that every manager, whatever may be
his function or status, should understand clearly the principles of
accounting and have a good working knowledge of its mechanics.
A manager must appreciate the extent and limitations of the
information which he may demand of the accountant, and he
should have a broad knowledge of the cost of producing it. Whilst
a good accountant will always help in the interpretation of figures,
the final assessment must rest with management. In the end the
value of accounting information depends on the action which it
calls forth from the managers of a business.

B. The First Principle

The Distinction between Capital and Revenue

1. General considerations

The income receivable and the expenditure incurred by a business must be allocated either: (*a*) to capital account, or (*b*) to revenue account. Capital may be defined as the wealth which is used
to produce income, and it must for this purpose be maintained
intact. The items which make up the capital of a business should
be recorded in accounts clearly identified as such, so as to show
whether capital has been lost or increased.

5

The remaining accounts record revenue items, comprising income and expenditure; they show in figures the day-to-day transactions of the business, and the difference between income and expenditure represents either profits or losses. Profits can be added to capital or withdrawn from the business, and losses represent deductions from capital.

In a complex business the distinction between the two kinds of transactions is in some cases rather fine and may involve differences of opinion. In such cases it is essential that the treatment be consistent from year to year so as to show a true picture of the *trend* of income, expenditure, profit or loss. There are certain principles which must be followed, and these principles are discussed in the following sections.

2. Capital

(a) *The meaning of "capital"*

The capital of a business consists of the assets (what is owned by the business) less the liabilities (what is owed by the business). The value of an asset will appear on the left-hand side of a double-sided account and the value of a liability on the right-hand side of an account. So as to complete the double entry (the theory of which is discussed in the succeeding section) the capital is treated as a liability of the business to the proprietor or proprietors and is therefore also shown on the right-hand side of an account.

If a man sets up in business as, for example, a boot and shoe repairer he requires a certain initial sum of money or money's worth to provide plant, tools, furniture, stocks of leather and ready cash. This initial sum represents his original capital, and he does not consider he has made a profit until he can withdraw cash from the business for his personal use and still show that the original total of capital remains intact. That is to say, there is no profit until income exceeds expenditure.

Income, in this example, consists of the charges made to customers for the work done; expenditure means the wages, cost of material and other expenses incurred in doing work. "Other expenses" include overheads such as rent, light, fuel, power, stationery and repairs to equipment and also include the loss of value which occurs in the machinery and furniture due to wear and tear and old age.

Original capital may be, and frequently is, increased either by: (*a*) the introduction of fresh funds on a permanent basis, or (*b*) the allocation of profits to a fund which it is not intended to distribute but which is retained in the business for the purpose of earning additional income and maintaining profits.

Thus, if the boot and shoe repairer, A, starts his business with an initial sum of £1,000 in cash, of which £250 has been borrowed temporarily from a friend, B, the original capital of A and of his business is:

Cash subscribed	£1,000
Less Owed to B	250
A's capital	£750

It should be noted that the loan in the above example is deducted from total funds in order to leave a sum representing the proprietor's capital which, as there is only one proprietor, also represents the capital of the business. B's loan is regarded as a debt due from A, but if B's loan was meant to remain with the business for many years it could be reckoned as part of the capital employed in the business.

Suppose that B's loan had been repaid and, with a view to increasing his income, A retained in the business £100 out of the first year's profits and then took into partnership C, who did not bring in cash but a motor van of an agreed value of £500, the capital position would be as follows:

A original capital	£750
Add Retained out of profit . . .	100
A total capital	850
C capital brought in	500
CAPITAL OF THE FIRM	£1,350

Thus the capital employed in a business is the capital owned by the proprietors, plus loans invested in the business on a permanent basis.

(*b*) Other uses of the term "*capital*"

(i) The expression "capital" is used in commercial spheres to mean money or money's worth invested in a business whether by the proprietors or by outside persons, in other words—the capital *employed* in a business. Thus investments in industrial undertakings in the form of loans and debentures or provided by banks and finance corporations are regarded as capital, although no rights of ownership of the assets of the undertaking may be conferred.

The authorised or nominal capital and the issued capital of a limited company must be distinguished from its real capital. The amount of capital which can be raised by a company is authorised and limited by its articles and memorandum of association, but not all such authorised capital is necessarily issued. A company's authorised capital may be, say, 1,000,000 shares of £1 each, but in fact only half of these may be issued, in which case its issued capital is £500,000 in shares of £1.

Again, the capital issued may be only partly called. If, in the above example, only 10*s*. a share had been called up by the directors the capital called up will be £250,000, and this amount may, in turn, be further reduced by any amounts which have not been paid by the shareholders under such calls. On 1,000 shares the call of 10*s*. may remain unpaid. The relationship of these terms referring to capital is illustrated in the following diagram:

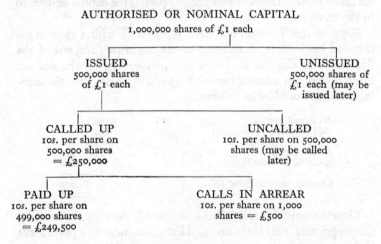

AUTHORISED OR NOMINAL CAPITAL
1,000,000 shares of £1 each

ISSUED	UNISSUED
500,000 shares of £1 each	500,000 shares of £1 each (may be issued later)

CALLED UP	UNCALLED
10*s*. per share on 500,000 shares = £250,000	10*s*. per share on 500,000 shares (may be called later)

PAID UP	CALLS IN ARREAR
10*s*. per share on 499,000 shares = £249,500	10*s*. per share on 1,000 shares = £500

Owing to the fact that it is the practice of most undertakings to retain part of the profits to meet contingencies or for development, the true value of shareholders' interests in a company is rarely indicated by the authorised or issued shares. The balance of value will be represented by reserve accounts.

The expression "capital employed" is often used to indicate owners', *e.g.* shareholders' interests only. A wider interpretation suggests, however, that the total capital employed in an undertaking is not always wholly owned by shareholders. Where part of the permanent funds of a company have been obtained by loans, such as debentures, the total capital in use consists of the sum of the issued and paid-up shares plus the debentures and the various reserve funds. It should be borne in mind, in this connection, that accounts recording shares, debentures, reserves and the balance of the profit and loss account merely show the classes of funds to which the real capital of the concern, *i.e.* the sum of assets less liabilities, has been allocated. The following illustration of a simplified Balance Sheet illustrates this point:

BALANCE SHEET

	£		£
Share capital . . .	150,000	Fixed assets . . .	200,000
Reserves	25,000		
Proprietor's capital =	175,000		
Debentures . . .	50,000	Current assets . .	50,000
Capital employed =	225,000		
Current liabilities . .	25,000		
	£250,000		£250,000

The capital employed might be expressed as the "net assets" or total assets *less* current liabilities, as follows:

	£
Total assets	250,000
Less Current liabilities . . .	25,000
Net assets or capital employed .	£225,000

Note. A Balance Sheet is a statement compiled from the accounts and is not in itself part of the double-entry accounting system. It is, therefore, quite immaterial which side is used for assets and which for liabilities, although assets are usually shown on the right in the U.K.

Capital in the sense of the difference between assets and liabilities is often termed "net worth". The figure of net worth or capital which can be calculated from the values shown in a Balance Sheet is not necessarily the same as the realisable value of the net assets if they were sold in the open market. Nor, in the case of a public company, is the capital as recorded in the accounts the same as the total to be arrived at by multiplying the number of shares and debentures by the respective prices at which they are quoted on a stock exchange. Briefly, the reason for these differences is that the accounts are supposed to record the value of an undertaking as a going concern, not as an accumulation of assets to be realised and liabilities to be discharged. The Stock Exchange prices are influenced by, among others, the following factors: (*a*) supply and demand for the securities; (*b*) changing money values; (*c*) the expectation or hope of a certain rate of return on money invested; and (*d*) prospects of capital profits. Stock Exchange prices of shares and debentures are not controlled by the company concerned, but merely represent the market price at which the securities change hands.

(c) The fixed and current elements of capital

(i) *Fixed and current assets.* Some part of the capital originally obtained or subsequently brought into a business is applied to the purchase of "fixed assets" which are intended to be held more or less permanently for the purpose of earning income. Land, buildings, plant and machinery and permanent investments in subsidiaries, or other companies, are of this nature, provided they are not held for the purpose of resale. Part of the capital is invested in items of a less durable nature, such as stocks of goods for sale and material for manufacture, temporary investments and a balance of cash for meeting day-to-day expenditure, and such items are termed "current assets". In the course of operating, the cash held for day-to-day expenditure, the stocks and the temporary investments will be partially converted into debtors as sales of goods or work take place. Thus debtors form an important section of current assets, as do bills of exchange, which may be obtained from debtors in respect of their obligations.

It should be noted that after the initial capital has been obtained for an enterprise the financing of day-to-day requirements should be met as far as possible out of its own resources and not out of further permanent capital. The development of a business may justify the directors obtaining further permanent capital for investment in fixed assets. Thus, fixed assets are often referred to as "capital assets".

(ii) *Fixed and current liabilities.* The net worth or net capital of a business is calculated by deducting liabilities (what is owed) from assets (what is owned). The accounts recording liabilities are, therefore, "capital accounts" for accounting purposes, and in a double-sided account they are shown on the right-hand side. As with assets, liabilities may be grouped as follows: (*a*) fixed liabilities—those which are likely to remain for a considerable time; and (*b*) current liabilities—those which are variable or likely to be soon discharged.

Fixed liabilities include long-term loans obtained by a business, such as debentures in a limited company. Current liabilities include trade creditors, bank or other short-term loans, taxation dues, dividends recommended for payment and bills of exchange payable.

(iii) *The necessity for distinguishing between fixed and current capital.* It is an essential precept of good accounting that (*a*) the fixed and (*b*) the current or variable elements of capital, whether assets or liabilities, should be clearly distinguished both in the accounting system and in any statements which are compiled from that system. This principle applies in particular to the Balance Sheet.

Whilst the maintenance of total capital is the guiding factor in the determination of profit or loss, fixed assets represent the source from which income is obtained, and they must be maintained in a condition to yield the desired income.

From the point of view of an investor in a business the ultimate security of the capital he has invested is represented by the value of the fixed assets less the fixed liabilities. If the investor's money is in the form of loan capital, such as debentures, his ultimate security consists of the gross total of the fixed assets subject only to such charges as may by law rank before his own. In many cases loan capital is secured on specific assets by way of mortgage.

Whilst attention is directed to fixed capital from the point of view of its intrinsic value and its capacity to yield income, the comparison of current assets and current liabilities will demonstrate the working capital of a business.

Lack of adequate working capital for day-to-day needs may bring an immediate halt to business activity. Working capital is generally calculated as the excess of current assets over current liabilities, and apart from its value as a guide to management, this figure is one of the first considerations by persons contemplating investment in a concern, granting substantial credit or lending it money.

The excess of current assets over current liabilities is not, however, by any means the sole criterion of the availability of funds for current needs. A large proportion of so-called working capital may be tied up in stocks, which may not be easily realisable and which may be subject to fluctuations in market prices. Furthermore, with a manufacturing business the value of work in progress, represented by partly finished goods or work performed, is often problematical.

In such cases an additional calculation is required for the purpose of arriving at liquid capital, that is the amount of cash which can be raised if necessary at short notice. Liquid capital normally consists of cash in hand, cash at bank on current account, good bills of exchange receivable, good debtors' balances and temporary investments valued certainly not higher than current market value. From these liquid assets there must be deducted money which may be demanded at short notice, such as short-term loans (*i.e.* bank loans), creditors' balances and bills of exchange payable. A flexible accounting system should be able to show the amount of liquid capital, although it may entail some adjustments to the totals normally shown in the accounts.

3. Revenue

Revenue may be defined as the surplus of income over expenditure after capital has been maintained. The second main division of an accounting system records revenue, that is it contains the accounts of income and expenditure. For accounting purposes a rather strict meaning is given to the terms "income" and "expenditure". Current income includes moneys due from customers for goods supplied or services rendered. Expenditure is the cost of doing the work, and includes not only payments due for labour, material and other current expenses of the business but also provision for maintaining capital intact.

The expressions "income" and "expenditure" must be distinguished from "receipts" and "payments". The latter refer to cash received and cash paid during a specified period, and include items which may refer to another accounting period, or receipts and payments on capital account.

The principle of separating accounting items into their fixed and variable elements is applicable to both income and expenditure.

Fixed income usually covers interest and dividends from investments, fees from royalties and licences, whilst variable income includes sales and other income directly resulting from the operations for which the business has its being.

So that management can measure efficiency and control costs it is essential for the accounts and for accounting statements to record the fixed and variable expenditure under separate headings. Frequently a third division, known as semi-variable costs, is found expedient.

Examples of the items falling within these groups are as follows:

Fixed Costs: staff salaries: administration expenses: rent and establishment charges; interest and other financial charges; and depreciation.

Semi-Variable Costs: indirect hourly labour, which varies more or less with output but not in direct proportion to it, for example, wages of maintenance men; indirect materials such as nuts and bolts, grease and oil; and other expenses of a semi-variable nature such as factory electricity.

Variable Costs: direct productive labour; direct materials; and direct expenses, the costs of which all vary closely with turnover or output.

The control of costs, and therefore, the correct accounting for costs, is a matter of major importance in any scheme of accounts which is to be used to assist management, and this aspect of the general subject will receive extended consideration later in the book.

4. Conclusion

The foregoing observations endeavour to set out the distinction between capital and revenue for accounting purposes in a simple form, and to give some indication of the further basic analyses which issue from these two major divisions of an accounting system. It is essential that these, perhaps, elementary matters should be clearly understood, for they lie at the root of all efficient accounting and, indeed, of efficient management. For such reasons the distinction between capital and revenue for accounting purposes has been used as an introduction to the subsequent studies.

C. THE NATURE OF PROFIT

It was stated at the beginning of this chapter that one of the basic objects of accounting was to show "the surplus or deficiency which has accrued during a specified period". This is, of course, another way of referring to "profit", but the latter term can take on a variety of meanings depending on the context in which it is used. It is, therefore, desirable to consider the nature of the "profit" which appears at the end of the Profit and Loss Account and is often the result of a protracted analysis of the business transactions, and the application of a number of accounting rules and conventions. These rules and conventions rest in part on law and in part on the accumulated experience of businessmen and accountants over the centuries. The reader will become acquainted with the more important conventions as he studies successive chapters of this book. One of the major conventions, which has been stated in the preceding section as a principle, is that transactions on revenue account must be distinguished from transactions on capital account.

The transactions on revenue account, which must include provision for maintaining the capital intact, will indicate how the profit has arisen, *i.e.* by deducting expenditure from income. In its most elemental form profit is the amount by which capital has increased over a period, and loss would be the loss of capital over the period. Thus the final profit made by a business in, say, a year could be calculated from the Balance Sheets at the beginning and end of the year, because from those Balance Sheets can be calculated the capital (or "worth") of the business at the beginning and at the end of the period. Profit is therefore basically an increase in worth.

It should be noted at this point that an accounting system does not, unless exceptional measures are taken, show the assets of the business in terms of the current purchasing power of the money in which they are expressed. This applies in particular to the fixed assets, which are normally stated at cost (*i.e.* the money paid for them) less provision for depreciation calculated on the basis of cost. The following discussion of the nature of profit in the accounting sense must be read with this qualification in mind. Many businesses have revalued their fixed assets to conform more closely to current values, but the resulting "book profit" is separated from the profit from trading by being placed in a Capital Reserve Account.

Consider the following Balance Sheets of Retailers Ltd. at the beginning and at the end of last year.

RETAILERS LIMITED

Balance Sheet as at the beginning of the year

Capital	£	Fixed Assets	£
Issued shares	100,000	Furniture, fixtures and fittings, less depreciation	60,000
Revenue reserves	50,000	Vehicles, at cost less depreciation	40,000
Current Liabilities			£100,000
Trade and other creditors	40,000		

Current Assets	£	
Stocks	45,000	
Debtors	35,000	
Cash in hand and at bank	10,000	90,000

	£190,000		£190,000

This balance sheet indicates that the capital employed in the business at the beginning of the year was:

	£
Fixed assets	100,000
Current assets	90,000
Total assets	190,000
Less: Current liabilities	40,000
Capital employed	£150,000

Or the same total derived from the accounts which record how the funds were obtained:

	£
Obtained by subscription from the shareholders	100,000
Obtained from profits retained in the business	50,000
Capital Employed	£150,000

Now consider the Balance Sheet of the Company after a year has elapsed:

RETAILERS LIMITED

Balance Sheet as at the end of the year

	£			£
Capital		*Fixed Assets*		
Issued shares	100,000	Furniture, etc., at cost less depre-		
Revenue reserves	60,000	ciation		54,000
Current liabilities		Vehicles, at cost less depreciation .		36,000
Trade and other				
creditors .	45,000			90,000
		Current Assets	£	
		Stocks . . .	55,000	
		Debtors . .	45,000	
		Cash . . .	15,000	
				115,000
	£205,000			£205,000

The capital employed at the end of the year thus becomes:

	£
Fixed assets	90,000
Current assets	115,000
Total assets	£205,000
Less Current liabilities	45,000
Capital employed	£160,000

The apparent profit made by the company during the year is, therefore:

	£
Capital employed at the end of the year .	160,000
Less Capital employed at the beginning of the	
year	150,000
Apparent profit	£10,000

If, however, the owners (the shareholders) had withdrawn any funds from the business during the year the amount so withdrawn would have to be added to the £10,000 apparent profit in order to arrive at the true profit. Let it be assumed that during the year the shareholders had been paid a dividend of, say, £5,000 in cash. The net profit would then have been:

	£
Apparent profit, as above	10,000
Add Funds withdrawn	5,000
Net profit for the year . . .	£15,000

Conversely, if further capital had been introduced into the business during the year (which has clearly not in fact occurred in this example) the amount of that additional capital would need deducting from the figure of apparent profit calculated as shown above.

Profit is therefore basically a question of putting a value on the assets and liabilities of a business, but it should be borne in mind that the value of the assets in accordance with accounting rules and conventions is not necessarily the same as the current saleable value of those assets. The business is looked upon as a going concern, and certainly the fixed assets are not held for resale but to earn income. In view of the prudent convention that profit must not be anticipated, stocks will be valued at the lower of cost or net realisable value. Investments outside the business will normally be shown at cost, but may be written down to market value if it is considered that a permanent fall in that value has occurred.

D. The Principle of Double Entry

1. The meaning of double entry

All methodical accounting is based on the principle of double entry, of which the first recorded use was amongst the Genoese in the fifteenth century. This simple theory is based on the assumption that there are two aspects to every transaction: one the surrender of a benefit and the other the gain of a corresponding benefit.

When the boot and shoe repairer, referred to earlier, buys leather from a supplier he will at some stage surrender cash and receive a stock of leather in return. When he repairs a shoe he will surrender the use of his time, that of his employees, his tools and his premises, and in return he will gain cash or a debt representing the price of his work.

Thus every transaction must be recorded twice in an accounting system, in the one case recording the gain of an asset and in the other the loss or liability.

Such a method of accounting enables a full record to be kept of every asset and liability and every gain or loss of assets or liabilities. It has the additional advantage of providing an automatic check on the arithmetical accuracy of the accounting, for the total assets must be made to agree with the total liabilities (including owner's capital). Capital will be treated as a liability of the business to the owner or owners for the purpose of this automatic check.

2. The mechanics of double entry

(a) *Entering capital transactions*

People unversed in the mechanics of accounting often find difficulty in understanding on which side of an account a particular entry should appear. Income is occasionally confused with liabilities and expenditure with assets. Some business-men cannot interpret the figures shown in their books without the aid of an accountant or a skilled book-keeper. It must be admitted that some of the difficulty is due to the confused state of certain systems of accounts, where, for example, capital accounts are not clearly segregated from those recording revenue transactions. The two kinds of transactions, though closely connected, must be considered separately if the double-entry system is to be understood. This was one of the reasons for preceding a description of the mechanics of double-entry accounting with observations on the distinction between capital and revenue.

Dealing first with accounts recording capital it is necessary to keep in mind that: (*a*) assets (what is owned by the business) appear on the left-hand side of a double-sided account, and (*b*) liabilities (what is owed by the business) appear on the right-hand side.

Thus, in the case of the boot and shoe repairer's initial capital the first accounts would appear in his books as follows:

CASH ACCOUNT
(an asset—something owned by the business)

Owner's capital	.	.	£750
B. loan account	.	.	250

B. LOAN ACCOUNT
(a liability—what is owed to B.)

	Cash account	.	.	£250

OWNER'S CAPITAL
(a liability of the business—what is owed to the owner)

	Cash account . . . £750

It will be observed that the sum of the totals on the right-hand side of the accounts agrees with the sum of the totals on the left-hand side, and the accounts are in balance, as they always must be if the entries have been made correctly.

(b) *Entering revenue transactions*

It has been stated that revenue transactions comprise: (*a*) income, and (*b*) expenditure. Income is shown on the right-hand side of a double-sided account and expenditure on the left-hand side. Thus, if the boot repairer had during the first year made sales of work to the value of £500, had incurred expenses of £100 and depreciation of tools was charged at £150, his revenue accounts would appears as follows:

SALES ACCOUNT
(income)

	Cash account . . . £500

BUSINESS EXPENSES ACCOUNT
(expenditure)

Cash account . . . £100	

DEPRECIATION OF TOOLS
(expenditure)

Tools account . . . £150	

So far as these accounts are concerned, however, the totals on the right-hand side do not agree with the totals on the left-hand side. This is because capital and revenue accounts have to be considered together; transactions on revenue account merely record gains or losses of capital.

The sales of £500 recorded in the revenue account would be accompanied by the receipt of assets such as cash or debtor's balances recorded in the Capital Accounts. The payment of expenses entered in the revenue accounts involves the loss of an asset or the creation of a liability; in this case either the loss of cash or the incurring of a liability in the form of creditors' balances. The writing off of depreciation involves the loss of part of the value of an asset; in this case a reduction in the value of tools.

(c) *The complete accounts*

With the above considerations in mind the complete set of accounts as they might exist at the end of a year may now be shown. It will be noted that part of the original cash balance has been spent in the acquisition of tools.

Capital accounts:

OWNER'S CAPITAL ACCOUNT

	Cash account . . . £750

B. LOAN ACCOUNT

	Cash account . . . £250

CASH ACCOUNT

	£		£
Owner's capital account. .	750	Business expenses account .	100
B. loan account . . .	250	Tools account . . .	300
Sales account . . .	500	Balance carried down . .	1,100
	£1,500		£1,500
Balance brought down .	.£1,100		

TOOLS ACCOUNT

	£		£
Cash	300	Depreciation account . .	150
		Balance carried down . .	150
	£300		£300
Balance brought down . .	£150		

Revenue accounts:

SALES ACCOUNT

	Cash account . . . £500

BUSINESS EXPENSES ACCOUNT

Cash account . . . £100	

DEPRECIATION OF TOOLS ACCOUNT

Tools account . . . £150	

(d) *The trial balance*

In order to test whether the accounts are in balance at this point a trial balance is drawn up in the following form. It is necessary to emphasise that the trial balance is nothing more than the book-keeper's device for checking the arithmetical accuracy of the entries and conveys no other information of any significance, although in some cases it may form a useful summary for preparing the final accounts.

TRIAL BALANCE

	£	£
Capital Accounts:—		
Owner's capital		750
B. loan		250
Cash	1,100	
Tools	150	
Revenue Accounts:—		
Sales		500
Business expenses	100	
Depreciation of tools . . .	150	
	£1,500	£1,500

The two sides of the trial balance being in agreement testify to the fact that the double entry has been carried out in each case. A trial balance will not disclose the following types of error:

1. Errors of omission—items completely omitted from the books of account.
2. Errors of commission—errors in posting to wrong accounts, or compensating errors.
3. Errors of principle—errors due to lack of knowledge of

accounting principles, *i.e.* treating revenue items as capital, and vice versa.

(e) *A diagram of entries*

At this stage the following diagram is introduced with the object of helping readers to visualise the correct side of a double-sided account to which entries must be posted:

	Left	*Right*
CAPITAL	Assets	Liabilities
REVENUE	Expenditure	Income

(f) *The recording of profit or loss*

The difference between income and expenditure, following the strict meaning of these terms, indicates profit or loss. Profit, so long as it is not withdrawn from the business, is an addition to capital, and loss is always a loss of capital.

The next stage in accounting for the boot repairer's business is accordingly to find his profit or loss as a result of the year's work. This operation is carried out by transferring the balances on the revenue accounts to a single account in order to find the net total of these items. In a complicated business, as will be explained later, the operation is carried out by stages, involving in some cases a Manufacturing Account, a Trading Account, a Profit and Loss Account and an Appropriation Account, the latter showing how the profit or loss is appropriated to the owner's and to reserve accounts. In the present simple example it is sufficient to use a Statement of Profit account. The book-keeping entries, still following the double-entry principle, will be as follows:

SALES ACCOUNT

Statement of profit account . £500	Cash account . . . £500

BUSINESS EXPENSES ACCOUNT

Cash account . . . £100	Statement of profit account . £100

DEPRECIATION OF TOOLS ACCOUNT

Tools account . . . £150	Statement of profit account . £150

STATEMENT OF PROFIT ACCOUNT

	£	Sales .	.	.	.	.	£500
Business expenses.	£100						
Depreciation of tools	150						
Profit .	250						
	£500						£500

To complete the double entry the profit of £250 or part of it must be transferred to the credit (or right-hand side) of either a drawing account, reserve account or the owner's capital account.

The accounts in the revenue section of the ledger are now closed. The accounts in the capital section of the ledger still have balances which are carried forward into the next accounting period. The financial position of the boot repairer's business can be ascertained at this point by extracting the balances of the accounts in the capital section, including the balance of profit, on to a statement usually termed a Balance Sheet, which can be prepared in the following form.

Balance Sheet as at ....

		£					£
Owner's capital	.	750	Cash .	.	.	.	1,100
Add Profit .	.	250	Tools .	.	.	.	150
		1,000					
B. loan	.	250					
		£1,250					£1,250

E. THE ORGANISATION OF ACCOUNTS

1. The elements of the ledger

The preceding sections set out to provide a general picture of principles on the basis of which an accounting system operates. One of the essential purposes of accounts is to show the extent to which capital has been maintained and to show the gain or loss on revenue account for a period. But the proprietor of a business will not be satisfied merely to learn that he has made a certain figure of profit over a period or has incurred a certain loss; nor is it sufficient for him to be informed that his capital stands at a stated total of money. If the affairs of the business are to be guided and controlled, the accounting system must be so organised that it will reveal the sources of movements in capital (assets and liabilities) and of revenue items (income and expenditure).

For such a purpose the accounting system—in a small business contained in one ledger—must be carefully planned so as to show the significant information required. The planning of the accounting system must also ensure that unwanted detail and unnecessary clerical labour are avoided.

The ledger must therefore be planned in accordance with certain broad classifications or headings available for extension or further analysis only if essential. There is an unfortunate tendency for ledger accounts to multiply until the significant information becomes lost in a mass of detail.

The overall divisions have already been discussed, and may be represented by the following diagram:

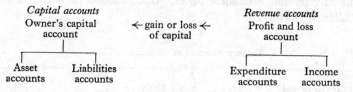

The accounting plan must now deal with further analysis of the headings shown above.

2. Asset accounts.—"What is owned"

The properties, equipment, stocks, debts, cash, etc., owned by the business are called the assets. These assets may be subdivided into: (a) "fixed assets"; and (b) "current assets".

(a) Fixed assets

Fixed assets are those which are held for the purpose of earning income and not for sale in the course of trading. In an industrial concern separate accounts under this heading will be established for:

(a) land and buildings, usually distinguished between freehold and leasehold property;

(b) plant and machinery;

(c) other fixed assets, such as investments, which are not intended to be disbursed in the course of business;
(d) deferred charges, such as heavy advertising expenditure incurred for the purpose of creating a market in a new product or other initial expenditure for development purposes,
   the benefit of which will be obtained in future years.

It should be borne in mind that although many assets are described as fixed, they are all, except possibly freehold land, subject
to depreciation or other loss of value, and the monetary total of
fixed assets continually requires replenishment out of income. The
method of accounting for such depreciation in value of fixed assets
is considered later.

(b) Current assets

Current assets are those which may be expended or consumed in
immediate day-to-day operations of the business. A very necessary
characteristic of current assets is that they shall be freely available
for conversion into cash. Cash balances and those current assets
which may be converted into cash almost immediately the necessity arises are known as "liquid assets".

Thus under the heading of current assets the following accounts
may be regarded as the minimum:

| Cash in hand. | Investments. | Debtors. |
| Cash at bank. | Stocks. | |

The assets section of the capital division of the ledger may be
shown diagrammatically thus:

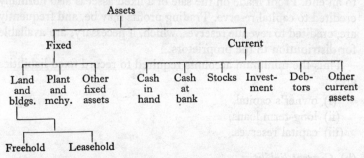

Note. Permanent investments are normally shown in balance sheets as a
separate item distinct from either fixed or current assets. Investments held for
short-term purposes are, however, normally treated as current assets.

B

3. Liability accounts—"What is owed"

Those from whom the business borrows or purchases on account are known as creditors. The creditors have a claim on the business until they are paid, and those claims are termed "liabilities".

Liabilities may also be divided into those which may be regarded as fixed or static, and those which are current.

(a) *Fixed liabilities*

The owners' capital is for accounting purposes regarded as a liability of the business, *i.e.* the amount owed by the business to the proprietors, although it is composed of the difference between the assets and the other liabilities, subject to the addition of profit and subtraction of loss represented by the balance in the profit and loss account.

In the case of a sole proprietor there will be an account recording his fixed capital, *i.e.* the amount which he will endeavour to maintain intact. In a partnership there will be separate accounts for each of the partners. In a company there will be accounts for each of the various classes of shares.

In addition to owners' capital, fixed capital will include long-term loans to the business such as, in the case of a company, debentures.

Where amounts are allocated out of surpluses with a view to increasing the permanent capital of the business, such allocations are credited to a "capital reserve" account, which henceforth forms part of the fixed capital of the concern and is not available for distribution to the owners except in the event of the business coming to an end. Profit made on the sale of a fixed asset is also normally credited to capital reserve. Trading profits may be, and frequently are, credited to revenue reserves, which, if necessary, are available for distribution to the proprietors.

Thus the minimum accounts required to record fixed liabilities are:

   (i) owner's capital,
   (ii) long-term loans,
   (iii) capital reserves.

(b) *Current liabilities*

Current liabilities are those which may need to be settled in cash at short notice, or in the normal operation of the business. They include trade creditors, short-term loans, such as loans from a bank, and bills of exchange payable.

(c) *Contingent liabilities*

It is considered appropriate at this point to refer to contingent liabilities, although they are not normally entered in an account forming part of the double-entry system.

Contingent liabilities are those which may become real liabilities and payable on the happening of a specified event. They include guarantees entered into by the business. Guarantees do not, of course, represent real debts until and unless the party guaranteed defaults. A contingent liability arises if, for example, a person or firm becomes a party to a bill of exchange. The contingent liability becomes a real liability if the principal debtor, the drawer or the acceptor of the bill, fails to pay.

Contingent liabilities have to be noted on the Balance Sheet of limited companies in accordance with the provisions of the Companies Act 1948, and the practice should be followed by other organisations.

(d) *A diagram of liability accounts*

The minimum accounts falling under the heading of liabilities may be expressed diagrammatically as follows:

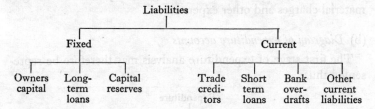

4. Income

In a trading organisation income may be considered under two headings of: (*a*) sales, and (*b*) other income. The income which arises from selling the products or services of the business forms the great bulk of "income", whilst "other income" comprises investment income, other interest and commissions, and exceptional receipts such as damages received in a legal action. Clearly the expression "sales" must be modified in the case of non-trading concerns so as to cover the main source of income to earn which the business exists: thus the main source of income for an insurance company is premium income, and for a transport company fares and freight charges.

5. Expenditure

(a) *Expenditure and "costs"*

The expenditure accounts are, perhaps, those which necessitate the most careful planning, for they are those from which stem detailed costing and many other methods of control. It is necessary at this point to emphasise that cost accounts, whether they set out to show unit costs, process costs or departmental costs, represent further analyses and breakdowns of the expenditure accounts which appear in the so-called Nominal or General Ledger. The illogical divorce between "cost accounts" and "financial accounts" has given rise to the modern technique of integrating cost and financial accounts. The use of the term "integration" in this context merely implies a reunion of the two systems which should never have been separated. An accounting system must be dealt with as one entity, not as several independent units.

Because of the temptation for indefinite and, in some cases, pointless analysis of expenditure in the ledger, it is essential for such accounts to conform to a concise plan. Business expenditure falls within three well-defined categories: personnel charges, material charges and other expenses.

(b) *Diagram of expenditure accounts*

The first stage of expenditure analysis may therefore be represented thus:

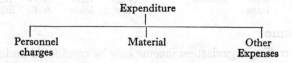

(c) *Personnel charges*

The expression "personnel charges" here means wages, salaries, national insurance, pensions and any expense directly incurred by the employment of people in the business. For a variety of reasons it is necessary to maintain at least three separate accounts recording personnel charges, and these accounts can be shown thus:

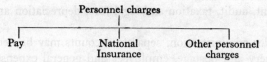

Personnel charges

| Pay | National Insurance | Other personnel charges |

For reasons which are shown later, in all but the smallest concerns the above headings will probably require to be expanded as follows:

Pay: (i) Hourly wages; (ii) weekly salaries; (iii) monthly salaries.

National Insurance: Subdivided as above.

Other personnel charges: (i) Pension contributions; (ii) pensions payable; (iii) other payments, such as welfare expenses.

(d) *Material*

Material in a manufacturing business should be shown under two accounts, one recording purchases of raw materials and the other bought-out parts. In a purely merchanting business "material" will, of course, represent the goods to be sold and classified as "Purchases". Diagrammatically shown:

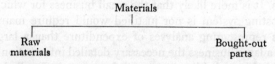

Materials

| Raw materials | Bought-out parts |

(e) *Other expenses*

So far the accounts required under the heading of expenditure present little difficulty. The heading of "other expenses" must, however, be considered with the greatest care because of the miscellaneous nature of expense which it comprises. One answer to the problem of classification is to record separately the largest identifiable groups of expense not being material or relating directly to personnel. The following broad headings may suffice and can be expanded as the need arises:

Financial charges,
Administrative charges,
Selling and distributive charges,
Exceptional charges, and
Sundries.

Under financial charges, separate accounts are normally extracted (depending on the nature of the business) for cash discount, audit, taxation and legal fees, depreciation and interest due.

Under administration, separate accounts may be necessary for stationery and postage, employees and general expenses, vehicle charges (petrol, licences, etc.) insurances, rent and rates.

Under selling and distribution charges, the accounts include advertising, warehousing, carriage outwards and commission. Commission payable to employed salesmen as part of their remuneration might preferably be included under the personnel heading, but in any event a separate account will be desirable.

Exceptional charges include compensation, damages, fines, losses on exchange, losses on sale of fixed assets and investments.

The analysis of "other expenses" is illustrated as on page 26.

In conclusion, the complete scheme of the planning and analysis of expenditure accounts is shown on page 33.

(f) *The economy of ledger accounts*

It is emphasised at this point that the growth of a business does not necessarily entail an increase in the number of main ledger accounts. It is more likely that the small business for which a detailed costing system is not justified would require many more accounts representing analyses of expenditure than a large concern. In a large business the necessary detailed information should be provided by subsidiary systems of accounts controlled by and agreeing in total with a limited number of main ledger accounts such as are indicated in the preceding section.

The main or control ledger is thus the chief accountant's personal instrument for watching the progress of the concern and reporting on the results to top management. He should be aware by a rapid scrutiny of the accounts of any trend or change in the financial position which requires immediate investigation; and by the use of a control ledger containing the minimum of accounts he would not be misled by masses of detailed information from which such accounts were made up.

The immediate source from which entries are made in such a control ledger are subsidiary books analysed so as to group items into, say, monthly totals for posting to the control accounts.

Detailed information is obtainable from subsidiary ledger systems, each self-balancing in itself and each controlled by an account in the main or control ledger.

Subsidiary ledger systems of this nature include a debtors' ledger with an account for each debtor, and analogous to the sales ledger, except that a debtors' ledger contains all debtors, not merely those resulting from sales. Similarly, a creditors' ledger includes all creditors' accounts and broadly corresponds to the "bought ledger", except that a creditors' ledger is not limited to suppliers' accounts. Further subsidiary ledger systems can, as necessary, be created to show various types of fixed assets, stocks, material purchases and any analysis of other expenses which may be required.

(g) *Preparation of financial statements*

If the accounts in the ledger are organised in the manner shown in the preceding paragraphs the preparation of financial statements for management is simplified. A trial balance can be extracted from the ledger under the main headings required on the financial statements: sub-totals are made for each heading, and the sub-totals extracted on to a summary financial statement. Before such a statement is prepared it will be necessary to ensure that outstanding expenses and accrued income have been taken into account. This latter matter is dealt with in detail in the next chapter on the subject of the preparation of the final accounts.

The advantage of using this method is that management is presented with information in a form which is readily understood, whilst the accountant can have before him the trial balance which contains the detailed information from which the summary financial statement was prepared. The accountant presenting the statement is thus enabled to answer any questions which may be put to him. The example which follows is a simplified one, and in practice the number of accounts may be greater than can conveniently be contained in one trial balance. If this is the case schedules of accounts could be prepared and summarised under convenient headings on the trial balance, before being extracted on to the financial statement.

It will be seen from an examination of the example that the profit for the current accounting period is included. To obtain this figure it will be necessary to total the revenue section first, obtain the profit or loss, and then enter it in the capital section. It will be noted that only the totals in bold type are taken on to the summary financial statement.

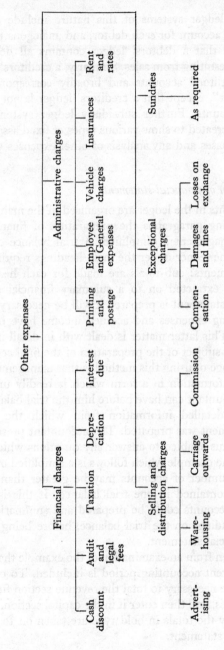

DIAGRAM OF OTHER EXPENSES

THE PLANNING OF EXPENDITURE ACCOUNTS

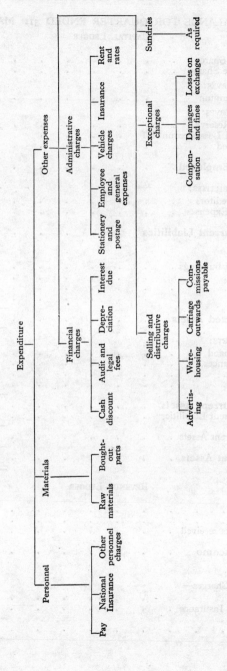

TRIAL BALANCE FOR QUARTER ENDED 31st MARCH 1958

CAPITAL LEDGER

	£	£
CAPITAL:		
Ordinary Shares		5,000
Preference Shares		5,000
CAPITAL RESERVES:		
Share Premium		1,250
REVENUE RESERVES:		
General Reserve		1,150
Profit and Loss Account b/f		4,000
This period		2,490
Capital Employed		**18,890**
CURRENT LIABILITIES:		
Trade Creditors		1,950
Accrued Expenses		200
Total Current Liabilities		**2,150**
FIXED ASSETS:		
Land and buildings	3,000	
Plant	1,530	
Fixtures	500	
Goodwill	1,500	
Total Fixed Assets	**6,530**	
CURRENT ASSETS:		
Cash in hand	260	
Bank balances	4,250	
Stock	4,500	
Debtors	5,500	
Total Current Assets	**14,510**	
Less Current Liabilities	2,150	
Net Current Assets	12,360	
Total Net Assets	**18,890**	

REVENUE LEDGER

	£
INCOME:	
Sales	30,350
Service	4,400
Discounts received	250
Total Income	**35,000**
EXPENDITURE:	
Personnel Charges—	
Pay	3,300
National Insurance	220
Total	**3,520**

Materials—	£	£
Raw materials	20,300	
Bought-out parts	8,050	
Total	**28,350**	

Other Expenses—		
Financial Charges:		
Depreciation	550	
Interest	200	
Total		750

Administrative Charges:		
Insurance	200	
Rent and rates	640	
Other	250	
Total		1,090

Selling and Distributive:		
Advertising	100	
Commissions	200	
Total		300

TOTAL EXPENDITURE AND INCOME	34,010	35,000
Stocks to begin and end	**3,000**	**4,500**
	37,010	39,500
Net Profit for Quarter	**2,490**	
	£39,500	39,500

SUMMARY FINANCIAL STATEMENT

FOR QUARTER ENDED 31ST MARCH 1958

	£	£
Capital Employed		18,890
Employment of Capital:		
Fixed Assets		6,530
Current Assets	14,510	
Less Current Liabilities	2,150	
Net Current Assets		12,360
		£18,890
Income		35,000
Increase in Stocks		1,500
		£36,500

Expenditure:

		£
Personnel Charges		3,520
Materials		28,350
Financial Charges		750
Administrative Charges		1,090
Selling and Distributive Expenses		300
		34,010
Net Profit for Quarter		2,490
		£36,500

F. THE SOURCE OF ENTRIES

1. The general purpose of subsidiary books

With the preceding broad picture of the principles of an accounting system in mind, consideration may now be given to the more detailed mechanics of the technique.

If the information provided by an accounting system is to be correctly assessed, and for the purpose of conducting detailed investigations into the results shown by the system, it is essential that the sources from which entries are made in the accounts be clearly understood.

Every entry made in an account forming part of the double-entry system should originate from a subsidiary book or, as it is otherwise known, a book of original entry. Examples of such books are:

> Day Books
> Journals
> Bill Books
> Cash Books (which can also be used as accounts).

The purpose of such books is to collect in chronological order, and if necessary classify transactions, so that totals are available for entry into the appropriate accounts. Thus in accounting for a retail shop the sales account in the ledger cannot be overburdened with every single sale, some perhaps for trifling amounts. A Sales Day Book or Journal is therefore maintained for the purpose of recording transactions on credit, analysing them by types of sales and providing daily, weekly or possibly monthly totals, for entry in the sales account. Following the principle of double entry, it should be noted that each subsidiary book constitutes the source of entries in at least two accounts. Thus the Sales Day Book or Sales

Journal not only provides totals for the credit of the sales account but also the individual debits to the debtors' account.

Each entry in the subsidiary books is in turn normally supported by a document to evidence the transaction, such as, for example, an invoice in the case of a sale.

The main subsidiary books and originating documents will now be considered in detail.

2. The Cash Book

(a) *The purpose of the Cash Book and the originating documents*

The Cash Book of a small business often performs the function of a cash account and a subsidiary book combined.

In many small businesses the receipt of money over the counter for small sales is not supported by any documentary evidence. It is, however, certainly desirable that some form of slip or receipt be issued, if only for the purpose of providing a check on the accuracy of cash receipts; it will be noted, for example, that bus conductors are required to issue tickets for fares. Money received in the form of cheques, postal orders, etc., should be paid into the firm's banking account, the counterfoil of the bank paying-in book forming the necessary evidence.

Payments of cash should in all cases be supported by a voucher. In the case of cash purchases the voucher will be the receipted bill if obtainable; if not, in common with other petty cash payments they must be evidenced by a petty cash voucher signed by the recipient and approved by an authorised superior. Cheque payments sent through the post should in the first instance be evidenced by a letter or more properly a remittance advice, of which a copy will be retained; later an official receipt may be received from the payee and filed with the copy of the remittance advice. The Cheques Act, 1957, Section 3, provides that: "An unendorsed cheque which appears to have been paid by the banker on whom it is drawn is evidence of the receipt by the payee of the sum payable by the cheque." As a result of this Act the practice of giving receipts for cheque payments, except where a formal discharge is required, has been largely discontinued.

The Cash Book should be written up, at least daily, from the supporting documents, and the procedure can be summarised thus:

Receipts

Cheque and Postal Remittance—from a remittance list.

Cash Sales—total of copies of counterslips or total rolls of cash registers.

Other Receipts—from suitable evidence.

Payments

Cheque Payments—from counterfoils of cheque book.

Cash Payments—from payees' receipted bills or petty cash vouchers.

(b) *The three forms of cash books*

Three forms of cash books may be found in use and these are:

Separate Cash and Bank Accounts.

The Double Column Cash Book.

The Bank Cash Book and Petty Cash Book.

(i) *Separate cash and bank accounts.* In the most simple form receipts and payments of money are recorded in one book, and a separate book is maintained for payments by cheque or receipts direct into the bank account.

(ii) *The double-column Cash Book.* In this case the entries are made in a similar manner as before, but with the use of tabular columns both accounts are recorded on the same page side by side. This method has the advantage of keeping all receipts and payments, whether by cash or cheque, in chronological order, and also showing the cash and bank balances adjacent to each other.

(iii) *The Bank Cash Book and Petty Cash Book.* The most methodical system of recording cash transactions depends on the rule that all payments shall be made by cheque and that all receipts shall be banked not later than the morning following the day of receipt. If this rule is enforced the Cash Book will contain an account of transactions with the bank only and will correspond with the bank pass book.

It will be necessary to maintain an independent record of individual cash receipts (including cheques received), since the bank account will show only totals of daily takings paid into the bank. Furthermore, the Cash Book being a medium for posting into the other accounts, an analysis will be required of the receipts by account headings. For this reason separate cash-received and cash-paid books are found convenient in any large business, and even the entries in such books may require further analysis for statistical purposes.

Small items such as postages and small local purchases are paid out of a cash balance kept for the purpose. The bank-cash system must therefore be combined with a petty cash system for small payments up to an authorised limit, say, £5.

The imprest or float which is held by the petty cashier should be sanctioned by a responsible executive. The initial imprest is recorded by drawing a cheque payable to "petty cash" for the amount sanctioned. This cheque is exchanged at the bank for the requisite coin and notes and the proceeds entered in the petty cash book and cross posted to a "petty cash" account in the ledger.

All disbursements made by the petty cashier are evidenced by a voucher signed by the recipient and countersigned by his superior. At stated intervals, say monthly, the sum disbursed, as shown in the Petty Cash Book, is reimbursed to the petty cashier by means of a further cheque for the amount required drawn payable to "petty cash".

The Petty Cash Book should be ruled so as to analyse the expenditure by headings corresponding to the ledger accounts. The following is a brief example of this method:

Transactions:							£
Jan. 1	Balance at bank	.	.	.	.	.	1,500
,, 1	Petty cash in hand	.	.	.	.	.	20
Cheques Received:							
Jan. 1	A. Jones	.	.	.	.	.	50
,, 1	T. Williams	.	.	.	.	.	70
,, 1	B. Evans	.	.	.	.	.	60
,, 2	R. Bright	.	.	.	.	.	20
,, 2	T. Boyle	.	.	.	.	.	90
,, 2	E. George	.	.	.	.	.	100
Cash Sales:							
Jan. 3	Per cash register	.	.	.	.	.	60
Cheques Drawn:							
Jan. 3	R. Green on account	.	.	.	.	100
,, 3	N.I. Co. for insurance	.	.	.	.	10
,, 3	Petty cash	.	.	.	.	.	11
Cash Disbursements:							
Jan. 1	Advertisement	.	.	.	.	.	3
,, 1	Stationery	.	.	.	.	.	2
,, 1	Stamps	.	.	.	.	.	2
,, 1	Petrol	.	.	.	.	.	3
,, 2	Oil	.	.	.	.	.	1

BANK RECEIPTS BOOK		£	BANK PAYMENTS BOOK		£
Jan. 1	A. Jones . .	50	Jan. 3	R. Green . .	100
,, 1	T. Williams .	70	,, 3	Insurance . .	10
,, 1	B. Evans . .	60	,, 3	Petty cash . .	11
		£180			£121
,, 2	R. Bright . .	20			
,, 2	T. Boyle . .	90			
,, 2	E. George . .	100			
		£210			
,, 3	Cash Sales . .	60			
		£60			

BANK CASH BOOK

		£			£
Jan. 1	Balance b/d . .	1,500	Jan. 3	Cheques . . .	121
,, 1	Deposits . . .	180			
,, 2	,, . . .	210			
,, 3	,, . . .	60			

PETTY CASH BOOK

Receipts			Payments			Stationery and Stamps	Adverts	Petrol and Oil	Etc.
		£			£	£	£	£	£
Jan. 1	Bal. b/d	20	Jan. 1	Advert .	3		3		
,, 3	Bank .	11	,, 1	Stationery	2	2			
			,, 1	Stamps .	2	2			
			,, 1	Petrol .	3			3	
			,, 2	Oil . .	1			1	
					11	4	3	4	
			,, 3	Bal. c/d .	20				
		£31			£31				
,, 3	Bal. b/d	20							

PETTY CASH ACCOUNT

		£			£
Jan. 1	Balance b/d . .	20	Jan. 3	Stationery and stamps .	4
,, 3	Bank . . .	11	,, 3	Adverts . . .	3
			,, 3	Petrol and oil . .	4
			,, 3	Balance c/d . .	20
		£31			£31
4	Balance b/d . .	20			

(iv) *The importance of correct cash accounting.* Some attention has been given to the mechanics of cash accounting, as it is the bedrock of efficient accounting in businesses of all sizes and kinds. A methodical system of recording and authorising cash transactions is essential for the prevention of fraud and petty pilfering and for the control of expenditure.

The methods outlined above should be reinforced by a system of internal cash audit with the object of checking not only the accuracy of the entries but also the efficiency of the system. In a small business such an audit may be carried out by the manager or his personal assistant; in a large concern it will be necessary to employ qualified staff for the purpose, and such staff should be free from any departmental responsibilities other than internal audit. The internal audit staff should report to top management, either the head of the financial department or preferably the managing director, in order that their independence shall be safeguarded. The work of the internal audit section is referred to in later chapters.

3. The Purchase Journal

(a) *The objects of the Purchase Journal*

So long as a business pays on delivery for everything it buys the purchases account or accounts could be written up from the entries in the Cash Paid Book or the cash paid side of a single Cash Book. Where purchases are obtained on credit it is necessary to operate a separate book of prime entry recording such transactions. This subsidiary book is variously called a Purchase Journal or Purchase Day Book.

The purpose of the Purchase Journal is to provide a medium from which entries can be made: (*a*) to the creditor's accounts recording the indebtedness of the business to its suppliers; and (*b*) to the purchases or material account, recording the cost of the material which has been obtained but not paid for immediately.

(b) *The basis of entries*

The entries in the Purchase Journal are made from the suppliers' invoices. Before an entry is made in the Purchase Journal the accuracy of the charge shown on the supplier's invoice must be verified. In the case of goods supplied the normal routine is for a goods inwards note to be made out by the goods inwards department after that department has checked that the goods supplied are in acceptable condition and that they correspond with the description shown on the delivery note. The goods inwards note is checked against the order, usually by the buying department, and the invoice, when it is eventually received is checked against both documents before it is passed for payment.

In a small business the order may be made out by the manager himself, or at least signed by him. In a large business an order will be preceded by an indent on the Buying Department made out by the departmental manager authorised to initiate ordering of goods. For stock items, where stock limits are set up, the stores may submit indents when the stocks have fallen to the ordering level. In the case of invoices for services supplied there will, of course, be no goods inwards note and the invoice will have to be approved by a responsible official who is in a position to certify that the services have been properly carried out.

Where a high standard and precise workmanship is called for from a supplier it may be necessary for the goods to be examined by the inspection department before the charges made for them are accepted. In such a case the indent and order should be marked to this effect so as to warn the staff concerned that a satisfactory inspection report must be received before the invoice can be passed for payment.

The procedure outlined above must be strictly followed in order to ensure that no unauthorised or incorrect charge is paid for or entered in the accounts. It should be noted, however, that in order to expedite the payment of invoices the practice is developing of paying known and trusted suppliers on the basis of their invoices immediately the latter have been checked against the goods inwards note. Any minor queries or discrepancies are dealt with subsequently. This method has the advantage of maintaining suppliers' goodwill and gaining cash discount as a result of the prompt payment. It may also obviate considerable accounting entries, since no account need be maintained for a supplier whose charges are paid for soon after receipt of his invoice.

Any system of paying on the basis of invoices as compared with the recorded balance on a supplier's account in the ledger requires, however, close supervision and a well-trained staff. In any event, the system of recording and paying suppliers should be subject to investigations from time to time by an internal audit section.

PURCHASE JOURNAL

		Total	Raw materials	Bought-out parts	Capital	General expenditure
		£	£	£	£	£
Jan. 1	Importers Ltd.	2,100	2,100			
,, 2	Manufacturers Ltd.	500		500		
,, 3	Thames Co.	50				50
,, 4	X.L. Ltd.	700	700			
,, 5	Tools Ltd.	400			400	
,, 5	Manufacturers Ltd.	300		300		
		£4,050	2,800	800	400	50
	Each item posted to respective creditor's account		Totals posted to raw materials and bought-out parts account		Individual items posted to asset accounts	Probably further analysed and total to expenditure account

(c) *The subsequent entries in the accounts*

From the point of view of the ledger keeper the entry in the Purchase Journal is tantamount to acceptance of the charge, and the remaining procedure is automatic. At convenient intervals, say monthly, the entries in the Purchase Journal against each supplier will be credited to that supplier's account in the ledger. The double entry will be completed at the end of, say, a month, by debiting the total of the entries to a purchases or material account.

The use of the Purchase Journal thus economises in book-keeping, since it avoids the necessity for entering every transaction in the expenditure accounts.

Where it is desirable to record suppliers' charges under different headings, the Purchase Journal will have to be analysed, preferably containing a separate column for each material or other account which is to be posted in the ledger.

A Purchase Journal used to be regarded as a book to be restricted to the entry of goods purchased for manufacture or re-sale. A more modern conception of the application of this book is that it shall be used to record every liability incurred, whether for material, capital items (fixed assets) services, or expenditure of any nature obtained on credit. There is otherwise considerable risk that a liability may be created which is not entered in the accounts until payment is made.

Such a use of the Journal necessitates the provision of analysis columns each representing an account or sometimes a group of accounts in the ledger. The following example, for which the Purchase Journal is shown on page 43, should be carefully studied:

Invoices Approved:—

Jan. 1	Raw materials from Importers Ltd.	2,100
,, 2	Bought-out parts from Manufacturers Ltd.. . .	500
,, 3	Thames Co. for warehousing charges . . .	50
,, 4	Raw material from X.L. Ltd.	700
,, 5	Milling machines from Tools Ltd.	400
,, 5	Bought-out parts from Manufacturers Ltd.. . .	300

LEDGERS

CAPITAL:	CREDITOR LEDGER:
Plant Account	Importers Ltd.

	£			£
Jan. 5 Tools Ltd. .	400		Jan. 1 Raw material	2,100

REVENUE:

Warehousing charges account

	£
Jan. 3 Thames Co.	50

Manufacturers Ltd.

	£
Jan. 2 Bought-out parts .	500
,, 5 Bought-out parts .	300

Raw materials account

	£
Jan. 5 Total .	2,800

X.L. Ltd.

	£
Jan. 4 Raw material	700

Bought-out parts account

	£
Jan. 5 Total .	800

Thames Co. Ltd.

	£
Jan. 3 Warehousing	50

Tools Ltd.

	£
Jan. 5 Plant .	400

A trial balance extracted from the ledgers for these transactions only will appear as follows:

Trial balance at 5th January

	£	£
Capital ledger:		
Plant account	400	
Revenue ledger:		
Warehousing charges account	50	
Raw materials account	2,800	
Bought-out Parts Account	800	
Creditors ledger:		
Importers Ltd. account		2,100
Manufacturers Ltd. account		800
X.L. Ltd. account		700
Thames Co. Ltd. account		50
Tools Ltd. account		400
	£4,050	£4,050

4. The Sales Journal

The Sales Journal or Day Book is intended to record individual sales on credit. The originating document for entries in the Sales Journal is a copy of the invoice sent to the customer.

A sales invoice is made out, normally by the sales department, (*a*) on notification from the works that the article required has been

completed and has been passed to the warehouse for despatch, or
(b) for stock items on the basis of the sales department's prior
knowledge of stocks held. In each case an order will have been
previously passed to the works or stores specifying the goods required and the customer's requirements as to packing and delivery.
A copy of the delivery note attached to the goods is passed to the
sales department for checking against the customer's order and as a
basis for preparing the sales invoice.

In the majority of businesses, large or small, it is necessary to
analyse sales by types. The Sales Journal requires to be similarly
analysed so that totals, say monthly, of each kind of sale may be
posted to the credit of the various sales accounts. The corresponding double entries are made to the individual customer's accounts
in the ledger. A brief example of a Sales Journal with analysis
columns follows:

SALES JOURNAL

		Total	Radios	Tele-vision	Radio-grams	Records
		£	£	£	£	£
Arcadia Ltd. .	Posted to	500	300	100	100	
Browns Co. .	individual	300		200	50	50
Emporea Ltd. .	customer's	1,000	500	200	250	50
Greenstreet Co.	accounts	100				100
Musicians Ltd.		100			50	50
		£2,000	800	500	450	250

Totals posted to
departmental sales accounts

5. The Journal proper

At least one further subsidiary book, sometimes called simply
"the Journal" is essential for the operation of any efficient accounting system. The purpose of the Journal is to record those entries
which cannot be made in the main books of original entry, such as
the following:

(a) *Opening entries*

   (i) To record initial assets, liabilities and capital taken over by
   a new business.
   (ii) In an amalgamation, to incorporate the assets and liabilities
   of the undertakings absorbed.

(b) *Transfer between one account and another*

Where, for example, an entry has been made in the wrong account; an item has been charged to expenditure or revenue account instead of to capital; the writing-off of bad debts, *i.e.* transfer from the customer's account to a "Bad Debts" account; transfer of profit to reserve or owners' accounts, etc.

(c) *Closing entries*

   (i) When a business is dissolved.

  (ii) To adjust accounts at the year end or other balancing period, *e.g.* the transfer of balances from the revenue accounts to the Trading and Profit and Loss Accounts; and various other end-of-period adjustments.

(b) *Other entries*

   (i) Where an analysed Purchase Day Book is not kept it will be necessary to record liabilities, such as capital items obtained on credit, in the Journal.

  (ii) Other entries, such as infrequent bill transactions, where it is considered unnecessary to maintain a special Day Book for the purpose.

Entries in the Journal should be strictly limited. The Journal should not be overburdened with many entries of a related nature: where this occurs such entries should be accommodated in a separate book of original entry.

Journal entries are made in the following manner:

	JOURNAL		£	£
Jan. 1	Office Equipment account	. Dr.	110	
	To Suppliers Ltd.			110
	Purchase of calculating machine.			
Jan. 10	Bad Debts account	. Dr.	50	
	To Johnson & Co.			50
	Writing off Johnson & Co.'s A/c.			
Jan. 10	Smythe & Co. Ltd.	. Dr.	25	
	To Smith & Co.			25
	Correction of error: amount posted to Smith & Co. instead of Smythe & Co.			
Jan. 10	Depreciation account	. Dr.	200	
	To Depreciation Suspense account—Plant .			200
	Being depreciation @ 10% p.a. on £2,000.			

G. Self-balancing Ledgers

1. General and subsidiary ledgers

So far it has been assumed that all entries are made in one ledger, but, as the volume of transactions and the number of accounts grow, it becomes more convenient to segregate groups of accounts into subsidiary ledger systems. Two subsidiary ledgers which come readily to mind are what are popularly called the Sales and the Purchases Ledgers, although it is more logical to widen the scope of these ledgers so that they contain in the one case accounts of all debtors and in the other accounts of all creditors, not only those arising from sales and purchases.

As a business develops it is necessary to create further subsidiary ledger systems, such as those recording the various classifications of stock and work in progress, leasehold and freehold property, plant and machinery and so forth. Each subsidiary ledger will be controlled by an account in the general ledger (sometimes called the "nominal" ledger). A subsidiary ledger should be self-balancing, that is to say the total of all the daily or monthly entries made in the various accounts which it contains are entered into a total account (variously called a "control account" or "adjustment account"), and this total account will be an exact replica of the corresponding account in the general ledger, although the entries will be on the opposite side.

The sources from which entries are made in the subsidiary ledgers are the same as those from which the general ledger account is made up, *i.e.* the normal day books, cash books, journals and other sources of first entry, but the control account in the general ledger and the adjustment account in the subsidiary ledger will contain only totals of each day's or month's transactions affecting the accounts concerned. In this way the person keeping the general ledger can "control" the subsidiary ledgers by ensuring that the adjustment accounts in those ledgers carry the same balance at any point as the balance in the general ledger control account concerned. The adjustment account in the subsidiary ledger also "controls" the detailed entries made in that ledger because the net total of the balances on all the individual accounts should agree with the balance on the adjustment account.

2. "Private" ledger

In some businesses a "private ledger" is maintained in addition to a general or nominal ledger. The private ledger is normally used to record figures which it is not considered desirable for the book-keepers to see, such as share capital, reserves and private accounts of directors. The private ledger thus becomes another subsidiary ledger, requiring a control account in the general ledger. In other systems the private ledger constitutes the ultimate controlling mechanism and contains a limited number of control accounts covering all transactions of the business.

3. Example of self-balancing ledgers

(a) *Books of first entry*

PURCHASE DAY BOOK

Date	Supplier	Folio	£
Jan. 1	B. Johnson	1	5·11
,, 1	G. Chaucer	2	6·42
,, 15	P. Plowman	4	7·34
,, 20	B. Johnson	1	3·13
,, 27	P. Sidney	3	2·41
	Total for January		£24·41

RETURNS OUTWARD BOOK

Date	Supplier	Folio	£
Jan. 8	B. Johnson	1	1·03
,, 26	P. Plowman	4	2·09
	Total for January		£3·12

CASH PAID BOOK (Extract)

Date	Name	Folio	£
Jan. 15	B. Johnson	1	4·08
,, 15	G. Chaucer	2	5·00
,, 31	P. Plowman	4	5·25
	Total for January		£14·33

(b) *Control account in General Ledger*

CREDITORS—Account No. 16

			£					£
Jan. 31	Sundries	ROB	3·12	Jan. 30	Sundries	PDB		24·41
„ 31	„	CPB	14·33					
„ 31	Balance	c/d	6·96					
			£24·41					£24·41
				Feb. 1	Balance	b/d		6·97

(c) *Creditors (or "Purchases") Ledger*

ADJUSTMENT ACCOUNT

			£				£
Jan. 1	Sundries	PDB	11·53	Jan. 8	Sundries	ROB	1·03
„ 15	„	„	7·34	„ 15		CPB	9·08
„ 20	„	„	3·13	„ 26	„	ROB	2·09
„ 27	„	„	2·41	„ 31	„	CPB	5·25
				„ 31	Balance	c/d	6·96
			£24·41				£24·41
Feb. 1	Balance	b/d	6·96				

B. JOHNSON—Account No. 1

			£				£
Jan. 8	Returns	ROB	1·03	Jan. 1	Purchases	PDB	5·11
„ 15	Cash	CPB	4·08	„ 20	„	„	3·13
„ 31	Balance	c/d	3·13				
			£8·24				£8·24
				Feb. 1	Balance	b/d	3·13

G. CHAUCER—Account No. 2

			£				£
Jan. 15	Cash	CPB	5·00	Jan. 1	Purchases	PDB	6·42
„ 31	Balance	c/d	1·42				
			£6·42				£6·42
				Feb. 1	Balance	b/d	1·42

P. SIDNEY—Account No. 3

			£				£
Jan. 31	Balance	c/d	2·41	Jan. 27	Purchases	PDB	2·41
				Feb. 1	Balance	b/d	2·41

P. PLOWMAN—Account No. 4

			£				£
Jan. 26	Returns	ROB	2·09	Jan. 15	Purchases	PDB	7·34
Jan. 31	Cash	CPB	5·25				
			£7·34				£7·34

TRIAL BALANCE at 31st January

	£	£
Adjustment account	6·96	
1. B. Johnson		3·13
2. G. Chaucer		1·42
3. P. Sidney		2·41
4. P. Plowman		
Totals . . .	£6·96	£6·96

H. A Specimen Set of Books

The following represents a simple but complete set of account books for a newly commencing business. The student is recommended to follow through all the transactions. For simplicity several things have been done:

(a) dates have been omitted;

(b) there are no individual personal accounts;

(c) no adjustments have been made.

Transactions

	£
Owner paid into bank as capital	5,000

He purchased on credit from Suppliers Ltd. a motor van costing 2,000

He received the following invoices for goods purchased on credit:

	£
X Ltd.	7,000
Y Ltd.	2,000
Z Ltd.	6,000

He sent out the following sales invoices:

	£
A Ltd.	9,000
B Ltd.	5,000
C Ltd.	5,900

He paid the following petty cash vouchers:

£

	£
Office expenses	5
Petrol and oil	6
Advertising	5
Office expenses	2
Advertising	5

His cheque-book counterfoils were:

	£
Petty cash	50
Equipment purchased	1,000
Office expenses	2,500
Advertising	2,000
Wages and salaries	1,700
Petrol and oil	500
Y Ltd.	2,000
Drew for self	100
Petty cash	23

He paid into the bank the following:

	£
Cheque from B Ltd.	5,000
Cash sales	100

At the end of the period his stock was valued at £3,000.

BANK RECEIPTS BOOK—J.1

	Folio	£
Capital	1	5,000
B Ltd.	9	5,000
Cash sales	13	100
	3	£10,100

BANK PAYMENTS BOOK—J.2

	Folio	£
Petty cash	5	50
Equipment	6	1,000
Office expenses	14	2,500
Advertisements	16	2,000
Wages and salaries	17	1,700
Petrol and oil	15	500
Y Ltd.	10	2,000
Drawings	2	100
Petty cash	5	23
	3	£9,873

PURCHASES JOURNAL—J.3

	Folio	£
X Ltd.	10	7,000
Y Ltd.	10	2,000
Z Ltd.	10	6,000
	12	£15,000

SALES JOURNAL—J.4

						Folio	£
A Ltd.	.	.	.	.	.	9	9,000
B Ltd.	.	.	.	.	.	9	5,000
C Ltd.	.	.	.	.	.	9	5,900
						13	£19,900

GENERAL JOURNAL—J.5

					Folio	£
Suppliers Ltd.	.	.	.	.	11	2,000
(Motor van)	.	.	.	7	£2,000

Note. In this exercise a "General Journal" has been created so as to show separately the transaction on capital account, *i.e.* the purchase of a fixed asset. This transaction could have been entered in a separate column in the Purchase Journal.

PETTY CASH BOOK

Receipts	£	Payments	Total £	Office Expenses £	Petrol and Oil £	Advertise- ments £
Bank	50	Office expenses	5	5		
Bank	23	Petrol and oil	6		6	
		Advertisements	5			5
		Office expenses	2	2		
		Advertisements	5			5
			23	7	6	10
		Balance c/d	50			
	£73		£73			
Balance b/d	50					

CAPITAL LEDGER

Owner's Capital Account—1

	Folio	£			Folio	£
Balance	c/d	5,000	Bank	. .	J.1	5,000
			Balance	.	b/d	5,000

Owner's Drawings Account—2

		Folio	£			Folio	£
Bank	. .	J.2	100	Profit and Loss a/c	18	1,277
Balance	. .	c/d	1,177			
			£1,277			£1,277
				Balance	. .	b/d	£1,177

Bank Account—3

	Folio	£			Folio	£
Receipts . .	J.1	10,100	Payments . .		J.2	9,873
			Balance . .		c/d	227
		£10,100				£10,100
Balance . .	b/d	227				

Petty Cash Account—5

	Folio	£			Folio	£
Bank . . .	J.2	50	Office expenses .		14	7
Bank . . .	J.2	23	Petrol and oil .		15	6
			Advertisements .		16	10
			Balance . .		c/d	50
		£73				£73
Balance . .	b/d	50				

Equipment Account—6

Bank . . .	J.2	1,000	

Motor Vans Account—7

Suppliers . .	J.5	2,000	

Stock Account—8

Trading a/c . .	18	3,000	

Sundry Debtors Account—9

A Ltd. . .	J.4	9,000	Bank (B) . .		J.1	5,000
B Ltd. . .	J.4	5,000	Balance . .		c/d	14,900
C Ltd. . .	J.4	5,900				
		£19,900				£19,900
Balance . .	b/d	14,900				

Sundry Creditors Account—10

Bank (R) . .	J.2	2,000	X Ltd. . .		J.3	7,000
Balance . .	c/d	13,000	Y Ltd. . .		J.3	2,000
			Z Ltd. . .		J.3	6,000
		£15,000				£15,000
			Balance . .		b/d	13,000

Suppliers Account—11

		Motor van . .	J.5	2,000

REVENUE LEDGER
Purchases Account—12

	Folio	£			Folio	£
Various . .	J.53	15,000	Trading a/c .		18	15,000

Sales Account—13

	Folio	£			Folio	£
Trading account .	18	20,000	Bank . . .		J.1	100
			Various . .		J.4	19,900
		£20,000				£20,000

Office Expenses Account—14

	Folio	£			Folio	£
Bank . . .	J.2	2,500	Profit and Loss a/c		18	2,507
Petty cash .	5	7				
		£2,507				£2,507

Petrol and Oil Account—15

	Folio	£			Folio	£
Bank . . .	J.2	500	Profit and Loss a/c		18	506
Petty cash .	5	6				
		£506				£506

Advertising Account—16

	Folio	£			Folio	£
Bank . . .	J.2	2,000	Profit and Loss a/c		18	2,010
Petty cash .	5	10				
		£2,010				£2,010

Salaries and Wages Account—17

	Folio	£			Folio	£
Bank . . .	J.2	1,700	Profit and Loss a/c		18	1,700

TRIAL BALANCE
(made up before transfers to Trading and Profit and Loss Account)

	Folio	Dr. £	Cr. £
Capital Ledger			
Owner's Capital . . .	1		5,000
Drawings	2	100	
Bank	3	227	
Petty Cash . . .	5	50	
Equipment . . .	6	1,000	
Motor vans . . .	7	2,000	
Stock (no opening stock) .	8	—	
Sundry Debtors . .	9	14,900	
Sundry Creditors . .	10		13,000
Suppliers Ltd. . . .	11		2,000
Revenue Ledger			
Purchases	12	15,000	
Sales	13		20,000
Office expenses . .	14	2,507	
Petrol and Oil . .	15	506	
Advertising . . .	16	2,010	
Salaries and Wages . .	17	1,700	
Total . .		£40,000	£40,000

Trading and Profit and Loss Account—18

	Folio	£		Folio	£
Purchases . .	12	15,000	Sales . . .	13	20,000
Gross Profit .	c/d	8,000	Closing stock .	8	3,000
		£23,000			£23,000
Office expenses .	14	2,507	Gross profit .	b/d	8,000
Petrol and Oil .	15	506			
Advertising . .	16	2,010			
Salaries and Wages	17	1,700			
Net profit . .	c/d	1,277			
		£8,000			£8,000
Drawings a/c .	2	£1,277	Net profit . .	b/d	1,277

Balance Sheet

	£	£		£	£
Owner's Capital			*Fixed Assets*		
Original Capital .		5,000	Equipment . .	1,000	
Profit . . .	1,277		Motor vans . .	2,000	
Less: Drawings .	100				
		1,177	*Total Fixed Assets*		3,000
		6,177	*Current Assets*		
			Cash in hand .	50	
Current Liabilities			Cash at bank .	227	
Sundry Creditors .	13,000		Debtors . .	14,900	
Suppliers Ltd. .	2,000		Stocks . . .	3,000	
Total Current			*Total Current*		
Liabilities .		15,000	*Assets* . .		18,177
		£21,177			£21,177

THE FINAL ACCOUNTS

A. THE OBJECTS OF FINAL ACCOUNTS

1. General considerations

The final accounts which were drawn up at the end of the year for the boot repairer's business considered in Chapter II were a Profit and Loss Account and a Balance Sheet. It should be noted that a Balance Sheet as distinct from a Profit and Loss Account does not form part of the double-entry system but is a statement compiled from the capital accounts included in that system. The objects of the final accounts may be simply expressed as: (a) to show the profit or loss for the period, and (b) to show the financial position at the end of the period.

These objects require, however, some further examination. The statement of profit or loss which normal revenue accounts disclose conveys little information as to the operating efficiency during a past period, and provides no guide to the future. It is necessary for the accounts to show clearly and simply the main headings of income and expenditure which gave rise to the profit or loss, and to compare these figures with some independent standard.

So far as the Balance Sheet is concerned the expression "financial position" which is nowadays applied to this statement is a rather vague term capable of various interpretations. It was probably introduced into accountancy terminology to remove any idea that a Balance Sheet purported to show the current value of the undertaking or its assets, especially in a period of changing money values. The problems involved in this perplexing subject are matters of recurring controversy which will be discussed later.

A Balance Sheet shows the assets and liabilities of the business at the values entered in the accounts. Some of the values may, however, bear little relation to the current values of the assets concerned at the date of the Balance Sheet whether such current values be interpreted as the amount of money the assets would fetch if sold in the open market or as the amount required to replace them at current prices. A building bought in, say, 1938 may be worth two and a half times as much in terms of monetary values twenty years later. Furthermore, the net total of real assets less liabilities as shown in the accounts does not necessarily represent the saleable value of the business, since many other factors are involved.

2. The uses of the Balance Sheet

In spite of these qualifications the Balance Sheet remains a valuable source of information to management and outside interests for two reasons in particular. It provides an informative picture of available funds, by comparing current assets with current liabilities, particularly the more liquid aspects of these items. The second main use of the Balance Sheet is for the purpose of computing net worth, net capital or capital employed, as it is variously described.

Whilst net capital as shown in a Balance Sheet may not altogether represent values in terms of current money, at least it will form a basis for comparison year by year, provided the accounts have been compiled on consistent principles. Net capital is especially valuable as a basis for calculating percentage profitability, again, not necessarily an exact figure but one of which the trend may be watched from period to period.

One may thus venture to suggest that the principal significance of the modern Balance Sheet is: (a) to show the current financial position in terms of available funds, and (b) to provide a picture of net capital.

Whilst these two uses of the Balance Sheet are clearly of great importance, both for domestic uses within a company and for interested parties outside a company, it is widely appreciated that a single Balance Sheet, even though drawn up to a recent date, is of limited use as a source of information. A Balance Sheet may be likened to a snapshot photograph of the finances of an enterprise at a particular point of time. Under modern economic conditions the financial position of any undertaking may be radically altered within a few months as a result of external changes in, say, the availability of credit, demand for the goods or services supplied, and in the cost of the materials required to produce the goods or services.

Thus a true view of a company's finances can be seen only by considering trends of events as shown by a succession of Balance Sheets, and future prospects of the enterprise and intentions of the management.

The Eighth Schedule of the Companies Act 1948 provides that comparative figures for the previous year shall be shown on every Balance Sheet to which the Act applies, thus giving some legislative authority to the principle of dynamic accounting. Any searching investigation into a company's finances will need, however, amongst other information, detailed consideration of the trends shown by considerably more than two years' results. For the domestic control of the finances by the directors and the chief executives it will, in addition, be essential for Balance Sheets (or similar documents) to be prepared at monthly or other frequent intervals, and be available soon after the end of each period.

Techniques for relating accounting results to future prospects and intentions is a subject for special study which will be considered later.

B. DRAWING UP THE FINAL ACCOUNTS

1. General considerations

The Profit and Loss Account shows for a particular period of time either: (a) the surplus which represents, until it is distributed to the owners, the amount by which capital has been increased as a result of the operations over the period: or (b) the loss, which represents a depletion of capital. Thus all accounting for past results tends towards a final objective of showing the capital of a business at a certain date, and this picture of capital is expressed in the Balance Sheet. The Balance Sheet records, therefore, the balances on all the capital accounts, i.e. the assets and liabilities after the profit for the period has been accounted for, and (the other aspect of the double entry) the way in which this capital has been allocated to funds, e.g. to owner's capital and reserve funds.

Expressed very briefly, the method of drawing up the final accounts is to transfer all the balances on the revenue accounts to a summary account such as a Profit and Loss Account, the balance of which is in turn either transferred to capital accounts such as reserve accounts, or distributed to the proprietors. The Balance Sheet is compiled from the remaining accounts, which for this purpose are called "capital accounts", including any balance left in the Profit and Loss Account. The balances on the "capital accounts" are not transferred to the Balance Sheet in the accounting system, but are carried foward to the next period. Thus, the Balance Sheet is not an account forming part of the double-entry system,

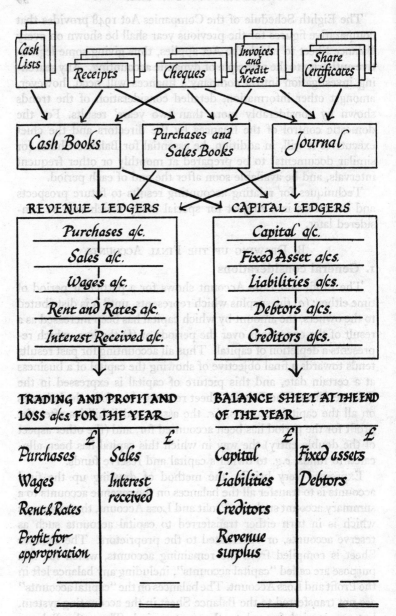

FIG. I

but is merely a record of the balances which remain in that system after the Profit and Loss Account has been compiled.

The life of the business

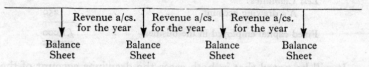

A simple form of balance sheet, showing the liabilities of the *business* (not necessarily of the proprietor) on the left, and the assets on the right, would appear as follows:

A. BOOT AND SHOE REPAIRER
Balance sheet as at the 31st December 19....

	£		£
A. Fixed capital . . .	750	Tools	150
A. Drawings account . .	250	Cash	1,100
B. Loan account . . .	250		
	£1,250		£1,250

This is the conventional form of Balance Sheet. A's fixed capital in the business might be more clearly shown by a statement in the following form:

Assets:	£
Tools	150
Cash	1,100
Total assets	£1,250
Less Liabilities:	
Loan by B	250
A's drawing account . .	250
Total liabilities . . .	£500
A's fixed capital	£750

If it is desired to show the capital employed in the business, as distinct from that of the proprietor, and assuming that the loan from B is not subject to withdrawal at short notice, the position might be expressed as follows:

Assets:						£
Tools	.	.	.	.	.	150
Cash	.	.	.	.	.	1,100
Total assets .		.	.	.	.	£1,250
Less Liabilities:						
A's drawing account			.	.	.	250
Fixed capital employed in the business				.		£1,000

It will be noted that in both cases the drawings account of the proprietor is treated as a liability, for this is an amount which represents a debt by the business to the proprietor and could have been drawn out. The same consideration applies to the amount recommended or appropriated for dividend in a limited company, including a dividend-equalisation reserve. Revenue reserves of limited companies are also, strictly speaking, available for distribution to the shareholders, and sometimes are so distributed, but in many large companies the revenue reserves are maintained and increased year by year, so that they may be considered as forming a part of the capital of the concern. Many companies, by the issue of bonus shares, convert reserves into fixed capital.

2. Subdivision of the revenue accounts

(a) *The principal forms of revenue accounts*

The revenue accounts, whose purpose is eventually to show the profit or loss for a period, and the way in which the profit or loss is disposed of, are normally subdivided where necessary as follows:

Manufacturing Account
Trading Account
Profit and Loss Account
Appropriation Account

Variants of these conventional headings are used for particular purposes and for particular types of organisations. Thus, Assurance Companies prepare Revenue Accounts for each main class of business; non-profit-making organisations prepare Income and Expenditure Accounts; Operating Statements are prepared, not necessarily for publication, by many industrial organisations to cover various processes or subdivisions of the main work of the concern.

(b) *The Manufacturing Account*

(i) *The objects of the account.* As the term implies, a Manufacturing Account is prepared by a producing organisation, and the object of the account is to show: (*a* the total costs of production during the period, and (*b*) the manufacturing cost of the finished output which is put into Finished Goods Store. The account is therefore essentially one which deals with workshop costs and not with questions of profitability.

In some companies, however, and for control purposes only, the Manufacturing Account is credited with a notional price for the finished output, either based on standard or assessed costs of the product or costs plus a small percentage. If standard costs are used for the purpose of pricing output and the Manufacturing Account shows a loss, that loss will indicate that costs are above the standard and merit investigation. In the same way, if the output is priced at costs plus, say, 5%, and the Manufacturing Account shows a notional profit of less than 5%, there is a presumption that some inefficiency is occurring. The notional manufacturing profit or loss which results from the use of this device will alter the profit which would otherwise have been shown in the Trading and Profit and Loss Accounts and must therefore be credited or debited, as the case may be, to one or other of those accounts. If this were not done the accounts would not balance nor would the true profit so far as the owners (*e.g.* shareholders) were concerned appear in the accounts.

The specimen, and simplified, Manufacturing Account set out on page 65 shows costs divided into the direct and indirect (overhead) categories.

Direct costs are those, such as direct labour (*e.g.* hourly wages) and direct material, which can be allocated to the different products with reasonable accuracy and convenience. Indirect costs are those which can only be applied to the products by a more or less arbitrary process of apportionment or on a percentage basis. This subject is dealt with in more detail in the subsequent chapters on costing.

It is desirable to bear in mind at this point that for control purposes it is often useful to group not only manufacturing expenses but also those of selling and administration into the variable and fixed classifications. Variable costs are those which, in theory at least, move in direct relation to movements in the volume of output. The direct costs would normally be of a variable nature, but a large element of the indirect costs or overheads will also vary in relation to output, *e.g.* indirect hourly wages, indirect material and power for the machines. Fixed costs are those which do not vary in relation to output except over long periods or as a consequence of substantial changes in the volume of output. The division between fixed and variable costs differs with the type of business concerned, but typical examples of fixed costs are rent, rates and other building occupation expenses, depreciation of machinery (if on the basis of a fixed rate per annum) and a substantial proportion of the works administration expense. Sometimes a third classification of semi-variable expenses is used, and this group will include the costs which vary in relation to output but not in direct proportion. The classification of expense into the variable and fixed elements is useful in assessing movements in the figures as between one period and another, and has a special application in Marginal Costing, which is discussed in Chapter X. It is, however, rather an arbitrary classification in the case of some items of expense, and it depends to a large extent on the time period envisaged.

The manufacturing account is rarely included in the published accounts of limited companies, and it is not mentioned in the Companies Act. It is therefore drawn up solely for the purpose of providing information to the management.

(ii) *The application of the Manufacturing Account for costing purposes.* If an industrial unit produces only one uniform product, then obviously the average factory or direct cost of producing that product can be ascertained by the simple process of dividing the total factory cost as shown in the Manufacturing Account by the number of articles produced during the period.

In this way a Manufacturing Account can be used as a basis for finding the unit cost of past production, for pricing purposes and for estimating the probable cost of future production. To the direct or factory cost so calculated it will be necessary to add a further sum to cover the remaining costs, mostly overheads or indirect costs, of the concern.

The usefulness of ascertaining past costs and estimating future costs by this method is, however, limited by: (*a*) the fact that the Manufacturing Account refers to past conditions and that in the future considerable changes may occur in cost, the volume of production, the nature of the production and the application of over-heads; and (b) the unlikelihood of one factory producing a single uniform product which is unchanging year by year.

These drawbacks may be partly lessened if the account is regularly drawn up for a short period, say at monthly intervals, and made available soon after the end of each period. Where the size or nature of the products can be grouped under a few headings, it may be possible to subdivide the Manufacturing Account so as to produce a unit cost for each group; or if such a procedure is impracticable some useful information may be derived from a Manufacturing Account which covers a diversity of products by using a unit of cost such as a man-hour, machine-hour or quantitative measurement which governs the cost of all types of products. In a jobbing works, for instance, it is often quite impracticable to attempt to find the cost of a single article for sale. But in all cases there will remain the problem of selecting the correct rate and method of applying overheads to the unit chosen to arrive at total cost.

Whilst periodic manufacturing accounts can be of great assistance in ascertaining the unit costs of a small business where an elaborate costing system is not justified, a more scientific method of ascertaining and controlling unit costs will be required in any substantial concern.

The manufacturing account is used by top management in a large producing unit as a broad picture of the cost of the factory, and by the cost accountant as a means of verifying the accuracy of predetermined unit costs.

(iii) *The form of the account.* The following account shows in summary form the headings of a manufacturing account suitable for a producing business:

MANUFACTURING ACCOUNT
for the (period) ending ....

	£	£	£
Raw materials:			
Opening stocks		1,000	
Add Purchases		500	
		1,500	
Less Stock at end		900	
Direct materials consumed		600	
Direct labour		450	
Direct expenses		100	
Total direct costs			1,150

			£	£	£
	Brought forward				1,150
Indirect materials:					
Opening stocks	. . . . . .	.	.	350	
Add Purchases	. . . . .	.	.	250	
				600	
Less Stock at end	. . . .	.	.	400	
Indirect material consumed	. . .	.	.	200	
Indirect labour	. . . .	.	.	200	
Indirect expenses	. . . .	.	.	300	
Total indirect costs	. . . .	.	.		700
Cost of production for the period	. . .	.			1,850
Change in work in progress:					
At beginning of period	. . . .	.	.	2,050	
At end of period	. . . .	.	.	1,900	
					150
Cost of finished goods, transferred to Trading Account	.				£2,000

The indirect expenses included in the above account would include the cost of works services, depreciation, building occupation costs and works administration. The total may also take into account a credit for sales of scrap.

With the object of setting out the information in the most readable and logical form the above account has been presented as a narrative leading to a definite conclusion. In the double-entry system the Manufacturing Account is compiled by means of transfers from the revenue accounts concerned and will appear as follows:

MANUFACTURING ACCOUNT

	£		£
Work in progress . .	2,050	Work in progress at end .	1,900
Direct raw-material stocks .	1,000	Direct material stocks at end .	900
Indirect material stocks .	350	Indirect material stocks at end	400
Labour, direct . . .	450	Cost of finished goods c/d. to	
Labour, indirect .	200	Trading Account . .	2,000
Direct expenses . .	100		
Indirect expenses. .	300		
Direct material purchases .	500		
Indirect material purchases .	250		
	£5,200		£5,200

(c) *The Trading Account*

(i) *The objects of the account.* The Trading Account is designed to show the gross profit on trading for the period covered. In some cases the Manufacturing Account is amalgamated with the Trading Account, and in others the Trading Account is amalgamated with the Profit and Loss Account.

Various forms of Trading Accounts will be met with, each designed to suit the needs of a particular organisation and its management.

TRADING ACCOUNT **for the (period) ended . . . .**

	£	£			£	£
Stock of finished goods at beginning . .		6,000	Sales . .	. 15,000		
Add: finished output for the period (from Manuf. a/c) .		2,050	*Less:* returns from customers	500		14,500
		8,050				
Less: stock at end of period .		4,500				
Cost of materials sold . .		3,550				
Selling and distribution expenses		1,950				
Gross Profit c/d to Profit and Loss a/c . . .		9,000				
		£14,500				£14,500

Generally speaking, it seems desirable that a Trading Account should show only: (*a*) the direct or factory cost of the goods produced for sale (this item is transferred from a Manufacturing Account in a producing business, or in a purely trading concern represents the cost of purchasing the goods to be sold); (*b*) the expenses of trading, *i.e.* those expenses which vary more or less directly with the selling effort; and (*c*) the value of sales. The inclusion of these items shows the gross profit before deducting establishment expenses of the organisation.

The problem in compiling a Trading Account following such principles is to decide which expenses vary with the selling effort as distinct from the manufacturing effort and which expenses represent general overheads of the organisation as a whole.

A simple form of conventional Trading Account is given on p. 67. The selling expenses included in this account would embrace salaries, commission and expenses of sales staff, and variable publicity costs; and the distribution expenses would cover packaging, warehousing and transport.

(d) *The Profit and Loss and Appropriation Account*

(i) *The purpose of the Profit and Loss Account.* The Profit and Loss Account is intended to show the final surplus available for appropriation, *i.e.* either for distribution to the proprietors or allocation to a reserve account.

The account must therefore contain all the remaining expenditure incurred over the period covered other than that which has been charged to the Manufacturing and Trading Accounts. Since the latter accounts normally show expenditure which varies in some relation to output and sales, the costs which appear in the Profit and Loss Account comprise administrative costs of the organisation.

Exceptional costs which do not form part of the normal overheads of the business are also shown in the Profit and Loss Account, and it is clearly desirable that such costs should be separated from those which are recurrent. Examples of such costs not strictly applicable to the normal operations of the business are: losses on exchange, losses on the sale of investments or fixed assets and damages payable in legal actions.

The costs which are shown in a Profit and Loss Account should be grouped, with sub-totals, under rational headings so that the trends shown by a succession of accounts may be followed more easily.

Income or sales from trading normally appear in the Trading Account, but most businesses receive miscellaneous income, such as interest on investments, profit on sales of capital assets, credits attributable to the operations of a prior period or are otherwise not directly attributable to current trading operations.

Taxation has been regarded for many years as an appropriation of profit, and as such is properly entered in the Appropriation Account, and not in the Profit and Loss Account, which is prepared for the purpose of showing the profit available for appropriation.

The relation between profit as interpreted for tax purposes and profit arrived at by the application of normal accounting principles is, however, nowadays often obscure. The tax provision made in the Profit and Loss Account will represent an estimate of the tax payable on the profits of the period and will be credited to a Tax account.

The Appropriation Account for accounting purposes may be considered as a capital account, since the balance forms part of the variable capital of the business and is included amongst the other liability balances in the Balance Sheet.

(ii) *Profit and loss under the Companies Act.* So far as limited companies are concerned, certain items of specific information are required to be shown in the Profit and Loss Account in conformity with the provisions of the Companies Acts 1948 and 1967. Some of the items required, such as auditor's fees, are often insignificant compared with the other outgoings of a company. Furthermore, there is an undoubted tendency for many companies, no doubt for good reasons, to regard the provisions of the Companies Acts as the maximum rather than the minimum information to be shown, with the result that the Profit and Loss Accounts prepared for publication are of limited use to the management either in measuring the efficiency of an undertaking or in controlling its affairs. In short, the final accounts prepared for internal uses are in many respects much more informative than those prepared in accordance with the Companies Acts or similar legislation applicable to other corporate bodies.

(iii) *The Appropriation Account.* The Appropriation Account is often treated as part of the Profit and Loss Account, although it serves the distinct purpose of showing how the profit or loss resulting from the operations of the period has been allocated. It is best, therefore, treated as a separate account to which will be transferred the balance of final profit obtained from the Profit and Loss Account.

The allocations or appropriation of profit normally shown in this account may be divided into the following four headings: (*a*) appropriations free for withdrawal by the proprietors, *e.g.* allocations to the drawings or current accounts of partners, and allocations to the dividend accounts of shareholders; (*b*) allocations to revenue reserves for strengthening the capital. Examples would be reserves for research and development, dividend equalisation reserves, reserves for possible losses on exchange. Revenue reserves may, even if not specifically earmarked for such a purpose, be distributed as dividends or other shares of profit to the proprietors; (c) capital reserves, *i.e.* those which may not be distributed to the proprietors, except on a winding-up of the business. Allocations are made to capital reserves from share premiums, capital profits and surpluses on the revaluation of fixed assets; (d) the balance carried forward to the next period of account. Such a balance is more strictly a revenue reserve available for distribution to the proprietors or other allocation at the end of the next period of account.

A conventional Profit and Loss Account and Appropriation Account, produced for internal management and NOT to satisfy the provisions of the Companies Act, is shown below.

PROFIT AND LOSS ACCOUNT for the (period) ended . . . . . .

	£		£
Administrative expenses .	6,850	Gross profit for the year from	
Exchange losses . . .	650	Trading Account . .	9,000
Royalties and interest pay-		Investment income . .	500
able	2,350	Profit on sale of fixed assets.	1,200
Pretax profit c/d . .	850		
	£10,700		£10,700
Provision for tax on the profit		Pretax profit b/d . .	850
for the period . . .	400		
Profit after tax c/d . .	450		
	£850		£850
Dividend recommended .	250	Profit after tax b/d . .	450
Transfer to General Reserve	300	Profit unappropriated from	
Balance of unappropriated		previous period . .	200
profit carried forward .	100		
	£650		£650

The administrative expenses shown in the Profit and Loss Account above would include salaries and expenses of administrative staff, executives and directors, and costs of space, building services, professional fees, depreciation, postage, stationery and other expenses not already charged in the Manufacturing or Trading Accounts.

(e) *The summarised revenue account*

The preceding sections have dealt with the conventional grouping of the revenue accounts which lead to the final profit. In a complex business the grouping of results into Manufacturing, Trading and Profit and Loss Accounts can be somewhat arbitrary. For the purpose of presenting the results for a particular period in a concise and logical form to top management all these accounts may be conveniently amalgamated into one account.

Thus, all the items may be fitted into a statement presented on the lines as set out on the next page.

The information to be derived from such a statement may be conveniently compared with budgeted expectations for the period and with past results; the figures may be shown with advantage as percentages of total cost or turnover, these percentages again compared with expectations or past results.

It is only by means of a logical, consistently applied, grouping of results that operating results may be effectively compared with either assessed standards or the past. It is also essential that exceptional items not related to the work or period under consideration or not within the control of the enterprise, should be separated from the working results.

C. Adjustments for Final Accounts

1. General considerations

The preceding sections of this chapter have aimed to give a broad picture of the objects of drawing up the so-called final accounts, and have indicated how a rationally organised accounting system can facilitate the preparation of final revenue accounts and Balance Sheets.

With the broad picture in mind, consideration may now be given to some of the adjustments or closing entries which must be made by the accountant in order that the final accounts may present the truest possible view of the events of the period and of the financial position at the end of the period. Only by understanding the mechanics of accounting can a manager thoroughly appreciate the story told by the figures.

It should be borne in mind that the final accounts now under consideration may either take the form of a simple Profit and Loss

Account and Balance Sheet for a small business, or may consist of numerous statements dealing with different aspects of the affairs and operations of a large concern. Further, the expression "final accounts" refers not only to the statements prepared at the year end but also to interim accounts which may be prepared half-yearly, quarterly or monthly according to the needs of the business and of its management. Rarely, if ever, is it sufficient for control purposes to prepare final accounts at yearly intervals only.

PROFIT AND LOSS ACCOUNT

for the period ....

	£	£
SALES		1,000,000
Less Cost of sales		475,000
GROSS PROFIT		525,000
Less Expenses:		
Selling and distribution	120,000	
Administration	130,000	
		250,000
OPERATING PROFIT		275,000
Add/deduct financial and exceptional charges, non-trading income, capital profits and capital losses . .		40,000
PRETAX PROFIT		235,000
Tax provision		127,000
NET PROFIT		£108,000

The adjustments which will be considered in the following sections comprise:

Outstandings   Provisions
Accruals   Reserves
Prepayments   Valuations

Strictly speaking the above list covers all the adjustments required except for depreciation, which is considered in a subsequent chapter. It is desirable for actual entries to be made in the accounts; and at the year's end the auditors will insist on such adjustments being made. In some cases, however, interim accounts may be prepared by the aid of schedules listing the adjustments which are not in fact entered in the accounts.

2. Outstandings

(a) *Outstanding charges*

At the balancing date there are in most concerns a number of charges incurred but not entered in the books. Thus, if the date to which accounts are being drawn up is, say, 31st December, it is unlikely that invoices for supplies received on that day—perhaps for some days previously—have been entered in the accounts. Until, therefore, such charges are entered the accounts will understate: (*a*) liabilities, and (*b*) either expenditure on revenue account or (where fixed assets have been delivered) expenditure on capital account. Outstanding invoices for goods delivered or services rendered by the date of balancing must therefore be listed and entered in the accounts as adjusting entries.

(b) *Outstanding credits*

Similarly, goods despatched, representing sales to customers, or services rendered up to the balancing period must be brought into the accounts by debiting debtors and crediting the appropriate income accounts.

(c) *Goods in transit*

It may be noted, in passing, that whilst Company A will credit its sales account with goods despatched to Company B on, say, 31st December, Company B (which will not receive such goods until, at earliest, 1st January), will not charge the cost of such goods in its accounts until the following period of account.

The point is of particular importance in drawing up a consolidated statement of the affairs of a group of companies where sales are made between members of the group. Of wider social interest is the fact that any statistical analysis of total company results for a particular period or at a particular point of time is likely to be inaccurate to the extent that it ignores the cost of goods in transit at that point of time.

(d) *Book-keeping entries*

The most efficient method of dealing with outstandings in the books is to open two or more special accounts for the purpose, usually known as "Debtors Suspense Accounts" and "Creditors Suspense Accounts".

Example

Company A has £1,000 of invoices outstanding at 31st December for raw material already supplied to it; and has despatched £500 of goods sold to customers but not yet entered in the accounts. The following entries will be made (after passing them through the Journal as the necessary subsidiary book or book of first entry):

Capital accounts

CREDITORS SUSPENSE ACCOUNT

	Raw material . . . £1,000	

DEBTORS SUSPENSE ACCOUNT

Sales £500	

Revenue accounts

RAW MATERIAL ACCOUNT

Creditors suspense . . £1,000	

SALES ACCOUNT

	Debtors suspense . . £500

The entries must be made before transferring the balances on the Materials and Sales Accounts to the Trading Account or such other final revenue account as may be used.

The balances shown on the two suspense accounts are included in the total of debtors and creditors to be shown in the Balance Sheet, and in the accounting system the balances on the suspense accounts are carried forward to the new period.

Early in the new period, probably, in the instance cited, some time in January, entries recording the purchase of £1,000 and the sale of £500 appear in the Sales and Purchases Day Books in the normal course. From the day books the entries are posted to the expenditure and sales accounts and to the Debtors and Creditors Account. A further Journal entry is therefore made at the beginning of the new period taking the entries out of the temporary Debtors and Creditors Accounts (the suspense accounts) and transferring these entries to the credit or debit of the normal Creditors or Debtors Accounts, thus nullifying the entries which are made from the day books.

Example

CREDITORS SUSPENSE ACCOUNT

		£			£
Dec. 31	Balance c/d . .	1,000	Dec. 31	Raw material a/c .	1,000
Jan. 1	Creditors account .	1,000	Jan. 1	Balance c/d . .	1,000

RAW MATERIAL ACCOUNT

		£			£
Jan. 10	Raw material (per Purchase Day Book)	1,000	Jan. 1	Creditors Susp. Account . . .	1,000

DEBTORS SUSPENSE ACCOUNT

		£			£
Dec. 31	Sales . . .	500	Dec. 31	Balance c/d . .	500
Jan. 1	Balance c/d . .	500	Jan. 1	Debtors account .	500

SALES ACCOUNT

		£			£
Jan. 1	Debtors Suspense Account . . .	500	Jan. 10	Sales . . .	500

The entries may appear over-simplified in the above example, and in any substantial concern numerous other entries will appear in the accounts represented. For the purpose of the example it has been assumed that the "Creditors" and "Debtors" Accounts are analysed by subsidiary systems into accounts for each supplier and sales customer.

The adjusting entries, indicated above, can be confined to the main or control ledger, and need not affect the subsidiary debtors or creditors ledgers.

3. Accruals

(a) *Accrued expenditure*

Invoices received from suppliers represent accrued expenditure in one sense of the term, but the expression is more strictly used to cover expenditure accrued but not yet evidenced by a formal invoice or bill from the creditor.

If accounts are made up to 31st December and rent payable quarterly has not been paid for the quarter ending on 31st December, clearly one quarter's rent has accrued and must be included in the account: (*a*) in the capital section of the accounting system as a liability, and (b) in the revenue accounts (expenditure division) as a charge.

Even where actual payment is not due to be made, expenditure may have accrued. If interest on a loan is payable annually on Lady Day, 25th March, annual accounts drawn up to 31st December must include approximately nine months' proportion of annual interest which is deemed to accrue from day to day and apportionable in respect of time accordingly (Apportionment Act 1870). Similarly, adjustments are required for such items as rates, fixed interest due on loans, and proportions of wages and salaries not yet paid.

The entries to be made in the accounts in respect of accruals follow precisely the same procedure as for outstandings, using the Suspense Creditors and Suspense Debtors Accounts or separate suspense accounts as may be convenient.

(b) *Accrued income*

Accrued income covers the appropriate proportion of income receivable but not paid and probably not evidenced by a bill or invoice. The kind of income to be included in this category includes for example, rents, interest and commission receivable. In this connection, however, it is necessary to point out that a sound accounting principle derived from experience is that whilst accrued expenditure must always be recorded as a charge and a liability in the accounts, accrued income must be reviewed in the light of the possibility that it may not be received. Thus, where a tenant was already in default with past rent and there was no guarantee that current rent would be forthcoming it would be incorrect to credit the rent account or the total of debtors with the rent due.

4. Prepayments

Prepayments cover payments received from debtors or payments made to creditors before due date.

Thus, if rent is paid for three months in advance on 31st December, the date to which accounts were made up, it is necessary to remove the charge of three months rent from the Rent Payable Account and to show the amount paid in advance as an asset or debtor of the business. Telephone rental and insurance premiums are other common examples of charges which are paid in advance.

Conversely, the business may have received a periodic payment in advance of the due date, and in such a case the credit should be removed from the income account and also be shown as a liability of the business.

In a small business prepayments of both kinds may be included in the Suspense Creditors and Suspense Debtors Accounts mentioned above, provided that the items so included are clearly set out in a schedule to the accounts. In any accounting system where the adjustments are numerous it will be found convenient to open separate suspense accounts for prepayments. In many large concerns prepayments are shown as separate items in the Balance Sheet.

The accounting entries are indicated by the following example:

Example

Company A makes up annual accounts at 31st December and at that date it has paid in advance £50 for rent of telephones and £10 for insurance premiums. It has received £25 rent in advance.

PREPAYMENT DEBTORS ACCOUNT

		£			£
Dec. 31	Insurance account .	10	Dec. 31	Balance c/d . .	60
,, 31	Telephone account .	50			
		——			——
		£60			£60
Jan. 1	Balance b/d . .	60	Jan. 1	Insurance account .	10
			,, 1	Telephone account .	50

PREPAYMENT CREDITORS ACCOUNT

		£			£
Dec. 31	Balance c/d . .	25	Dec. 31	Rent receivable account	25
Jan. 1	Rent receivable account	25	Jan. 1	Balance c/d . .	25

5. Provisions

The Companies Act 1948, 8th Schedule, Part IV, Article 27, defines a provision as: "Any amount written off or retained by way of providing for depreciation, renewals or diminution in value of assets or retained by way of providing for any known liability of which the amount cannot be determined with substantial accuracy."

It will be noted that a provision is a charge against profits, but as distinct from a charge outstanding for payment or an accrued charge of which the precise amount can be ascertained, a provision is a charge of which the amount has to be estimated.

Thus, if a firm or a company has accepted responsibility in an action for damages, pending whilst the accounts are being made up, the amount of damages which will be payable must be estimated and included as a charge in the revenue accounts and as a liability in the capital accounts.

Similarly, where a loss is anticipated under a contract for work in progress at the date of drawing up the accounts, an estimate of the amount of the loss must be made and included in the accounts. In such a case, whilst all the anticipated loss may not be attributable to operations in the period under review, it is considered good accounting and prudent business practice to allow for the whole of the loss in such accounts. This follows the established accounting principle that anticipated losses must be accounted for but anticipated profits should not be shown in the accounts until such profits are realised. Provisions for possible bad debts are frequently required, and should always be made either as a result of detailed examination of each account or as a percentage of debtors, where any doubt exists as to the value of the debts.

Provisions, where material, should be shown separately in the Balance Sheet, and such disclosure is obligatory for Balance Sheets drawn up in compliance with the Companies Act 1948. It will therefore be necessary for at least one separate "Provisions" account to be opened.

Example

Company A at 31st December, when it makes up its accounts, has discharged as redundant an executive who has two years of his contract to run. Pending the result of negotiations, it is decided that a sum of £2,000 shall be provided to meet payments to the executive for compensation for loss of office.

The book-keeping entries are as follows:

PROVISIONS ACCOUNT

	Profit and loss account . £2,000

PROFIT AND LOSS ACCOUNT

Provision for compensation . £2,000	

The balance of the Provisions Account is carried forward to the next period and is shown separately as a current liability in the Balance Sheet.

If during the following period the sum finally agreed to be paid to the retiring executive is £1,500, the balance of £500, representing the provision not required, may be dealt with in any of the following ways:

(a) Credit back to the Profit and Loss Account, thus becoming available for appropriation in the new period.

(b) Transferred to a reserve account.

(c) Retained in the Provisions Account to meet some further specific commitment which has arisen and of which the precise amount cannot be ascertained with reasonable accuracy.

The amount not required should not be left in the Provisions Account as a kind of indefinite reserve against contingencies. The Provisions Account should at all times contain exclusively estimated charges for specific commitments.

6. Reserves

Reserves are usually divisible into two kinds—specific and general reserves. These again may be classified as either revenue reserves or capital reserves.

An essential point to note is that a reserve is not a charge to be deducted before arriving at the profit for the period under review, but it is an appropriation of profit, and a reserve account represents the fund to which part of the profits has been allocated. The reserve account will accordingly be credited as a result of a debit to the Appropriation Account, not to the Profit and Loss Account or other revenue account.

Whilst, therefore, in a broad sense all allocations to reserve represent additions to capital, some of such allocations are intended to meet commitments which are expected to arise in the future, and some are made for the purpose of permanently increasing the capital of the concern. The former are revenue reserves and the latter capital reserves.

Examples of revenue reserves are: reserves for research, development, to replace fixed assets beyond the amount of depreciation charged in the accounts, to cover possible future losses on exchange, to equalise dividends.

The foregoing are specific reserves. A tendency has been observed for large industrial companies to replace a number of specific reserves by one bulk account, known simply as the "General Reserve".

In a limited company the revenue reserves may, if necessary, be credited to the Profit and Loss a/c. In some companies fortunes may fluctuate considerably year by year, and it is considered desirable to prevent dividends fluctuating in like manner. In such cases a dividend-equalisation fund is set up, so that by this means shareholders have a reasonably clear indication of the funds which have been specifically allocated for the payment of dividend on their capital.

The necessity for distinguishing between capital which is held to earn income and the income itself has been emphasised in the early chapters of this book.

Capital reserves are such as are specifically allocated to the fixed capital of the concern and are not therefore available for distribution as dividends, except in a winding-up when the concern is dissolved.

It is desirable that profits arising out of transactions on capital account should be placed to a capital reserve. Such profits will include profits on the sale of fixed assets, sales of investments, etc. Premiums received on the issue of shares must be credited to a capital reserve in accordance with the provisions of the Companies Act 1948.

7. Valuation of stock

Valuations of stock are made for two main purposes: one, to find the value of the asset represented by stock for entry in the Balance Sheet as at the date to which the accounts are drawn up; the other, to find the cost of stock used during the period concerned.

(a) *Valuations for Balance Sheet purposes*

Stocks in the sense used here may cover stocks of raw materials, loose tools, bought-out goods, finished parts, partly made goods and work in progress.

So far as raw materials are concerned, the generally accepted method of valuing stock is on the basis of cost or market value, whichever is the lower. Neither cost nor net realisable value is in all cases easy to ascertain, and numerous problems, discussed in a later chapter, arise with regard to valuations. Whatever may be the precise method of valuation adopted, the essential principle of consistency must be emphasised, so that the same method must be used at the end of each period.

The problem of valuing bought-out goods, including loose tools, is usually much more simple of solution, since it is usually practicable to find the price paid for each individual item.

Where, however, articles have been fabricated by the business both the ascertainment of cost and market price involve the use of certain conventions.

Where finished goods have been made and are ready for sale the market price will usually be higher than the cost. The latter figure should therefore be used, otherwise the profit included in the market price will have been anticipated.

In a business where no form of unit costing is undertaken the value of finished goods can be calculated by deducting average or estimated profit from the market price. This method may be dangerous in unskilled hands, but with proper safeguards against inaccuracy is a quick and economical aid to drawing up interim accounts without undertaking the work, expense and possible delays of a complete stock-taking.

Where unit costs are available, however, the direct or variable costs of labour, material and direct expenses may be applied to the stock of finished and partly finished goods.

The cost of production does not, however, rest with direct or variable costs. It is usually considered proper to add at least a proportion of the overheads of the concern. The overheads must in the long run be covered by the sales if the business is to continue. Furthermore, it is pertinent to mention that in calculating profits for income-tax purposes the value of stocks should include overheads, although the method of accounting for tax may well be different from those shown in accounts.

In view of the fact that the amount of fixed costs applicable to each sale depends on the volume of turnover in a particular period, it is usually considered unwise in valuing stocks to add to variable costs any other overheads than those relating to the factory. Thus, strictly semi-variable costs, such as indirect wages, material and factory indirect expenses, may be apportioned to products for the purpose of valuing stocks of finished goods and work in progress. Many companies also include in the calculation of the works overhead rate applied to products the fixed overheads applicable to the manufacturing function, but it is desirable that the amount of fixed overheads thus applied to product costs shall be at a standard rate based on the achievement of a reasonable level of activity.

It is necessary to note that considerable variations in the methods of valuing such stocks exist in practice. The principle of consistency must, however, be emphasised again.

(b) *Valuation for revenue accounts*

The valuation of stocks for use in the revenue accounts is necessary for the purpose of finding the cost of goods or material sold in the period covered. The final revenue accounts should be charged only with the material actually used in the production of the period, whatever may be the value of purchases.

Again, the goods sold during the period may have been produced partly in the previous period; some of the goods used in the production of the current period may not be sold until a future period. In the Manufacturing Account the cost of raw material or bought-out parts used in manufacture will be ascertained in the following manner:

	£
Stock of raw material or bought-out parts at the beginning	5,000
Add Purchases during the period	10,000
Material or bought-out parts available	£15,000
Less Stock at end	7,000
Material or bought-out parts used	£8,000

The cost of material used in production forms part of the cost of production for the period. The cost of production includes the cost of completed articles and also the cost of partly finished goods or work in progress. The value of unfinished work must therefore be deducted from the cost of production for the purpose of arriving at the cost of completed production for sale.

Part of the cost of completed production may consist of work done and costs incurred in the previous period of account, and such amount will be represented by the work in progress or stock of unfinished goods which existed at the beginning of the account period. This opening figure of stocks of work in progress must therefore be added to the current cost of production. Reference should be made to the section headed "Manufacturing Account" for an example of the procedure.

Having in this way arrived at the cost of completed production during the period (the sum to be credited to the Manufacturing Account and debited to the Trading Account) there remains the question of finding the cost of sales; for profit consists of the difference between sales and their cost.

To the cost of completed production transferred to the Trading Account from the Manufacturing Account there must be added the stock of finished goods not sold at the end of the previous period. Similarly, the stock of completed goods not sold at the end of the period under review must be deducted from the total of costs now appearing in the Trading Account.

The book-keeping entries required for dealing with all these adjustments may be expressed by means of the following Journal entries:

		£	£
(a)	*Stock at the beginning of the period*		
	Revenue Account	100	
	Stock Account		100
	Being opening stock trfd to *Mfg/Trading/P. and L.* Account .		
(b)	*Stock at end of period*		
	Stock Account	50	
	Revenue Account		50
	Being closing stock trfd to *Mfg/Trading/P. and L. Account* .		

8. Further matters for final accounts

(a) *Contingent liabilities*

Contingent liabilities are those which may become real liabilities on the happening of some specified event. Thus, if a business guaranteed the repayment of a loan made, say, to a customer for his own purposes, there would be a contingent liability to pay the loan which would become an actual liability if the customer defaulted. The endorsement or drawing of a bill of exchange normally gives rise to a contingent liability which will become a real liability if the drawer, acceptor or prior endorsers default.

Contingent liabilities should be noted on the Balance Sheet but need not be entered in the accounts until they become real liabilities. It is, however, desirable that some provision or reserve should be made out of profits to meet contingent liabilities where they are considerable.

(b) *Capital commitments*

It is also desirable (and in fact obligatory under the Companies Act) that the Balance Sheet should contain a note of the value of commitments which have been entered into for the purchase of fixed assets or other commitments on capital account. Whilst such commitments do not affect current results they will clearly have an effect on future costs and available cash.

D. THE ROUTINE SUMMARISED

1. The Balance Sheet as the ultimate objective

The ultimate objective of the final accounting procedure is the preparation of a Balance Sheet. A Balance Sheet is not an account forming part of the double-entry system; it is a statement prepared from the accounts. The object of the Balance Sheet is to show the financial position of a business or venture at a particular point of time. The financial position is demonstrated by a statement of assets and liabilities, including also the funds to which the net capital of the business has been allocated.

The Balance Sheet is drawn up from the "capital" accounts in the ledger after the profit or loss has been arrived at by transferring the balances on the revenue accounts to a summary account such as the conventional Trading and Profit and Loss Account. The balance of profit not withdrawn from the business is part of the capital of the business, and thus the Profit and Loss Account (or its extension in the form of an appropriation account) becomes a capital account. The balance on this account must, therefore, appear on the Balance Sheet.

2. Stages in the routine

The procedure for compiling the final accounts at the end of an accounting period may now be summarised as follows:

1. Test the arithmetical accuracy of the book-keeping by preparing a trial balance.
2. Prepare a schedule of adjustments to the accounts, journalise these adjustments and post from the journal to the accounts.
3. Transfer through the Journal the balances now shown on the revenue accounts to the appropriate account, *e.g.* one or

more of the following: manufacturing, trading and profit and loss account, thus arriving at the profit available for appropriation, which is transferred to an Appropriation Account.

4. Transfer through the Journal the appropriations decided by the management, from the Appropriation Account to the relevant dividend, tax and revenue accounts.

5. If the adjustments are very numerous, as they will be in a large and complex organisation, it is desirable to prepare a second trial balance in order to ensure that the final Journal entries have been posted correctly.

The Appropriation Account now represents a capital account, and no balances will now appear on the revenue accounts. In other words, the balances now remaining will all be shown on the Balance Sheet or statement of the financial position, and carried forward as opening balances for the new period. The final stage is, therefore:

6. Draw up a Balance Sheet or statement of the financial position from the remaining accounts. If the entries have been made correctly this statement will balance in the manner shown by the simplified examples given below.

Note. Many Balance Sheets, particularly those of American companies are drawn up so as to show assets on the left-hand side and liabilities, including capital funds, on the right-hand side.

First method

XYZ COMPANY LIMITED
BALANCE SHEET as at ....

	£	£		£	£
Authorised and issued capital:			Fixed assets:		
1,000 ord. shares of £1 each		1,000	Land and buildings	750	
General reserve	400		Plant and machinery	300	
Undistributed profits	100		Fixtures and fittings	200	
		500	Total fixed assets	—	1,250
Total issued capital and reserves		1,500	Current assets:		
			Cash	200	
Current liabilities:			Debtors	250	
Creditors	250		Stock	300	
Dividend recommended	250		Total current assets	—	750
Total current liabilities	—	500			
		£2,000			£2,000

Second method

XYZ COMPANY LIMITED
BALANCE SHEET as at ....

	£	£			£	£
Authorised and issued capital:			*Fixed assets:*			
1,000 ord. shares of £1 each		1,000	Land and buildings .	750		
			Plant and machinery .	300		
General reserve . .	400		Fixture and fittings .	200		
Undistributed profits .	100		*Total fixed assets* . .	—	1,250	
		500	*Current assets:*			
			Cash . .	200		
			Debtors . .	250		
			Stock . .	300		
					750	
			Less: Current liabilities:			
			Creditors. .	250		
			Dividend recommended .	250		
					500	
			Net current assets .		250	
		£1,500			£1,500	

Third Method

XYZ COMPANY LIMITED
Statement of net assets

	£	£	£
Fixed assets:			
Land and buildings		750	
Plant and machinery		300	
Fixtures and fittings		200	
Total fixed assets		—	1,250
Current assets:			
Cash	200		
Debtors	250		
Stock	300		
		750	
Less: Current liabilities			
Creditors	250		
Dividend recommended	250		
		500	
Net current assets			250
Total net assets			£1,500

The net assets shown above are represented by:

	£	£
Authorised and issued capital		
1,000 ordinary shares of £1 each		1,000
General reserve	400	
Undistributed profits	100	
		500
		£1,500

CHAPTER IV

DEPRECIATION

A. Objects of This Chapter

It is necessary to set aside a chapter for the consideration of depreciation, not only because of the intrinsic importance of the subject but also because of recurrent controversy as to the meaning of the expression for accounting purposes. Until the meaning and purpose of depreciation are decided there are bound to be variations of treatment in different concerns and, as a result, unit costs, prices, profit and appropriations may not be comparable between different undertakings or even between those in the same line of business.

The following sections endeavour to set out as simply as possible the main points of view on the subject. For those who wish to study the matter more deeply the following publications are recommended: *Accounting for Inflation*, published by the Association of Certified and Corporate Accountants, and *The Accountancy of Changing Price Levels*, published by the Institute of Cost and Works Accountants. It will be observed from the titles of these pamphlets that recent discussions on the subject have focused on the effect of inflation on profits.

B. The Physical Nature of Depreciation

Depreciation is a term applied to fixed assets, *i.e.* those which are expected to last for a considerable period, certainly for longer than a year. Fixed assets, such as buildings, plant, machinery and vehicles, suffer natural deterioration in the course of time, and such deterioration can rarely be wholly arrested by regular maintenance. Physical depreciation is accelerated by use, and this aspect of the subject is more precisely called "wear and tear".

The first accounting problem to be considered is therefore the assessment in monetary terms of the value lost by depreciation, both that due to natural deterioration and that due to wear and tear. Such loss in value must be made good out of profits, that is, the amount of loss must be charged to the revenue accounts in order that the monetary total of capital may be maintained intact. The mere charging of depreciation to the Profit and Loss Account does not, of course, arrest the physical deterioration which is taking place in the assets, it simply means—or should mean—that wealth of an amount equal to the depreciation has been retained in the business and that the net capital of the business has not been reduced.

It must not be forgotten that physical deterioration occurs in stocks held for a long time, but such loss in value should be automatically accounted for by the process of valuation described in the preceding chapter.

C. Assessing the Monetary Loss caused by Depreciation

1. The straight-line method

The monetary loss of value caused by depreciation can only be estimated. Where it is known by experience that a fixed asset will in the course of time become useless and lose all value, a simple approximation of the annual loss of value is to divide the initial cost, say £50, by the number of years of its estimated life, say ten years, charging the sum of £5 against profits each year; and an appropriate proportion for shorter periods.

Where, as is usual, the asset may be expected to have a scrap value at the end of its useful life, the sum to be charged in each accounting period will be the figure arrived at after dividing the initial cost *less estimated scrap value*, by the life. Thus, a machine purchased for £100 with an estimated life of eight years and an estimated scrap value of £20 would be depreciated by this method at the rate of:

$$\frac{£100 - £20}{8} = £10 \text{ a year}$$

2. The reducing-balance method

In many cases the cost of maintenance increases towards the end of the life of an asset. For this reason it is sometimes considered desirable to calculate depreciation so that the charge lessens towards the end of the asset's life, thus roughly equalising the combined charge of depreciation plus maintenance over the period.

The method used for this purpose is to charge to the revenue account in the first year a percentage of the cost of the asset. In the following year the same percentage will be calculated on the reduced value of the asset after the first year's depreciation has been deducted, and so on year by year until the value of the asset has been virtually reduced to nil.

3. The two methods compared

Example: Identical machines are purchased for £120 on 1st January by companies A and B respectively. The estimated useful life of the machines is five years and the scrap value is estimated at £20. Company A uses the straight-line method, and company B the reducing-balance method with an approximate depreciation rate of 30 per cent. The depreciation charged by each company may be compared as follows:

	Company A (straight-line method)	Company B (reducing-balance method)
	£	£
Cost . . .	120	120
Less:		
1st year's depn. . .	20	36
	£100	£84
2nd year's depn. .	20	25
	£80	£59
3rd year's depn. .	20	18
	£60	£41
4th year's depn. .	20	12
	£40	£29
5th year's depn. .	20	9
Scrap value . .	£20	£20

4. Other methods

The straight-line and the reducing-balance methods of calculating depreciation are the two methods most widely used. Both have the advantage of simplicity in conception and execution. Other methods may be used for specific purposes, many of them designed not only for the purpose of calculating depreciation but also to provide cash for replacing the asset when it is worn out.

The remaining methods are briefly summarised below:

(a) *Annuity method*

The theory supporting the annuity method is that since a fixed asset is held for the purpose of earning income, the basic amount of

D

annual income which may be expected from it may be expressed as a percentage of its value. Such a percentage is therefore credited to the revenue account and the depreciation, calculated as a fixed sum each year, is debited to the revenue account. The interest credited to revenue decreases annually as it is calculated on an asset value which diminishes each year. The net sum thus charged in the revenue account increases year by year, having the opposite effect to the reducing-balance method. The annuity method is often applied to leases involving heavy initial expenditure.

(b) *Sinking-fund method*

The basis of the sinking-fund method is to charge annually to revenue account such sum as, with compound interest, will amount to the net cost of the asset at the end of its useful life. This method is normally used in combination with the accumulation of a fund in easily realisable and secure investments, so as to provide for cash to replace the initial cost of the asset at the end of its life. The interest rate used corresponds with the expected return on the investment. This method is also frequently used to provide for the amortisation of leases. The amount of the annual charge may be obtained from tables drawn up for the purpose.

(c) *Insurance-policy method*

The insurance-policy method is analogous to a sinking fund in that an annual sum, in this case a premium, is invested in a form of endowment policy assuring payment of a sum equal to the initial cost of the asset at the end of its estimated useful life. In strictness the amount to be charged to revenue in respect of depreciation, as distinct from the premium payable to the insurance company, should exclude the interest, bonus or other benefit credited to the policy by the insurance company in addition to the principal sum assured.

This method, like the sinking-fund method, is more suitable as a device for ensuring the availability of cash to replace the asset, rather than as a method of calculating the loss of value due to depreciation or wear and tear.

5. Accounting entries

Whatever method of calculating the depreciation charge is adopted, the amount so calculated must be debited to the revenue account, normally to the Profit and Loss Account. In a substantial business holding a number of fixed assets of various kinds it is advisable first to collect the various amounts of depreciation applicable to each asset or group of assets in an intermediate depreciation account. The balance accumulated in the depreciation account is then transferred by means of a journal entry to the Profit and Loss Account at the end of the accounting period.

The corresponding credit aspect of the double entry may be dealt with in one of two ways. It may be credited to the asset account concerned, thus reducing the value of the asset as shown in the books. The better method is for the credit to be entered in a capital account, sometimes called a "Depreciation Reserve" or "Depreciation Fund" account. It may be expedient to maintain a number of such accounts, corresponding to the main groups of assets. The amounts credited to the depreciation fund account are carried forward from period to period until the useful life of any particular asset is at an end.

The balance on the asset account representing original cost will, meanwhile, have been likewise carried forward from period to period.

In a simple case where depreciation exactly equals the original cost of the asset it is merely necessary to extinguish the asset from the books and the accumulated depreciation on it by a transfer of that amount, crediting asset account and debiting depreciation fund account.

Any amounts received as scrap value are credited to the asset account. Where the depreciation charged is insufficient to cover the cost of the asset less scrap value received, a further allocation out of profits must be made to the depreciation fund (which would not otherwise suffice to cover the net cost of remaining assets).

Where the depreciation charged exceeds the net cost of the asset the surplus may be dealt with in any of three ways:

(i) Credited to Profit and Loss Account as a capital profit available for appropriation or distribution to proprietors. But this procedure is contrary to good accounting and prudent business principles, particularly in an inflationary period, where such profits are often not attributable to the efficiency of the business.

(ii) Retained in the depreciation fund account to meet possible deficiencies in the provision made for depreciation of other fixed assets. Whilst this procedure may be considered prudent, consideration should be given to its possible effect in obscuring the accuracy of the depreciation fund and hence of the net capital of the concern.

(iii) Transferred to a specific revenue reserve, such as that for the replacement of fixed assets, to the extent that depreciation is inadequate. Little criticism can be directed at this procedure save, perhaps, from those who maintain that excess replacement costs should be provided out of profits on revenue account, not on capital account.

(iv) Transferred to a capital reserve, *i.e.* one expressed to be not available for distribution to the proprietors except on a dissolution of the business. This method would add to the monetary value of fixed capital and would appear to meet all the possible objections to the other devices.

D. DEPRECIATION IN THE FINAL ACCOUNTS

1. The revenue account

Depreciation of fixed assets is normally regarded as a fixed charge, since it depends on fixed assets, and it should therefore be shown under the heading of fixed charges in any operating account prepared for management. Where the formal succession of Manufacturing Trading and Profit and Loss Accounts are drawn up, depreciation should appear in the Profit and Loss Account, and it is usually desirable to show the charge as a separate item, not grouped with other sub-headings.

For the purpose of depicting the cost of the factory, depreciation on factory plant, machinery, premises and equipment is often included in the manufacturing account. Similarly, for a non-producing unit an account showing the direct operating costs, whether such costs refer to a selling activity or the provision of a service, often includes depreciation on the fixed assets involved. Such an account showing the cost of a function of the business must be distinguished from an account intended to show the income, expenditure and surplus relating to the business as a whole. For any subdivision of depreciation by functions of the business it will be necessary to make arrangements for segregating fixed assets by departments, as well as by type.

2. The Balance Sheet

The Eighth Schedule paragraph 5, of the Companies Act 1948, has established the proper method of showing fixed assets in a Balance Sheet for concerns governed by that Act, and this method is suitable for other businesses. The paragraph states that a fixed asset shall be shown at cost or a valuation less the aggregate amount provided since the date of acquisition or valuation for depreciation or diminution in value.

Whilst, therefore, the depreciation charge for the year concerned appears in the Profit and Loss Account, the Balance Sheet shows the aggregate depreciation charged during the whole period since the acquisition or last valuation of the assets. The statement in the Balance Sheet may be expressed in the following form:

FIXED ASSETS	Cost	Aggregate depreciation	Net value
	£	£	£
Land and buildings . .	10,000	1,000	9,000
Plant and machinery . .	5,000	2,500	2,500
Total fixed assets . . .	£15,000	£3,500	£11,500

E. THE PROBLEM OF DEPRECIATION

1. The general argument

So far the depreciation charge has been dealt with from the traditional standpoint of an amount based on what is called "historical cost", that is, on the actual money paid out for the asset.

Where money values change, and it is probably true to say that they have always been changing in some degree, depreciation based on historical cost has the following disadvantages:

(a) The present value of the asset may be quite different from that shown in the accounts and entered on the Balance Sheet.

(b) The depreciation being calculated on historical cost distorts true profitability, for it is expressed in money values when money had greater (or possibly less) purchasing power.

(c) The depreciation charged on the basis of historical cost will not suffice to replace the asset at the end of its useful life.

2. The effect on asset values

The value of the asset concerned, after depreciation of its historical cost has been deducted, does not necessarily correspond to its current value. Current value in this sense may be interpreted in three ways: (i) the value of the asset to the business as a source of income; (ii) the saleable value of the asset in its present state; (iii) the cost of replacing the asset at current prices.

The consequences of charging depreciation on historical cost so far as Balance Sheet values are concerned may be indicated by the following example:

A manufacturer A buys a machine tool for £1,000 in 1945 and, using the accepted depreciation rate of 5 per cent on a straight-line basis for the tool, shows it in his Balance Sheet at the end of 1955 at a value of £500. Owing to the rise in prices, the machine tool could be sold in 1955 at a second-hand value of, say, £750; but it would cost £1,600 to replace it by a new tool.

Manufacturer B, who operates exactly the same kind of business, purchased an identical machine tool in 1954 for £1,500. After charging one year's depreciation at 5 per cent his Balance Sheet shows a value of £1,500−£75=£1,425 against the asset, but in his case the second-hand value of the tool is £1,400.

The manufacturers are equally efficient, and the value of the asset in terms of the income yielded by it is the same in each case.

If the values to be placed against fixed assets in Balance Sheets is to signify merely historical cost less depreciation based on that figure, the conventional methods of depreciation adopted by the two manufacturers are correct. In each case, however, and particularly for manufacturer A, the total of net assets to be obtained from the Balance Sheets is expressed partly in monetary language of a former period (the fixed asset portion) and partly in terms of current monetary values (the net current assets portion).

In the case of A the break-up value of his business, and probably the total value if it were sold as a going concern, is probably far higher than the figure of net assets obtainable from his Balance Sheet.

It has been questioned whether it is feasible or even desirable for Balance Sheets to indicate the current worth of fixed assets or even of the concern as a whole; and that Balance Sheets should merely set out to show the way in which money injected into a business, or retained out of profits, has been allocated to the property held.

It cannot be denied, however, that investors and other interested parties expect a Balance Sheet to provide at least some idea of the worth of the business and of its assets in terms of current monetary values and purchasing power. It is because of the fact that asset values based on historical cost are continually becoming out of line with current monetary values that many companies have arranged for their fixed assets to be revalued. The revalued totals are thereupon incorporated in the accounts (the contra credit entry being to a capital reserve account) and are shown in the Balance Sheet.

3. The effect on cost, prices and profits

Reverting to the two manufacturers cited above, A will charge annually to revenue 5 per cent of £1,000 = £50, and B will charge 5 per cent of £1,500 = £75. On the assumption for the sake of the argument, that the two manufacturers are equally efficient and their operations are similar in all other respects, A's profit for the year will be £25 greater than that shown by B. There is thus a tendency for either A's price for exactly the same quality of work to be lower than B's, or the dividend paid to the proprietors of A's business to be greater than that of B's.

In such a case, therefore, percentage net profit will be misleading as a gauge of efficiency, and for this purpose comparisons between the net profits, overall costs or prices of the two firms will be equally illusory.

Furthermore, the situation will be reversed when A's machine tool is worn out and he has to replace it by one costing at least £1,600 if the upward trend of prices continues. At that point the respective amounts charged against profits will be:

A 5 per cent of £1,600 = £80
B 5 per cent of £1,500 = £75.

A consideration of the greatest importance to each firm is that in neither case with a rising trend of prices does depreciation on historical cost retain out of profits sufficient capital to provide for the replacement of the asset. Thus, by 1955 A will have provided by means of depreciation for the original money paid out for the asset, *i.e.* £1,000, but he will have to find a further £600 out of capital or profits for its replacement. The inadequacy of depreciation based on historical cost for replacement purposes is accentuated by reason of the additional prices resulting from the continual improvement of machinery and the trend towards greater mechanisation.

The high and increasing proportion of capital which must for many undertakings be invested in fixed assets, and the need for continual modernisation, means that the provision of adequate finance for replacing buildings, plant and machinery represents an important function of top management.

4. A possible solution of the problem

The problems centering on depreciation and the replacement of fixed assets have been debated so extensively that any dogmatism on the subject is extremely unwise. Some broad lines of policy are, however, discernible from the actions of many leading companies, and may lead to some generally accepted principles for dealing with the matter.

As mentioned above, many large companies have revalued their fixed assets in terms of current monetary values. Whilst such revaluations soon become out of date as a result of continuing inflation, they at least bring asset values much nearer to current realities than if, for instance, buildings and land were shown on the basis of purchase prices in, say, the 1920s or before.

In some cases current depreciation is charged on the new values with, possibly, an adjusting charge or appropriation for the deficiencies of previous allocations. More frequently *an appropriation of profits* to a reserve, specially set up for the purpose, is made with the object of providing funds to meet such replacement costs as are in excess of the depreciation charged in the accounts.

The situation has been confused in some cases by the use in accounts of capital allowances, *e.g.* wear and tear, initial allowances and the investment allowances obtainable for tax purposes. These allowances are always based on historical cost, but, on the other hand, usually have the effect of depreciating the asset completely before its use to the business is at end. The effect of using capital allowances for tax purposes in the accounts is thus: (a) to charge to revenue a greater sum than would probably have been charged (on historical cost) as a result of an independent assessment of the life of the asset, and (b) to accumulate a fund towards excess replacement costs.

The principal reason for the use of taxation capital allowances in the accounts appears to be to ensure that the additional surplus (after charging taxation) is not distributed to the proprietors. This matter could, however, be dealt with by means of a reserve, *i.e.* an appropriation of profits, rather than a charge against profits in the form of depreciation.

The use of taxation capital allowances as depreciation in the accounts may therefore be considered a mixed blessing. Capital allowances for taxation purposes are, however, essentially an instrument of government financial policy. It seems arguable that industry should find a more scientific method of charging depreciation and providing for the replacement of its fixed assets.

Undoubtedly the first essential of a scientific method of depreciating fixed assets is an expert assessment of the probable useful life of the asset. The important question that then arises is whether the percentage rate so obtained should be applied to the original cost (less scrap value) or the probable cost of replacement.

There is no decided answer to this question. The trend of thought on the subject seems to point to:

(a) charging depreciation on the basis of original cost; and
(b) either charging against profits or appropriating from profits a further sum to cover the cost of replacement which is in excess of the depreciation on original cost already charged.

5. The effect of the solution

(a) *Appropriation or charge*

There remains the important question as to whether the excess cost of replacement is to be regarded as a charge against profits or an appropriation. The distinction may appear to be unduly fine to a business man unversed in the conventions of accountancy. Whichever way the excess cost of replacement is shown in the accounts, that sum will not be available for distribution to the proprietors.

One important aspect of the matter lies in the fact that if there are no profits to be appropriated the excess replacement cost cannot be allowed for in the accounts. Similarly, a small profit may tend to induce management to refrain from making the appropriation in respect of excess replacement costs in order to pay a reasonable dividend. The amount of an *appropriation* lies in the discretion of management, but a proper *charge* must be entered in the accounts whether management like it or not.

(b) *Effect on costs and prices*

Assuming the management have decided that it is necessary to make some allocation whether of the nature of a charge or an appropriation to cover replacement costs, they will have presumably accepted the necessity for recovering such charge or appropriation in the prices to be charged to customers.

If excess replacement costs take the form of an appropriation the amount will not normally be incorporated in the unit cost prepared by the financial department. It will be difficult, to say the least, for the sales or estimating department to assess the additional sum per sale which must be allowed for excess replacement costs. Whilst prices are not wholly dependent on costs, they are obviously affected by past, present or anticipated future costs. This is particularly so where, as in many nationalised industries, and those providing a service to the State, conditions tantamount to "cost plus" apply. This further aspect of the problem is introduced as a matter for consideration at this point. It will be dealt with more fully in the chapters bearing on unit costing.

F. THE ACCOUNTING ENTRIES

The following is an example of the accounting entries required in dealing with depreciation and in accounting for profit or loss on the sale of a fixed asset.

Assume that a business purchased two machines, A and B, at the beginning of its financial year and it was decided that each machine was to be depreciated on the straight-line method, the estimated useful life of each machine being five years. The estimated scrap value of the machines at the end of the five years was: Machine A—£150; Machine B—£100. The annual rate of depreciation was, therefore, calculated as follows:

$$Machine\ A.\ \frac{£600 - £150}{5} = £90$$

$$Machine\ B.\ \frac{£400 - £100}{5} = £60$$

Machine B was in fact sold at the end of the third year for £200. The ledger accounts appear as set out below.

Revenue accounts

DEPRECIATION (charge) ACCOUNT

Year		£	Year		£
1	Depn. provision a/c .	150	1	Profit and Loss a/c .	150
2	,, ,,	150	2	,, ,,	150
3	,, ,, .	150	3	,, ,, .	150

SALE OF FIXED ASSETS ACCOUNT

Year		£	Year		£
3	Machine a/c . .	400	3	Depn. provision a/c .	180
			3	Cash (or debtors) .	200
			3	Profit and Loss a/c or	
				Capital Reserve a/c .	20
		£400			£400

Capital accounts

MACHINES ACCOUNT

Year		£	Year		£
1	Machine A . .	600			
1	Machine B . .	400			
			3	Sale of Fixed Assets a/c	400
			3	Balance c/d . .	600
		£1,000			£1,000
4	Balance b/d . .	600			

DEPRECIATION PROVISION ACCOUNT

Year		£	Year		£
			1	Depn. (charge) a/c. .	150
			2	,, ,, .	150
3	Sale of Fixed Assets a/c	180	3	,, ,, .	150
3	Balance c/d . .	270			
		£450			£450
			4	Balance b/d . .	£270

In the balance sheet at the end of year 3 the relevant entries will appear as follows:

FIXED ASSETS

		£
Machinery, at cost:		
At beginning of year		1,000
Less: Sales during year		400
At end of year		600
Less: Accumulated depreciation . . .		270
Book value at end of year		£330

In year 4 and year 5 depreciation will be charged in the accounts at the rate applicable to machine A, *i.e.* £90 per annum. No further depreciation will be charged in respect of machine A after the 5th year and the balances on the Machine Account and the Depreciation Provision Account will remain as they stand until the machine is sold or scrapped.

CHAPTER V

ACCOUNTING AIDS

A. MANUAL METHODS—FOR USE IN THE SMALLER BUSINESS

1. Simplification

It will have become apparent that in the accounting department there is a large amount of routine work to be performed. Cash accounting must be strictly controlled, and the various day books and ledgers must be entered. In a small business it may be possible for the proprietor to make the necessary entries day by day and, perhaps, leave the final accounts to be written up by a professional accountant. As the size of the business grows the entering of the books of account becomes an increasing burden, and if conventional double-entry books continue to be written up by hand, every increase in business involving additional transactions adds still further to the amount of routine work in the accounts department. At the end of the accounting period balancing the books will become an extended process, and the preparation of the final accounts may be delayed. The importance to management of prompt financial information has been emphasised, and with this object in view simplification of the accounting routines is essential.

Simplification of accounts, particularly in the smaller firm, does not of necessity mean the purchase of expensive equipment or machines. Consider first the question of balancing the ledger accounts. This must be completed at least monthly for the collection of debts and payment of suppliers, and also at the end of the accounting period to produce the necessary schedules of debtors, creditors, expenses, etc. In connection with the ledger the first simplification which might be considered is the adoption of the three-column ledger—debit, credit, balance. Under this method the balance of the account is thrown out after each entry, thus eliminating the necessity at the end of the month or accounting period of ruling and balancing. An account in the Sales Ledger under this system would appear as follows:

S. Smith and Son   Credit limit £800   Folio 84

Date	Details	F.	Dr.	Cr.	Balance
Jan. 1	Balance	b/f			20. –. –.
,, 6	Sales		15. –. –.		35. –. –.
,, 8	Sales		10. –. –.		45. –. –.
,, 10	Returns			5. –. –.	40. –. –.
,, 15	Bank			20. –. –.	20. –. –.

This method forms the basis of machine accounting.

2. The slip system and batch posting

It has already been stated in Chapter II that the purpose of Sales and Purchases Journals is to provide a medium from which the customers and suppliers accounts can be posted, and also to provide totals for the various sales, purchases and materials control accounts. If these are the sole reasons for keeping the Journals, then consideration should be given to the possibility of eliminating the writing up of these books by the introduction of the slip system or "file posting", as it is sometimes called. Taking the example of a day's sales invoices, a copy of each invoice will be sent to the accounts department, and a total of the invoices will be made on an adding-listing machine. Departmental totals can be obtained on a special analysis machine. The total of the invoices will be entered in the sales account, and the personal accounts of the customers in the Sales Ledger will then be entered direct from the copies of the invoices. This procedure is shown diagrammatically opposite.

An additional advantage of the slip system is that invoices can be sorted in the required order for entering in the ledger. It must be emphasised that where use is made of simplified methods a strict control must be kept since the normal book-keeping checking methods cannot be used.

The sales accounting system indicated in the previous paragraph is relatively easy to inaugurate since the sales invoice originates in the firm and can be suitably designed for the purpose; also a routine can be introduced to facilitate its adoption. When the Purchase Journal is being considered, other factors must be borne in mind. For example, the invoice must be accepted, in most cases, in the manner in which it is sent by the supplier. Again, on receipt it must be checked for accuracy, pricing and against goods received. Since the number of suppliers is often less than the number of sales customers, consideration might be given to the method known as batch posting. Under this method when a purchase invoice is received it will be registered and put through the appropriate checking routine. When it is passed as correct for payment it will be placed in a special file under the supplier's name. When the supplier's statement of account is received at the end of the month it will be checked against the invoices and if correct the latter will be attached to the statement. Thus only one entry (the total of the statement) is made for each supplier each month. It

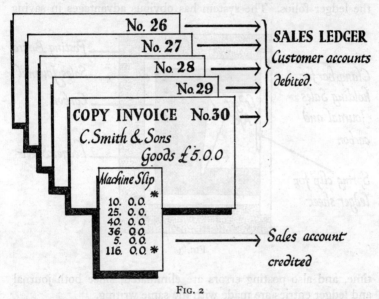

FIG. 2

will be recalled that in Chapter II, when discussing the payment of suppliers' invoices, it was mentioned that suppliers' accounts need not be maintained in some circumstances, and such a system might be incorporated with the batch method.

3. Posting boards

Under the double-entry system each transaction necessitates two entries, one in a subsidiary book and one in the ledger. In connection with the Sales Ledger the two entries required are in:

1. The Sales Journal
2. The Sales Ledger.

With the use of manual posting equipment these two entries can be performed at one writing. The diagram below illustrates the principle of the manual posting board.

The method to be adopted is as follows. The Sales Journal sheet and carbon paper are placed on the posting board under the clamp bar. Each ledger sheet is inserted as required under the spring clip; this sheet must be so aligned that the writing line in the ledger coincides with the next vacant line on the journal sheet. When the entry is written it will appear on both the journal and the ledger folios. The system has obvious advantages in saving

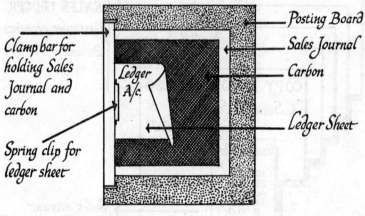

Fig. 3

time, and also posting errors are eliminated, since both journal and ledger entries are made with the same writing.

With posting boards additional documents or records can be produced whilst the entry is being made. If a statement form is filed with each ledger account it can be inserted under the spring clip at the same time as the ledger sheet; thus one writing will produce the Sales Journal, the Ledger, and the entry on the Statement. At the end of the month all that is necessary is to extract the statements and mail them to the customers.

Although, as an example, a detailed description has been given of the sales section of the accounts department, it should be realised that the posting-board method can be adopted for other entries. In dealing with cash received it is possible to produce at the same time the receipt, the Cash-Book entry and the bank paying-in-slip. Whilst writing a cheque entries can be made in the Cash Book and Purchase Ledger. Throughout the accounting system, and indeed for other purposes, wide use can be made of manifold posting equipment.

4. Bookless book-keeping

For many businesses the cycle of business operations is to purchase supplies and materials from a relatively small number of suppliers, and to sell or distribute the resulting products or services to a great number of consumers. The effect on the accounting department of this cycle of events is to create a very large number of customers' accounts in the Sales Ledger. Taking the argument a stage farther most productive and distributive firms buy materials in bulk and sell to customers in much smaller quantities and at much more frequent intervals. This again greatly increases the amount of routine book-keeping to be completed in the Sales Ledger section of the accounts department. There have been evolved systems of "bookless book-keeping" which are designed to eliminate the ledger, as such. The systems are particularly suited to firms with regular customer connections where frequent periodic sales are made.

What are the reason for maintaining customer accounts in the sales ledger? They may briefly be stated as follows:

1. To have a record of transactions with each customer.
2. To ensure accounts are paid when due.
3. To enable the total amount of debts to be ascertained for financial purposes.

Methods of bookless book-keeping are based on similar principles to those of the slip system of posting, in other words, copies of the sales invoices are filed under customers' names, and these files of invoices replace the written ledger account.

When considering the actual installation of such a system there are alternatives. The first method requires the maintenance of a separate flat-top file for each customer. As an invoice is prepared one copy is placed in the appropriate customer's file. When accounts are paid the invoices are clearly marked. If required a card may be slotted into position in the front of the folder on which brief particulars may be noted, or an analysis of sales recorded. On the visible top edge of the folder can be signalled a variety of important facts about each customer; thus in addition to the name and address there can be information about credit limits, overdue accounts, etc.

The second system of bookless book-keeping requires the use of specially designed cabinets and a spring clip for each customer. Under these clips are kept copies of the documents relating to the transactions with the customer—invoices, credit notes and receipts. The documents are designed and prepared so that the amount of the balance shows clearly on each document. Thus, as each document is prepared, the balance owing is picked up from the last copy under the customer's clip, the current particulars are entered in the usual manner, the new balance is then computed and entered at the foot of the document. At any time the total amount owing can be found by extracting the last balance shown under each customer's clip, in a summary or on an adding machine. Since a strict control must be kept, it is a simple matter to record the total amount owing, and at the end of each day to extract the total of the new balances, and through a control account to check the accuracy of the sales records.

B. Mechanised Methods—For Use in the Larger Business

1. The types of machines

The accounting aids described in the foregoing section may find suitable application in the small and medium-size concerns, but in the large undertaking the amount of routine work in the accounts department will necessitate the use of mechanical methods.

The advantages of mechanical accounting are economy, speed, accuracy and improved records. In addition to making the records machines can produce a variety of documents at one operation and compute and accumulate totals and balances.* Among the applications of accounting machines are the following: sales ledger, purchase ledger, cash recording, payroll, stores records, costing, analysis and statistical work.

A great variety of machines are available, but the main types are the following (references to any particular methods of mechani-

---

* For further information see *Machine Accounting*, price 42*s*., and *The Students Machine Accounting Tutor*, price 15*s*., both by Owen Sutton and both published by Macdonald and Evans Ltd.

cal accounting are only given as a general appraisal and without prejudice to any particular make):

1. Those with full-figure sterling keyboards which have been developed from the adding machine. They have mechanism for accumulating a number of different totals in separate registers. The keyboard is split with sections for dates, folios and fixed characters for descriptions. There is also the addition of an automatic carriage to accommodate the records and cards on which the information is printed.

2. Those with typewriter keyboards with the addition of a full-figure adding keyboard. As well as the features mentioned in the preceding paragraph, these machines have the advantage of greater flexibility in writing, since they are not restricted to certain fixed narrations.

3. The twelve-figure keyboard machine is developed from an adding machine which has twelve numeral keys with additional keys for dates, descriptions, etc. These machines, because of their abbreviated adding keyboard, are less bulky than some of the other types.

4. The cash-register type of accounting machine is capable of printing, in original print, on several records at one operation; it is also capable of both addition and subtraction, and is especially useful for dealing with receipting and public-utility billing.

5. Specially designed accounting machines of a type developed from the typewriter with the addition of special rows of keys to actuate the calculating mechanism.

In addition to the above types of machines there are the punched-card machines which work on entirely different principles and which will be discussed later in this chapter.

2. Mechanical ledger posting

It will be impossible in the space available to give a full description of mechanised accounting, but since a great amount of work will be in the debtors or sales ledger, this will be used for the purpose of illustration. Many of the principles stated will be of application to other tasks which the accounting machine will be called upon to perform.

The ledger will consist of account cards housed in special trays or binders designed to aid the speedy selection and return of cards. To save the time of the trained machine operator it is usual for a junior to offset those cards on which entries have to be made.

For the actual operation the posting media (in this case invoices, credit-notes, receipts, etc.) are made into convenient batches, and sorted into account order to facilitate posting. The size of the batch or run of media will depend on the type of work being done, but the runs should be of reasonable size to enable frequent checks to be made as the work proceeds. In many systems the posting medium will consist of Day Book or Journal sheets which have been prepared already from the original documents.

Assuming a run of documents is being posted, the batch must be pre-listed on an adding machine. The accounting machine will accumulate the total of the debits posted, and at the end of the run this total can be posted on to a control or proof cards and compared with the pre-listed total or day book total. If the two totals agree, then this will be a check that the correct amounts have been posted on the ledger cards (a similar procedure will be followed with other types of posting media).

The carriage of the machine will have a dual feed, that is, sheets or cards can be inserted independently from the front or the back of the platen. The journal sheet will be inserted in the back as in a typewriter, and this will accumulate line by line details of all the items posted to the various accounts, thus forming the Sales Journal. The ledger cards will be fed in separately at the front of the platen, the feed being so arranged that the cards can be inserted or withdrawn without disturbing the journal sheet. After the operator has depressed the necessary keys the machine automatically prints the entries and balances.

An important point is that for each entry the old balance on the account must be picked up before the posting is made. There is no automatic proof that the right balance has been picked up. There are several kinds of proof, known as visual proof, double pick-up proof, direct proof and cypher proof. The principle of the old balance proof is usually that the old balance is picked up twice, once at the beginning of the operation and once at the end. If the two pick-ups agree, then it is assumed that the correct balance has been used; if the pick-ups disagree, then the machine record will disclose the fact and the operator must check to see which is correct.

When the total of the amounts posted has been agreed with the pre-list it is posted to the control or proof card, the posting being done in the same manner as for an individual account. The balance on the control account is thus the net total of all the balances in the ledger or ledger section.

3. Punched-card systems

Two outstanding features of the business world to-day are the growth and integration of the large groups of companies, and the development of public corporations. The scale of operations of these organisations necessitates the use of punched-card systems in their financial departments.

The main cycle of operations in punched-card systems is as follows:

1. Punching the cards.
2. Verifying the cards.
3. Sorting the cards.
4. Tabulating the required information.

The basis of the system is the card on which information is recorded by punching holes having numerical or alphabetical significance according to their positions. Cards may be of various sizes, and their recording capacity is governed by the number of vertical columns they contain. The columns are grouped in "fields", and the headings of each section of the card shows the information which the field contains. The positions of the holes determine the information which is contained on the cards. Punched cards can serve in the dual capacity of original documents if provision is made for writing on the cards the information which can be subsequently punched into them.

Since the punched card replaces the original media, and is the basis of all subsequent operations, it is vital that the holes should be punched in their correct places. After the original punching by one operator, the posting media and cards are passed to another operator for verifying. The second operator punches the information on a somewhat similar machine, inserting the original cards. Incorrect punching is automatically indicated.

The second principal operation is sorting the cards. This is done on an automatic sorter which arranges the punched cards in any desired sequence (account number, department, job number, etc.).

The machine groups all cards of a similar classification and arranges them in numerical sequence. The cards are placed in the receiving magazine and a pointer is set against the particular column to be sorted. The cards are deposited by the machine in numbered pockets agreeing with the position of the punched hole in the column. The operation is repeated for each column in the particular field being sorted. The sorting is extremely rapid, and speeds of about 40,000 cards an hour can be obtained.

The final operation in the cycle is tabulation. After the cards have been sorted into the required order they are ready for the tabulator which automatically produces from these documents accounts or statistical statements in clear, legible characters. All the columns on a card are sensed simultaneously, and in one completed line of type all the information contained on the card can be printed at one stroke. Whilst the tabulator is printing, adding and subtracting mechanism is accumulating totals and balances which may subsequently be printed.

In addition to the punch, verifier, sorter and tabulator, a full range of punched-card equipment will contain a number of other units such as the interpreter, the interpolator and the multiplier.

4. Integrated data processing

Integrated data processing is a term applied to a planned effort to devise a system of paperwork in offices which will eliminate much needless copying and recopying of information. Integrated data processing aims to reduce costs by producing only such information as is necessary for the efficient operation of the business, by increasing the speed of the administrative functions and by avoiding the errors which are associated with many manual methods.

The basic idea behind integrated data processing is not new. The concept that one writing of information should produce all necessary documentation is applied by means of carbon paper, duplicating machines and accounting machinery. Reference to the previous section will show that punched-card systems represent a form of integrated data processing in that the punched card is used to activate machines for the preparation of subsequent documents, records and statistical information.

The term "integrated data processing" indicates, however, a wider concept than the devising of new methods for producing information. There is an increasing tendency for all business records to be produced by means of key-driven machines such as typewriters, accounting machines, calculating machines or cash registers. If such a machine operation is introduced at the earliest stage in the recording process, then the information which is required at a later stage can be recorded in "machine language" as a by-product of the original recording operation. Such "machine language" may be recorded on punched cards, perforated paper tape or on magnetic media. The "by-product" recordings can be used in subsequent mechanised operations of the office system.

As an illustration of the practical operation of a system of integrated data processing the following description assumes the use of perforated (or punched) paper tape as a medium.

The basic raw material is a roll of paper tape about half an inch wide. A commonly used size is five-channel tape, but wider tape could have six, seven or eight channels, the larger sizes giving greater flexibility in coding. A machine called a "tape punch" can punch holes on the paper tape according to a pre-designed code.

The information punched on the paper tape is subsequently read by a "tape reader". Tape punches and tape readers can be attached to conventional office machines, either to record data or to reproduce it. In addition, tape-to-card converters, and card-to-tape converters, make it possible to intermingle punched cards and perforated paper tape in one integrated system.

In the following example it is assumed that orders are received in an Order Department which prepares various carbon copies on a typewriter (or manually), one copy being sent to the warehouse to authorise despatch of the goods from stock and another copy going to the Accounts Department. In suitable applications a copy of the original document can also be made to serve as an invoice or, alternatively, the Accounts Department (or invoicing section) will prepare an invoice on notification that the goods have been despatched and send one copy to the Punched Card Section for statistical analysis.

A traditional method of dealing with the routine could be as follows:

Step 1. Order arrives in the Order Department and is typed on a carbon set of various copies one of which is sent to the warehouse.

Step 2. The warehouse clerk writes out despatch notes by hand also in carbon sets, and sends one copy to the Accounts Department.

Step 3. The Accounts Department types the customer's invoice also in a carbon set, and sends one copy to the Punched Card Section.

Under an integrated data-processing system, a tape punch would be attached to the typewriter in the Order Department. As the warehouse copy is being typed, perforated paper tape would be produced as a by-product of the typing operation, the paper tape being sent to the Accounts Department. On a check from the warehouse the paper tape would be fed into an automatic typewriter, and at the same time this machine would select other standard information, *e.g.* prices, from a second tape. Thus the invoice would be produced automatically with the minimum of human intervention. It should also be borne in mind that, as a further simplification for suitable applications, it is possible to produce delivery note, invoice and advices to all departments by one typing from the customer's order. As a by-product of the invoicing operation a further tape could be produced which could be fed into a tape-to-card converter for the purpose of producing information on a punched card.

This particular example is shown in diagram form below, but it is necessary to point out that, according to the circumstances of a particular business, other systems can effectively cover the situation envisaged.

It will be appreciated from the following example of a particular business operation that integrated data processing is an approach to accounting work which has innumerable applications. If, furthermore, in the example used it could be arranged for the customer to send his order in machine language (*e.g.* on a punched card) the automatic process could begin earlier in the procedure. When an electronic computer forms part of the system then integrated data processing (IDP) becomes electronic data processing (EDP). It is important to observe that whilst reference has been made above to various mechanical means of speeding up and simplifying administrative processes, the IDP concept does not merely imply the use of office machinery. It implies that a business shall first decide with as much precision as possible what information is required for successful and efficient operations. The second step is to organise the simplest and most economical means of obtaining that information, having due regard to the ever-present requirement of speed. In general, the most efficient means of obtaining information is to make one reproduction of essential facts at the earliest point in the process. This requirement

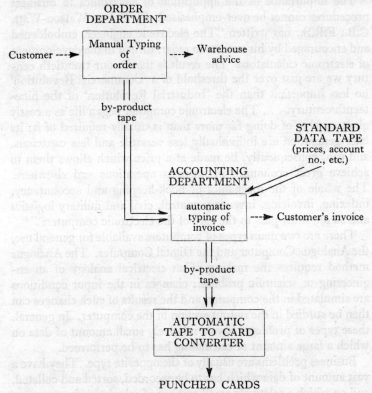

is usually best satisfied by the use of mechanical aids, but in a very small business the benefits of integrated data processing can be achieved by the intelligent use of carefully designed forms for manual reproduction of information through carbon paper, or paper which allows reproduction without the insertion of carbons.

5. Electronic data processing

No description of mechanised aids to accounting would be complete without some reference to the use of electronics in accounting procedures. The term "electronics" refers to the use of electrons moving in thermionic tubes and electrical circuits, and the devices which depend on the movement of these electrons. This is quite distinct from the electro-mechanical accounting machines in which electricity is used as a driving force to actuate the mechanical action.

The importance of the application of electronics to business procedures cannot be over-emphasised. Sir Robert Watson-Watt, C.B., F.R.S., has written "The electronic engineer, emboldened and encouraged by his success in radar, turned to the development of electronic calculators. The result is that in our twentieth century we are just over the threshold of a 'Commercial Revolution' no less important than the 'Industrial Revolution' of the nineteenth century. . . . The electronic computer began life as a costly giant capable of doing far more than is usually required of it; its later generation are individually less versatile and less capacious, and can, consequently, be made at a price which allows them to achieve great economies in business operations and elsewhere. The whole of the mechanics of book-keeping and accountancy, indexing, invoicing, inventory control, civil and military logistics and so on, must pass to the care of the electronic computers."*

There are two main types of computers available for general use, the Analogue Computer and the Digital Computer. The Analogue method requires the making of an electrical analogy of an engineering or scientific problem: changes in the input conditions are simulated in the computer, and the results of such changes can then be studied in the output section of the computer. In general, these types of problems have a relatively small amount of data on which a large amount of calculating has to be performed.

Business problems are usually of the opposite type. They have a vast amount of data which has to be recorded, sorted and collated, and on which a relatively small amount of calculating is necessary. This has led to the development of digital computers, in these machines numbers, letters and characters are represented in the form of a chain of electric pulses; thus these pulses represent our normal "digits" of information. The remarks which follow refer to digital computers which are the type of computers used for accounting purposes.

* "Adapting Electronics to Peace", *Financial Times Annual Review of British Industry*, 1954.

The operation of a computer can be divided into the following five functions:

1. *Input.* The receipt of information into the computer in a form which is acceptable to an electronic machine. This "machine language" may be in the form of punched cards, perforated paper tape or magnetic tape, wire or film. To avoid unnecessary operations it is important that this "machine language" should be produced during an early stage of the accounting system. It may often be produced as a by-product of some other operation carried out in an electric typewriter, adding machine, cash register, etc. Future developments in computer input will undoubtedly take the form of producing electrical-pulse input for the computer from some original operation or transaction.

2. *Storage.* Since the arithmetical circuits are capable of performing calculations at electronic speeds, *i.e.* speeds reckoned in millionths of a second, it is necessary to have a working store inside the machine which will provide the processing units with information at comparable speeds. Such storage devices consist of magnetic drums and cores, acoustical delay lines and magnetic discs. In addition to the working stores it is also necessary to have external storage for information which will require to be re-introduced into the computer for further processing. For some purposes the external store may be in the form of punched cards or perforated paper tape. In other cases it will be preferable to store the information in a form which will re-introduce the information in electronic form; for such purposes the external storage can be in the form of magnetic-tape spools or electronic discs.

3. *Processing.* These units of the computer contains the circuits which perform the arithmetical and logical processes. The arithmetical circuits can add, subtract, multiply and divide, as well as performing specialised operations, such as shifting and instruction modification. The logical circuits perform operations known variously as jumping, branching or looping. This is the decision-making part of the machine. It can be made to distinguish between two distinct courses of action and select the one most appropriate to the data under consideration.

4. *Output*. The function of these units is to translate the results of computing into "human language", that is, into printed results. This can be achieved either by producing punched cards or perforated paper tape which can subsequently be handled by tabulating machinery, or by connecting the computer direct to a printing machine. (Since the computer produces its results at electronic speeds, much research is being carried on in respect of this aspect of computers.) Until suitable devices are available it is usually necessary to hold the answers in "buffer stores" until the output machines can deal with them.

5. *Control Unit*. The above devices work under the control of this component part of the computer. It receives the instructions and brings the various units into action in their correct order. It also provides the operator with a means of communicating with the computer. A "control console" is fitted with visual indicators in the form of neon tubes or cathode-ray tubes, which are an additional aid in showing the operator what is happening in the various parts of the computer, and enabling him to check on errors or stops.

In order to complete an accounting procedure the computer must first be given "instructions". These instructions are in the form of a coded programme which guides the computer through each individual step of its operation. The programme is the key to efficient computer operation, and is the result of highly skilled work, which includes methods analysis, knowledge of computer codes and computer operation. A great amount of forethought, analysis and planning is necessary before an accounting task can be successfully carried out on a computer. An electronic computer is not a "giant brain" but a complex machine which puts emphasis on human brainwork.

In addition to performing "data processing" operations, the speed at which computers work makes it possible for them to produce a much greater amount and variety of information for management purposes. The complex business factors of to-day make management demand more and more information from the office, but too often they are baulked in this demand because of the cost of providing this information. In many cases an electronic computer will be able to provide the information sought. To realise fully the potential of computers, management must place itself in the position of being able to utilise more detailed and faster figures. If it does not, the benefits to be derived from using computers will prove largely illusory.

The advent of the "electronic office" demands a new approach to the whole question of office procedures. No longer will office routines be dependent upon paper-work and individual operations; office managers will need to re-adjust their way of thinking so that the tasks of recording, calculating, selection and presentation of information are regarded as one comprehensive operation. There is a danger that when electronic data-processing equipment is acquired it will be considered as "just another office machine" and tasks which are already efficiently done by punched-card equipment transferred to the computer in much the same form. This is one method of approaching the transfer from electro-mechanical to electronic equipment and has the advantage that known routines are being used. But wider horizons should be scanned than those of knowing how to do to-day's job better; then more progress will be made by concentrating on what the job ought to be.

C. THE ORGANISATION OF THE DEPARTMENT

Two factors will dominate the organisation of the accounting department: (a) Speed—the necessity of providing management with up-to-date information regarding the progress of the business. (b) Cost—the necessity of keeping the expenditure of the department within reasonable limits. Orthodox book-keeping calls for accurate entering and posting; normal procedure is complex and calls for experienced staff. There are two main obstacles to be overcome, the high cost of experienced staff and the shortage of labour. Accountants take pride in the usefulness of the information they provide, but as business operations become more complex, there are increasing demands from management for more information. Because of this and because the salaries of clerical staff continue to rise, accountants will always be faced with the challenge of preventing costly administrative practices. Clerical cost reduction is an integral part of their work.

A large amount of the work in connection with accounts is of a routine nature, and it is this routine work which lends itself to the introduction of new procedures and accounting aids. The general effect of modern methods is to break the work down into a number of simple operations which can be carried out by junior members of the staff. The introduction of simplified routines and modern office equipment causes significant changes in the staffing of offices. A larger proportion of the staff tends to be female operators skilled in the use of particular machines, whilst the smaller ratio of male staff needs to be more highly specialised in interpreting and using the information made available. Thus the general pattern in the modern accounts office is as follows: a qualified accountant at the head in the capacity of office manager, various sections under specialised supervisors, with batteries of machines dealing with routine entries.

One of the main tasks of the accountant in connection with the organisation of his department is the smooth flow of work through the machines. By the general nature of the work there tends to be peaks and troughs in the flow. The number of staff must be sufficient to cope with the work at peak periods, but obviously there should not be too great a gap between busy and slack times. As an example, consider, once again, the sales or debtors' ledger section. The normal procedure is for a statement to be sent to each customer at the end of the month. Prompt despatch of statements assists in the prompt receipt of money, but the effect of this is to cause a peak at the end of the month. The arrival of the remittances from customers in the early days of each month causes a peak in the cashier's section, and in posting the cash credits to the ledger account cards. These peaks can be smoothed out by what is known in the U.S.A. as "cycle billing" (in America billing refers to the despatch of statements). Under cycle billing, the sales ledger is split into sections; during the first week of the month statements would be sent to customers in the first section of the ledger, during the second week to customers in the next section, and so on. Thus the work is spread equally over the whole month.

The foregoing is only one method of controlling the flow of work, and it must be emphasised that clerical cost reduction is a wider subject than the installation of modern office equipment and piecemeal changes in routine. These are important, but the reduction of clerical costs demands a planned programme which extends beyond the bounds of the accounting department into the clerical procedures of every section of the business.

CHAPTER VI

ACCOUNTING FOR PARTNERSHIPS

A. The Nature of Partnerships

Modern business is conducted by a wide variety of organisations which include sole proprietors, partnerships, and corporate bodies such as limited companies, societies, chartered bodies, associations and public corporations. Each body is controlled by its own domestic rules, and the main types are subject to differing legal regulations.

Individual proprietorship is still a widely used form of business in this country; it holds, for example, a prominent place in the retail trade, and many small engineering firms are owned by one person. The management of the small firm is in the hands of the owner, who makes his own decision and carries the entire risk if his business fails—he has "unlimited" liability, which means that if his business is unsuccessful his private property may be taken to satisfy his business debts. The fact that the owner can manage his business as he pleases, perhaps largely on the basis of intuition, does not mean that an intelligent application of modern methods will not be advantageous, and although there are no legal provisions as to the precise form of his accounting, he must benefit by using modern techniques.

The important factor limiting the expansion of a one-man business is normally the provision of sufficient capital to finance the expansion. For a time the expansion may be financed by borrowing or by extended credit facilities, but the time will come when the owner must seek further permanent capital. For this purpose, and probably also to divide the responsibilities of management, the business may be converted into a partnership, the new partner or partners bringing in the further funds required.

A partnership may be defined as the association of persons who carry on business in common with a view to making a profit. The law governing partnerships is contained in the Partnership Act 1890. It is not here proposed to survey the legal obligations of partnership, but in general it may be said that the Partnership Act comes into effect in the absence of agreement among partners, or when the rights of third parties are affected. Except in the case of a Limited Partnership, all partners have the right to share in the management, and it is advisable to have a partnership agreement which will clearly state how the firm is to be managed and the form which the accounts will take.

B. Partnership Accounts

The actual accounting organisation and procedures will follow the general lines outlined in the preceding chapters in so far as they are appropriate to the size and type of the firm. The only matters which require special attention are those which concern the partners individually. Although there is no legal obligation to do so, it is advisable that the capital accounts should be kept at fixed amounts, and that all other items relating to the partners—shares of profit, remuneration, etc.—should be dealt with in separate accounts, called the Partners Current Accounts. This procedure will accord with the principle described in Chapter I, of distinguishing between the fixed and variable elements of capital. The partners' capital accounts will show the fixed element, and the current accounts the variable element. The items should appear in the Balance Sheet as follows:

		£	£
Capital accounts:			
R. Brown	. . . .	10,000	
B. Smith	. . .	5,000	
			15,000
Current accounts:			
R. Brown	. . . .	2,500	
B. Smith	. . .	1,000	
			3,500

Since the accounts will have been prepared for the information of the proprietors, it may be desirable to give additional information under the heading "Current Accounts" to show the derivation of these amounts.

The method of remuneration of partners should be decided by the partners and included in the partnership agreement. This point is important, since in the absence of agreement the Partnership Act provides:

(a) Partners shall share profit and losses equally.

(b) Partners are not entitled to interest on capital before profit is ascertained, or to be charged interest on drawings.

(c) A partner may not receive a salary for acting in the partnership business.

(d) Partners are entitled to interest on loans at 5 per cent per annum.

It must be emphasised that the above provisions apply only if there is no agreement among the partners. They may, if they wish, remunerate themselves by a regular salary, by receiving interest on capital and so on. As has been stated, these items will be dealt with through the current accounts, and thus a current account may contain the following items.

PARTNER'S CURRENT ACCOUNT

DEBITED WITH	CREDITED WITH
Share of loss (if any).	Share of profits.
Drawings, and interest thereon.	Interest on capital.
Goods charged to him.	Salary (if unpaid).
Expenses paid on his behalf.	Loan interest.

When preparing the final accounts it is preferable for the net profit to be ascertained before the personal items of the proprietors are transferred. It will be remembered that final accounts should facilitate comparisons from year to year, and enable operating budgets to be compiled for the future. The figures to be used for these purposes do not normally include appropriations showing how the surplus has been distributed. Since the remuneration of partners may be varied by considerations outside the business, an additional section should be added to the Profit and Loss Account after the net profit has been struck (sometimes called the appropriation account); this final section of the Profit and Loss Account will show how the revenue surplus has been disposed of. The following example shows the method to be adopted when completing the final section of the Profit and Loss Account:

PROFIT AND LOSS ACCOUNT
(final section)

	£		£
Salary:		Net profit b/d . . .	3,730
R. Brown . . .	700		
Interest on capital:			
R. Brown . . .	500		
B. Smith . . .	250		
Share of profits:			
R. Brown . . .	1,140		
B. Smith . . .	1,140		
	£3,730		£3,730

E

C. Goodwill

One advantage of a partnership is that the constitution of the firm can be changed quite easily. A partnership is merely an agreement among individuals. If additional capital is required a new partner can be brought into the business; but the admittance of a new partner means that a new "firm" has come into being. If the original partnership was "Brown and Smith", the admittance of Jones really created a new firm of "Brown, Smith and Jones", although the name of the firm need not be altered; indeed, speaking generally, partners can carry on business in any name or style they please subject to registration where necessary under the Business Names Act, 1916, when the firm name is not composed of the names of all the partners. In deciding the terms under which Jones shall be admitted, a new factor comes into the picture, namely "goodwill". As a simple change has been described in this case, it will probably be arranged that Jones shall pay a premium on account of goodwill; this sum will be paid directly to Brown and Smith and no entries will be necessary in the partnership books.

Assume that after the expiry of a few more years of continued prosperity, "X. Company Ltd." decides to make an offer to buy the business. What price shall the company pay? Suppose the simplified Balance Sheet of the partnership is as follows:

Brown, Smith and Jones
BALANCE SHEET
as at date of proposed purchase

	£				£
Capital Accounts:					
Brown	10,000	Fixed assets	.	. .	13,000
Smith .	5,000	Current assets	.	. .	8,000
Jones . . .	5,000				
Creditors . . .	1,000				
	£21,000				£21,000

X. Company Ltd. will be acquiring a business the net worth of which is £20,000, i.e. the value of the assets less the amount of the creditors; but the company will be acquiring something much more valuable than net assets worth £20,000. The company will be acquiring a business which is a "going concern", that is, an already established and profitable business; not only will it buy the net assets, but it will acquire the business connection and reputation, "the probability that the old customers will resort to the old place" (per Lord Elton, *Crutwell* v. *Lye* 17 Ves. 346). It is these intangible, but substantial, rights which are usually referred to as "goodwill". That goodwill has been built up by the past efforts of Brown, Smith and Jones, and the results of these past efforts will continue to earn profits for the company in the future.

The negotiations which precede the transfer of the business will have to cover the question of the valuation of the goodwill. The value which X. Company Ltd. will place on the intangible item of goodwill must be related to the profit-earning capacity of the business of Brown, Smith and Jones, and the only yardstick which can be applied is that of the net profits of the most recent years. The rough-and-ready method of valuation of goodwill which is often applied is three to five years purchase of the average net profits of the recent past. Suppose that during the three years immediately preceding the proposed purchase the partnership net profits were £3,400, £3,100 and £3,700, and it is agreed that goodwill shall be valued at four years purchase. The calculation would be:

				£	
Net profits Year 1	.	.	.	3,400	
,, 2	.	.	.	3,100	
,, 3	.	.	.	3,700	
				£10,200	
Average net profit	.	.	.	£3,400	
4 years purchase	.	.	.	£13,600	Value of goodwill

A more scientific method of valuing goodwill is by a calculation of "super profits". Continuing the previous example, it is assumed that X. Company Ltd. has surplus funds which it wishes to put to a profitable use. The company could, by making a good investment, expect to get a reasonable rate of interest without risk or effort. It will use its money for the purchase of the partnership business only if it can earn above this "normal" rate, *i.e.* what are known as "super-profits". In calculating the value to be placed on the goodwill, it will eliminate the "normal" rate, and purchase the "super-profits". It is not proposed to examine in detail the factors which will affect the "normal" rate, since these will vary in different circumstances and in differing businesses. In this case let the normal rate be taken at 10 per cent of the net assets. The purchase price may now be calculated as follows:

		£
Net Assets:		
Assets	. . . . . .	21,000
Deduct liabilities	. . . . .	1,000
Net assets	. . . . . .	£20,000
Goodwill:		
Past net profit, Year 1	. . . . .	3,400
„ 2	. . . . .	3,100
„ 3	. . . . .	3,700
		£10,200
Average for 3 years	. . . . .	3,400
Deduct "normal" rate of 10 per cent (10 per cent of net assets of £20,000)	. . . .	2,000
"Super-profits"	. . . . .	£1,400
4 years purchase	. . . . .	£5,600
Purchase price:		
Net assets	. . . . . .	20,000
Goodwill	. . . . . .	5,600
		£25,600

It will be appreciated that the question of goodwill will arise whenever there is a change of ownership of a business, when a sole owner sells his business, when a partnership changes its personnel or is taken over by a company or when one company is acquired by another company.

D. Termination of Partnership

A serious defect of partnership is that (in common with the case of individual proprietorship) there is "unlimited liability" of the partners; should the assets prove insufficient to meet the claims of the creditors, then each partner is jointly liable for all the debts of the firm; for wrongful acts, or "torts", the partners are severally liable. The disadvantage of unlimited liability may be greater than it seems, since should one or more partners be unable to meet their share of any deficiency, then an additional burden will fall on the private estates of the remaining partner or partners. Although the ultimate risks of business fall on the members of a partnership, it is still a popular type of business organisation. The legal requirements are few, and since there is no obligation to publish accounts (as there is with limited companies), a partnership is eminently suitable for professional purposes, and in fact is the only form of organisation available for doctors, lawyers, dentists, practising accountants and others subject to professional regulations. It is also suitable for the distributive trades if the business is not too large.

More serious defects arise so far as concerns the management and continuity of the enterprise; as all partners are entitled to take part in the management, important decisions cannot be taken without the consent of all of them. Although the maximum number of partners is limited by law to twenty (except in the case of a banking business, where it is ten *), the difficulties of obtaining agreement among partners often make a more practicable limit four or five.

A partnership is simply an agreement among individuals, and if one dies or wishes to withdraw, then the existing agreement comes to an end. Since the personalities of the partners will be a dominant factor in the business dealings, a change of partners may cause the business to suffer.

The books of account will necessarily be maintained on double-entry principles to ensure accuracy and to facilitate equitable distribution of profit. In the event of the partnership being dissolved, it will be necessary to close the books of the firm. In closing the books of a partnership a Dissolution Account is opened to deal with the disposal of the assets and the costs of the dissolution. The assets may realise more or less than their book value so that the Dissolution Account will show either a surplus or a deficiency. This balance will be transferred to the partners' capital accounts in the same ratio as they share profits and losses. After the creditors have been paid off the amount of cash available will be shared among the partners, and the transfer of these amounts from the Cash Book will close the remaining accounts in the ledger.

* By virtue of the Companies Act, 1967, the number of partners may be unlimited in certain professional firms.

CHAPTER VII

ACCOUNTING FOR COMPANIES

PART 1—COMPANY ACCOUNTS

A. THE NATURE OF COMPANIES

As the size of a business grows and the scope of its operations widens so the need arises for more capital and greater stability of the capital structure.

Individual proprietorship and partnership forms of organisation no longer suffice. To obtain the capital necessary for large-scale production or operations appeal must be made to a wider class of investor, and for this purpose the limited-liability company is of particular importance. Even in the case of smaller organisations, the risk of unlimited liability may be so great as to deter enterprise, and as a result many small concerns also seek the protection and facilities gained by the formation of a limited company.

In the case of a sole owner or a partnership, although it is necessary to keep business affairs separate from the owner's personal affairs, there is no such distinction in law, and the ultimate risks of the business fall on the owner or partners—there is what is known as "unlimited liability". When a company is formed in accordance with the provisions of the Companies Act, a "body corporate" is created; this means that in the eyes of the law the company has a separate existence quite apart from the members of of whom it is from time to time composed. The company can, in its own right, own property and enter into contracts—for the purposes of law it is a "person". The liability of its members is limited, that is to say, once a member has paid or been credited with the nominal value of the shares for which he has agreed to subscribe, then his liability is at an end. If, in a "winding-up" of the company its assets are insufficient to meet its debts, the personal property of the members of the company cannot be pursued.

The principle of limited liability was first introduced in Great Britain by Act of Parliament in 1855; since then there have been many other Acts and amendments, the law as it stands at present being contained in the Companies Act 1948.* In addition, there are

* This Chapter refers to Companies Act, 1948. *See* Appendix IV for Companies Act, 1967.

special kinds of companies which have been formed under Royal Charters, and others which have been formed under special Acts of Parliament. Even under the Companies Act 1948 there are several kinds of companies which may be formed. The following diagram shows the various types of companies which are in existence:

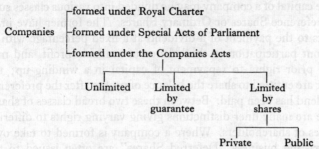

B. COMPANIES FORMED UNDER THE COMPANIES ACT 1948

The most important group of companies in the industrial and commercial world is that formed under the Companies Acts. Unlimited companies are few in number. Companies limited by guarantee are those in which the raising of share capital is not so important; many professional associations make use of this form of incorporation. It has the advantage of giving the members limited liability, the memorandum containing a provision which states the amount which members agree to contribute in a winding-up if the assets are insufficient to meet the debts and other liabilities.

By far the most important group is that in which the liability of the members is limited by shares. Since the members cannot be called on to pay more than the nominal value of their shares (plus any premium), once a shareholder has contributed the full amount (his shares being then "fully paid up") his liability ceases. It is largely this protection which has encouraged investors to provide the capital for large industrial and commercial companies. The growth of the limited-liability company is one of the most striking features of the period since the industrial revolution. New and existing companies are, as a result of the introduction of limited liability, able to draw on a wide variety of sources for their capital requirements. These sources include not only individual investors and companies but also insurance companies, finance houses, investment trusts and other bodies with large funds available for investment in industry.

In considering the advisability of taking up or buying shares in a particular company, various factors influence different investors. Some are willing to speculate in the hope of large dividends and possibly capital appreciation, whilst others seek a more certain income with greater security of capital. For these reasons the total share capital of a company may be divided into various classes such as Preference Shares or Ordinary Shares. The former have prior rights to the payment of a dividend at a fixed percentage with or without participation in the balance of available profit, and may have prior rights to repayment of capital in a winding-up; the latter are entitled to share the balance of profits after the preference dividend has been paid. Between these two broad classes of shares there are many finer distinctions giving varying rights to differing classes of shareholders. Where a company is formed to take over an existing business "Deferred Shares" are often issued to the owners of the original business, whose faith in the concern is shown by their agreeing that others shall come first in the division of a limited share of the profits in consideration of such deferred shareholders having any balance, which they expect will be at a higher rate. Deferred Shares frequently carry the controlling interest in the new company.

C. PRIVATE COMPANIES

It will have been noted that a distinction was made between private companies and public companies. Private companies are by far the most numerous, although not necessarily the most important. In return for certain restrictions they have certain privileges. A private company restricts the right to transfer its shares, limits the number of its numbers to fifty, excluding employees, and prohibits any invitation to the public to subscribe for any of its shares or debentures. The main advantage accruing to a private company, if it has been registered as "exempt", is that it does not have to file accounts, *i.e.* a Balance Sheet and documents relating thereto, with its annual return. Company files are maintained by the Registrar of Companies and are open to inspection by the public on payment of a fee of one shilling. Thus one important advantage of an exempt private company is that its affairs remain confidential to the company. The formation of a private company is particularly suitable to a family business, the proprietors having the protection of limited liability without the necessity of making their accounts public.

Prior to the passing of the Companies Act 1947 (later consolidated into the Companies Act 1948) there was no obligation on private companies to file accounts and balance sheets with the Registrar; but since the passing of that Act, to obtain this benefit a company must show that it is an "exempt private company". The basic conditions of exemption are:

(a) That no body corporate is the holder of any of its shares or debentures.

(b) That no persons other than the holder has any interest in the shares or debentures.

(c) That the number of persons holding debentures is not more than fifty.

Public companies are those which have no restrictions on the number of members or the transferability of shares. The shares can be freely bought and sold, and the main market for such transactions is the Stock Exchange. Large issues of share capital are accordingly offered to the public by public companies. Although there are fewer public than private companies, the majority of the large industrial and commercial concerns are public companies.

D. Formation of a Company

Any seven or more persons, two in the case of a private company, associated for any lawful purpose, may form an incorporated company by satisfying the conditions of the Companies Act. The promoters decide the necessary details and objects of the proposed company and enter into any negotiations which may be necessary, such as for the acquisition of property. The actual formalities of incorporation are relatively simple. It is necessary to pay stamp duties and file with the Registrar of Companies the following documents:

1. A Memorandum of Association.
2. Articles of Association.
3. A list of persons who have consented to act as directors.
4. A statement of the nominal capital of the company.
5. A statutory declaration that the requirements of the Act have been complied with.

The memorandum and the articles are the most important of these documents. In brief, the memorandum sets out the objects for which the company is being formed; it is in the nature of a "charter" and cannot be altered without following special procedures laid down in the Act. The articles of association are the regulations for management of the company, and since they deal with the rights of the shareholders, they can be altered by the company in general meetings. The Companies Act 1948 provides, in the First Schedule appended to the Act, forms of memorandum of association and model sets of articles. The schedule contains the following tables:

TABLE A. Regulations for Management of a Company Limited by Shares, not being a Private Company.

TABLE B. Form of Memorandum of Association of a Company limited by Shares.

TABLE C. Form of Memorandum and Articles of Association of a Company limited by Guarantee, and not having a Share Capital.

TABLE D. Memorandum and Articles of Association of a Company limited by Guarantee, and having a Share Capital.

TABLE E. Memorandum and Articles of Association of an unlimited Company having a Share Capital.

It is a popular practice for companies to adopt "Table A" as their articles of association with such modifications as are necessary in particular cases—although a company may if it so wishes adopt its own set of articles. The provisions of Table A will apply except to the extent that they are specifically excluded by the company's own regulations.

When the conditions of incorporation have been satisfactorily complied with, the Registrar issues a Certificate of Incorporation. It is with the issue of this certificate that the company comes into existence as a body corporate. The promoters must then raise the capital to commence business. The invitation to apply for shares is in the form of a Prospectus; this contains a statement of the objects for which the company is formed and, probably, its future prospects. The Fourth Schedule to the Companies Act 1948 specifies the matters to be set out in a prospectus. Where shares are offered to the public for subscription the prospectus must state the minimum amount which, in the opinion of the directors, must be raised to cover:

1. The purchase price of any property to be defrayed out of the proceeds of the issue.
2. The preliminary expenses of the company.
3. The repayment of moneys borrowed for the foregoing.
4. Working capital.

It is usual practice for the detailed arrangements for an issue to be undertaken by an "issuing house", which also underwrites the shares. Underwriting means that in return for a commission the issuing house agrees to take up any shares for which the public does not apply. In some cases issuing houses buy outright the whole of an issue and then make an "Offer for Sale" to the public, or the house might arrange a private "placing" of the issue with interested investors.

E. Formation of a Company—the Accounts

Where shares are not issued to the public some of the formalities might be dispensed with, since the cash will be received in a few large amounts. In the case of a public issue, then it is probable that only a proportion of the price of issue will have to be sent with the application. A special bank account is opened and arrangements usually made for the amounts payable to be sent direct to the company's bankers. By this means the entries in the company's Cash Book are restricted to the various totals notified by the bank. An application for shares makes no contract with the company; the applicant is signifying his willingness to take up a certain number of shares; but until the directors decide to allot shares to specific investors there is no creation of capital. In the ledger the entries are made in a special account called "The application and allotment account".

Illustration

A company whose nominal capital is £150,000 Ordinary Shares of £1 each, proposes to make an issue of 100,000 Ordinary Shares of £1 each payable 10s. on application and 10s. on allotment. Application for 110,000 shares were received on 10th January, the closing date.

CASH BOOK

		£	
Jan. 10	Ordinary Share Capital Application and Allotment Account 110,000 shares at 10s. each .	55,000	

APPLICATION AND ALLOTMENT ACCOUNT

			£
	Jan. 10	Cash . . .	55,000

It will be seen that applications have been received for more shares than are on issue. The directors will hold a meeting to decide how the 100,000 shares on issue shall be allotted among the applicants. This allotment may be in any form the directors wish: they may scale down all the applications, reduce the larger ones or refuse the smaller. When the decision has been made "Letters of Allotment" will be sent to the successful applicants, and "Letters of Regret", with cheques, to the unsuccessful ones.

In the example being used, assume that the directors proceed to allotment on 12th January; the letters were sent on 13th January and the allotment moneys were received by 17th January. As soon as the allotment is made share capital is created and the necessary transfer is made to capital account, the other entries then follow in chronological order.

CASH BOOK

		£			£
Jan. 10	Applications .	55,000	Jan. 13 Oversubscription moneys returned on 10,000 shares at 10s. . .		5,000
,, 17	Allotment 100,000 shares at 10s. .	50,000	,, 17 Balance c/d .		100,000
		£105,000			£105,000
,, 17	Balance b/d .	100,000			

APPLICATION AND ALLOTMENT ACCOUNT

		£			£
Jan. 12	Ordinary Share Capital Account .	100,000	Jan. 10 Cash applications.		55,000
,, 13	Cash (oversubscription) . .	5,000	,, 17 Cash allotment .		50,000
		£105,000			£105,000

ORDINARY SHARE CAPITAL ACCOUNT

		£
Jan. 12	Application and Allotment Account	100,000

The application and allotment account is simply a collection account which is opened to deal with the details of the issue. The capital account is in the nature of a total account, since the detail of the shareholdings will appear in the register of members.

Assuming no other transactions have been made, a Balance Sheet of the company will now appear as follows:

BALANCE SHEET
as at 17th January

Share capital:	Authorised £	Issued £	Current assets:	£
Ordinary Shares of £1 each	150,000	100,000	Cash at Bank	100,000
		£100,000		£100,000

Shares need not be issued at their nominal value. Only in special circumstances set out in the Companies Act can shares be issued at below nominal value, *i.e.* at a discount. But an issue may be made at such a higher price as the company can command, the excess over the nominal value being known as a premium. Factors which affect the price of issue are:

1. The dividend prospects.
2. The amount by which the issue is covered by net assets.
3. The probable demand for the shares as influenced by the company's standing.
4. Other market factors such as general rates of interest and security price levels.

The Act contains regulations for dealing with share premiums in the accounts. Where a company issues shares at a premium, the amount of the premium must be transferred to an account to be called "The Share premium Account", and the provisions of the Act relating to the reduction of share capital apply as if the share premium account was paid-up capital of the company. In other words, the Share premium Account is a capital reserve and is not available for distribution through the Profit and Loss Account. The premiums may be used for certain specified purposes, such as writing off preliminary or formation expenses, or be applied in paying up unissued shares of the company to be issued as fully-paid bonus shares.

A company may also raise capital funds by means of an issue of debentures. The word "debenture" has been used in a variety of senses, but the term is usually applied to the document evidencing a loan of money to a company on security. If a company issues mortgage debentures, then these give a charge over whole or part of the property of the company and should be secured by a trust deed. A debenture holder does not become a member of the company; he has simply loaned money to the company under the preferential rights and terms laid down in his debentures.

The entries for debentures in the books of account are of a similar nature to those for share capital. If a composite issue is being made for, say, Ordinary Shares, Preference Shares, and Debentures, separate accounts must be opened in the Ledger for each class of shares or debentures.

Example

A company whose authorised capital is 100,000 Ordinary Shares of £1 each, and 100,000 6 per cent Preference Shares of £1 each, makes an issue of 50,000 Ordinary Shares at 25s. (£1·25) per share, 50,000 6 per cent Preference Shares at 30s. (£1·5) per share, and 500 5 per cent First Mortgage Debentures of £100 each at 95. The full price was payable on application in all cases, the exact number of shares and debentures was applied for, application money was received on 10th January, and allotment was made on 12th January. The expenses of the issue were £1,000.

CASH BOOK

		£			£
Jan. 10	Ordinary Share Capital Application and Allotment Account . . .	62,500	Jan. 10	Issue expenses .	1,000
„ 10	6% Preference Share Capital Application and Allotment Account .	75,000	„ 12	Balance c/d . .	184,000
„ 10	1st Mortgage Debentures Application and Allotment Account .	47,500			
		£185,000			£185,000
12	Balance b/d . .	184,000			

Capital Ledger
Ordinary Share Capital
APPLICATION AND ALLOTMENT ACCOUNT

		£			£
Jan. 12	Ordinary Share Capital Account .	50,000	Jan. 10	Cash . .	62,500
,,	Share premium a/c .	12,500			
		£62,500			£62,500

Six per cent Preference Share Capital
APPLICATION AND ALLOTMENT ACCOUNT

		£			£
Jan. 12	6% Preference Share Capital Account . .	50,000	Jan. 10	Cash . . .	75,000
,, 12	Share premium Account . .	25,000			
		£75,000			£75,000

Five per cent Mortgage Debentures
APPLICATION AND ALLOTMENT ACCOUNT

		£			£
Jan. 12	5% First Mortgage Debentures Account . .	50,000	Jan. 10	Cash . .	47,500
			,, 12	Debenture discount account . .	2,500
		£50,000			£50,000

SHARE PREMIUM ACCOUNT

		£			£
Jan. 12	Balance c/d . .	37,500	Jan. 12	Ordinary Share Application and Allotment Account	12,500
			,, 12	6% Preference Share Application and Allotment Account . .	25,000
		£37,500			£37,500
			,, 12	Balance b/d .	£37,500

DEBENTURE DISCOUNT ACCOUNT

		£		
Jan. 12	Debentures Application and Allotment Account .	2,500		

ISSUE EXPENSES ACCOUNT

		£
Jan. 10 Cash . . .		1,000

ORDINARY SHARE CAPITAL ACCOUNT

		£
	Jan. 12 Application and Allotment Account	50,000

SIX PER CENT PREFERENCE SHARE CAPITAL ACCOUNT

		£
	Jan. 12 Application and Allotment Account	50,000

FIVE PER CENT FIRST MORTGAGE DEBENTURES ACCOUNT

		£
	Jan. 12 Application and Allotment Account	50,000

BALANCE SHEET
as at 12th January

	Authorised £	Issued £		£
Share capital:			*Current asset:*	
Ordinary Shares of £1 each .	100,000	50,000	Cash at bank . .	184,000
6% Preference Shares of £1 each .	100,000	50,000	*Formation and issue expenses:* Issue expenses . .	1,000
			Debenture discount .	2,500
	£200,000	100,000		
Capital reserve:				
Share-premium Account		37,500		
Debentures:				
500 First Mortgage Debentures of £100 each		50,000		
		£187,500		£187,500

F. STATUTORY AND OTHER BOOKS

There are certain books and records which a company must keep under the provisions of the Companies Act 1948. A list of these follows with a reference to the appropriate section of the Act. For more complete details the Act should be consulted:

1. *Register of members.* This contains names and addresses of members, details of their shareholdings and their tenure

(S.110). It is usually kept at the registered office of the company, but it may be kept elsewhere provided the Registrar is kept informed of its whereabouts. In some cases the share registration duties are performed by some other organisation which specialises in this work.

If a company has more than fifty members it must keep an index to the register of members, unless the Register is in such form as to constitute itself an index (S.111).

The register must be open for inspection by members at reasonable hours, the fee payable being one shilling (S.113). At the end of financial periods the share registration department has much work to complete in regard to dividends, etc., and it is usual for the register to be "closed" during such periods. During the period it is closed there is usually a restriction on the registration of transfers.

2. *Register of charges.* This must contain details of any charges affecting property of the company (S.104).

3. *Register of debenture holders.* It must be open at reasonable times for inspection by debenture holders or shareholders without payment of a fee and by other persons on payment of one shilling.

4. *Register of directors and secretaries.* This must contain full details of the persons concerned, and must be open for inspection by members without charge, and other persons on payment of one shilling (S.200).

5. *Register of directors' share and debenture holdings.* This must show as respects each director full details of holdings of shares and debentures (S.195).

6. *Minute books.* Every company must keep minute books of general meetings and directors meetings. The minutes of general meetings are open to inspection by members without charge.

It is possible to obtain from company printers and stationers books which contain specially printed pages to conform with all the above requirements, and these are particularly useful for use by the smaller company.

G. Books of Account

The Companies Act 1948 contains the following provisions (S.147).

Every company shall cause to be kept proper books of account with respect to:

(a) All sums of money received and expended by the company and the matters in respect of which the receipt and expenditure takes place.

(b) All sales and purchases of goods by the company.

(c) The assets and liabilities of the company.

Section 147 goes on to say that the "proper books" must give a "true and fair view" of the company's affairs and explain its transactions. In view of what was said in Chapter V on accounting aids, it may be asked whether some of the methods explained in that chapter could be said to be "proper books of account". This point, however, is covered in Section 436 of the Act, which states, "Any register, index, minute book or book of account required by the Act to be kept by a company may be kept either by making the entries in bound books or by recording the matter in question *in any other way.*" Where such records are not kept in bound books "adequate precautions shall be taken for guarding against falsification and facilitating its discovery". Thus simplified or machine accounting methods may be used, and in the Ninth Schedule to the Act, an obligation is laid on the company's auditors to state in their report whether in their opinion "proper books of account" have been kept.

H. REPORTS TO SHAREHOLDERS

There are important provisions in the Companies Act which lay upon the directors the duty of placing before the company at the annual general meeting a Balance Sheet and Profit and Loss Account. Attached to these accounts must be a copy of the directors' and auditor's reports.

In previous chapters revenue accounts and balance sheets were discussed from the point of view of providing information for management; in this chapter it is the accounts which have to be provided for the members which are under discussion. The Act and the Eighth Schedule do not specify a particular form which the accounts and Balance Sheet shall take, but state the information they must contain.

It is not proposed here to quote in full the provisions of the Eighth Schedule, but to state briefly the information required.

1. The Balance Sheet

(a) The authorised and issued share capital, liabilities and assets shall be summarised.

(b) The following must be specified:

(i) Redeemable Preference Shares and earliest date of redemption.

(ii) Interest paid out of capital and the rate of such interest unless shown in the profit and loss account.

(iii) The share premium account.

(c) The following shall be stated under separate headings:

(i) Preliminary, formation and issue expenses of shares and debentures, so far as they are not written off.

(ii) Capital reserves, revenue reserves, provisions, liabilities, fixed and current assets.

(iii) Investments, distinguishing between trade and other investments.

(iv) Goodwill, patents and trade-marks, so far as not written off.

(v) Aggregate amount of bank loans and overdrafts.

(vi) The amount, after deduction of tax, which is recommended for dividends.

Other paragraphs in the Eighth Schedule state that the method of arriving at the value of the fixed assets and the aggregate amount of depreciation written off shall be shown. Other information which may be shown by way of notes or in appendices to the Balance Sheet include such items as contingent liabilities, capital expenditure not provided for, market value of investments and corresponding figures for the immediately preceding financial year.

It will be obvious from the foregoing that a large amount of information is required to give a true and fair view of the financial position of a company. This is a great advance on previous practice, since before the Companies Act 1947 the provisions were much less stringent.

The Balance Sheet in its published form is intended primarily for the information of the shareholders, but naturally, many of them will have had little or no training in financial matters. Within the limits available, the presentation of the actual Balance Sheet should be as simple as possible, the more detailed information being relegated to appended statistical tables and reports. By this means a shareholder will be able to look at the Balance Sheet and see a clear picture of the main facts; if he wishes to delve more deeply the detailed data is there for him to consult. In this way the supporting statistical information can be more comprehensive than if the attempt is made to confine it within the bounds of a Balance Sheet. Comparative figures, for example, can cover a number of years and not be limited to the immediately preceding year. Other people besides shareholders may require comprehensive information as to the finances of a public company.

The merits of the respective methods of presentation, whether in conventional form or columnar form, have already been discussed. In the context of this chapter it is the published accounts which are being dealt with, and the principles which have been stressed are:

1. The Balance Sheet should be simple, straightforward and have clear headings.
2. The supplementary statistical information should be relegated to supporting schedules, and should be comprehensive, going much beyond the minimum statutory requirements.

2. The Profit and Loss Account

The provisions of the Companies Act 1948 relating to the Profit and Loss Account differ from those relating to the Balance Sheet. The published Balance Sheet does not differ in essence from that drawn up under normal accounting methods. In the case of the Profit and Loss Account, however, the Act specifies certain information which must be shown, and an account will have to be specially prepared to contain this information. Some of the items specified by the Act are charges against profits and some are allocations of profit. This will be evident from the following brief analysis of the main information required.

The Eighth Schedule states that the following shall be shown:

(a) Depreciation of fixed assets.
(b) Interest on debentures and fixed loans.
(c) Taxation—distinguishing between income tax and other forms of taxation, if possible.
(d) Amounts provided for the redemption of capital or loans.

(e) Amounts allocated to, or withdrawn from, reserves and provisions.

(f) Income from investments.

(g) Dividends paid or proposed, whether or not subject to tax.

(h) Auditor's remuneration where not fixed by general meeting.

(i) Corresponding figures for the immediately preceding financial year.

In addition to the foregoing, Section 196 contains important provisions regarding the disclosure of amounts paid to directors. It states that in the accounts laid before the company in general meeting or in a statement annexed thereto, the following information shall be shown (again this is a brief summary of a complex section of the Act).

1. Directors' remuneration, distinguishing between fees and other emoluments.

2. Directors and past directors' pensions.

3. Compensation paid to directors and past directors in respect of loss of office.

In considering the presentation of all the aforementioned information in the accounts to be presented to the shareholders, once again the principal object should be clarity and simplicity. The directors' report should contain a well-tabulated statement which shows the profit for the year after deduction of all charges. Then should follow concise details of recommendations for appropriations and distribution of dividend. The Profit and Loss Account can then show the full detailed information required by the Act and the statistical tables can include more comprehensive information. It is felt that the foregoing is a better method than the presentation of a brief Profit and Loss Account, with details relegated to notes or appendices, where, perhaps, some information of interest to shareholders might escape notice. Thus the method of dealing with information relative to the Profit and Loss Account should be:

1. A concise statement of net profit and appropriations in the directors' report.

2. A fully detailed Profit and Loss Account.

3. Further information in statistical tables appended.

3. The Directors' report to the shareholders

With the Balance Sheet laid before the company in general meeting the Companies Act 1948 requires, in Section 157, that there shall be attached a report by the directors. This report must deal with the state of the company's affairs, the amount which they recommend should be paid by way of dividends and the amount which they propose to carry to reserves. Directors' reports are often short formal statements strictly within the minimum legal requirements, perhaps supplemented by a statement from the chairman of the board of directors. It is undoubtedly desirable that something more than the minimum legal requirements should be given, and it is equally important to consider the form in which this additional information is provided.

In the previous paragraphs in this chapter the point was stressed that shareholders are not necessarily accountants or business-men, so that the wording and presentation of the directors' report should be within the understanding of ordinary people. The written statement of the company's position should be simple and free from technicalities. Descriptions of technical activities can be made more real and acceptable by photographs which illustrate the text.

When facts and figures are being discussed charts and diagrams can be used to advantage. These charts will not necessarily be the same as those prepared for use by management. The most simple forms of charts will be those which show areas to represent quantities or amounts. The most useful of these are:

1. *The circle graph.* This is useful for presentation of costs or distribution of net revenue. In principle, it shows a circle which represents the total amount, and this is divided into segments, the area of which gives the proportion each item bears to the total. A circle graph is often thought of as a pie, and the segments as slices of that pie, thus they are often referred to as "pie-charts". A clearer representation can often be achieved by adding an additional dimension to the circle, as shown in Fig. 5.

2. *Rectangle graphs.* In these the area of the rectangle represents the total sum concerned, and the divisions of the rectangle the proportion of the parts to the total. By this means the growth of a business can be presented pictorially as shown in Fig. 6.

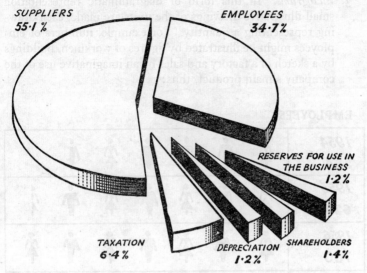

FIG. 4

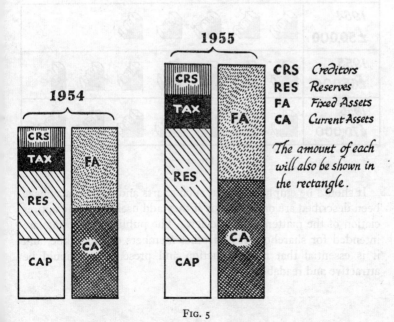

FIG. 5

3. *Pictograms.* In this form of diagrammatic representation small illustrative drawings of the units are made, each drawing representing a quantity. For example, numbers of employees might be illustrated by figures of workmen, buildings by a sketch of a factory and sales by an imaginative use of the company's main product, thus:

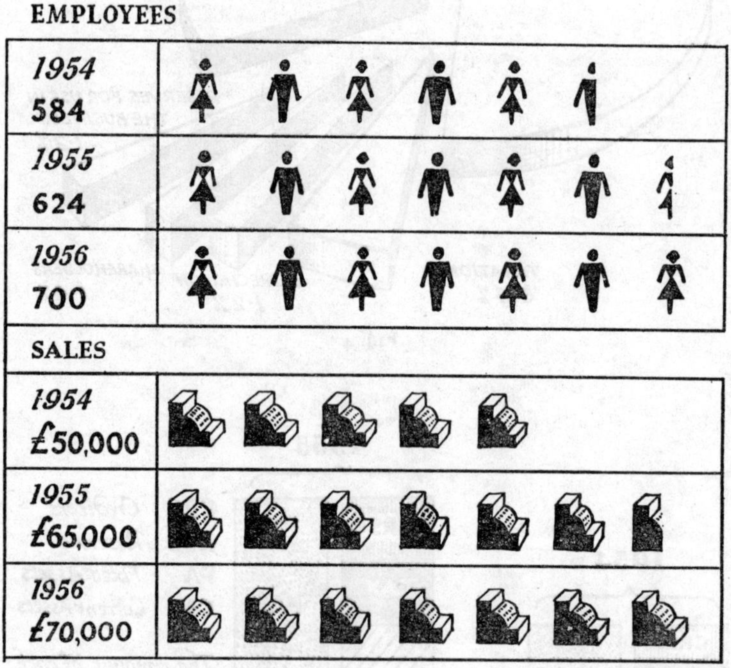

EMPLOYEES

Fig. 6

It should be emphasised that such charts and diagrams as have been described are only of value if they add usefully to the appreciation of the matters under review. The published accounts are intended for shareholders and other members of the public, and it is essential that the production and presentation should be attractive and readable.

PART 2—GROUP ACCOUNTING

A. The Nature of Holding Companies

One of the outstanding features of modern industrial organisation is the existence of large integrated groups of companies. There are various methods of amalgamation, but the most important is the relationship between holding company and subsidiary company. As the management of a company is vested in the board of directors, one company can obtain control of another by controlling the composition of its board of directors. The usual method of acquiring such control is the purchase of a sufficient amount of share capital to enable the acquiring company's nominees to constitute a majority on the board of the other company. When this is the case the company whose shares have been purchased is called a subsidiary company. The Companies Act 1948 defines a subsidiary company as follows:

"For the purposes of this Act, a company shall . . . be deemed to be a subsidiary of another if, but only if—

(a) That other either:

(i) is a member of it and controls the composition of its board of directors; or
(ii) holds more than half in nominal value of its equity share capital.

(b) the first mentioned company is a subsidiary of any company which is that other's subsidiary."

The position of holding company and subsidiary can, therefore, arise in two ways.

1. Assume that Company A holds sufficient of the voting shares in each of Companies B and C to control both the latter's boards of directors; B and C are therefore subsidiaries of Company A. This relationship could be shown diagrammatically as follows:

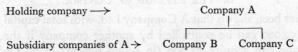

Holding company ⟶   Company A

Subsidiary companies of A →   Company B   Company C

2. Now suppose that the foregoing arrangement still holds good, but that Company C itself has control of Company D.

In this case Company D would be a subsidiary of both Companies A and C. This situation can be illustrated as follows:

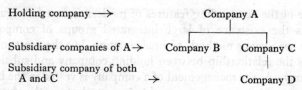

Holding company ⟶   Company A

Subsidiary companies of A→   Company B   Company C

Subsidiary company of both
    A and C   ⟶   Company D

It is important to note that to obtain control it is only necessary for sufficient shares to be acquired to ensure a majority vote at the annual meeting when the directors are appointed. It is a fairly general rule that the voting rights of a company, or a substantial majority of the votes, are vested in the Ordinary Shares, although in some cases a much smaller number of shares, called Deferred Shares, may carry the majority vote. Whichever is the case, the company which wishes to obtain control need only interest itself in the shares which carry the major voting rights. As an example of this assume that the capital of A Company Ltd. has been raised as follows:

Share capital: £
     100,000 Ordinary Shares of £1 each   .   .   .   100,000
     100,000 6% Preference Shares of £1 each   .   .   100,000
Debentures:
     50,000 5½% First Mortgage Debentures of £1 each   .   50,000

                                              £250,000

For the purposes of this example it is assumed that the right of voting at meetings of the company is conferred by the holding of Ordinary Shares. Then if another company can acquire by purchase 50,001 of the Ordinary Shares it will have a majority vote at the meetings of A Company Ltd. and will be able to control the composition of the board, thus establishing the relationship of holding and subsidiary companies.

B. The Pyramid of Control

It has been shown that A Company Ltd. with total capital funds of £250,000 can be controlled by another company if the other company can acquire 51,000 (in round figures) of its Ordinary Shares. B Company Ltd. is formed with a capital of £51,000 in Ordinary Shares of £1 each with the purpose of acquiring ordinary shares in A Company Ltd. When B Company Ltd. has acquired the shares it will become the holding company of A Company Ltd.

Any company which could now acquire a majority of B Company Ltd.'s shares, say, 26,000, will obtain control of B Company Ltd. and through it the control of A Company. C Company Ltd. is now formed with a capital of £26,000 in Ordinary Shares of £1 each, for the purpose of acquiring Ordinary Shares in B Company Ltd. and through these shares obtains control of both B and A Companies.

The above process can be continued and can be illustrated in the following table (the number of shares necessary to acquire control has to be kept in round figures for the sake of simplicity, but it must be realised that a simple majority of one would be sufficient):

A Company Ltd. Total capital funds	£250,000
B Company Ltd. Capital (invested in 51,000 Ordinary Shares of A Company Ltd.)	£51,000
C Company Ltd. Capital (invested in 26,000 Ordinary Shares of B Company Ltd.)	£26,000
D Company Ltd. Capital (invested in 14,000 Ordinary Shares of C Company Ltd.)	£14,000
E Company Ltd. Capital (invested in 8,000 Ordinary Shares of D Company Ltd.)	£8,000

At this point a company owning £4,001 in Ordinary Shares of £1 each in E Company Ltd. would control, through a pyramid of companies, A Company Ltd., whose total capital funds are £250,000. If the capitals of companies B to E had been raised in part in non-voting Preference Shares, then the amount of capital necessary for E Company Ltd. would, in fact, have been very much smaller.

C. The Accounts of Holding Companies

The Companies Act 1948 contains detailed provisions regarding the accounts to be laid before the members of holding companies. The introductory section 150 commences as follows:

"Where at the end of its financial year a company has subsidiaries, accounts or statements (in this Act referred to as 'Group Accounts') dealing as hereinafter mentioned with the state of affairs and profit and loss of the company and the subsidiaries shall, subject to the next following subsection, be laid before the company in general meeting when the company's own balance sheet and profit and loss account are so laid."

The commencement of section 151 states:

"Subject to the next following subsection, the group accounts laid before a holding company shall be consolidated accounts comprising:

"(a) a consolidated balance sheet dealing with the state of affairs of the company and all the subsidiaries to be dealt with in group accounts.

"(b) a consolidated profit and loss account dealing with the profit or loss of the company and those subsidiaries."

There are a number of alternatives and options which may be made in special circumstances, but in general the two quoted sections give a general picture of the law regarding the group accounts.

D. The Preparation of Consolidated Balance Sheets

It is not within the scope of this book to give detailed instruction for the preparation of Consolidated Balance Sheets, which, in practice, can be a complicated matter; but it is possible to show simple examples in which the general principles can be illustrated. In the examples given, for the sake of brevity, a holding company is designated "H Co. Ltd." and a subsidiary company is designated "S Co. Ltd."

Example I

In this example H Co. Ltd. has acquired all the shares in S Co. Ltd. at their nominal value. The simplified Balance Sheets of the two companies are as follows:

H CO. LTD		£		S CO. LTD.		£
Capital .	10,000		Investment in S Co.		Capital .	5,000	Sundry assets	6,000

H CO. LTD		£			S CO. LTD.		£
Capital .	10,000		Investment in S Co.		Capital .	5,000	Sundry assets	6,000
Creditors	2,000		Ltd., 5,000 shares	5,000	Creditors	1,000		
			Sundry assets .	7,000				
	£12,000			£12,000		£6,000		£6,000

The object of the Consolidated Balance Sheet is to show to the members of H Co. Ltd. what their capital represents in assets and liabilities. The assets and liabilities of both companies are therefore brought in, and the investment held by H Co. Ltd. is set off against the share capital of S Co. Ltd. (The inset column of figures is shown to illustrate the working: in practice only the total would be shown.) The Consolidated Balance Sheet of the two companies to be laid before the members of H Co. Ltd. would be as follows:

CONSOLIDATED BALANCE SHEET OF
H CO. LTD. and S CO. LTD.

	£	£		£	£
Capital (H Co. Ltd.)		10,000	Sundry assets:		
Creditors:			H Co. Ltd. . .	7,000	
H Co. Ltd. . .	2,000		S Co. Ltd. . .	6,000	
S Co. Ltd. . .	1,000				13,000
		3,000			
		£13,000			£13,000

Example II—Cost of acquiring control

It rarely happens in practice that shares are acquired at the nominal value. More frequently they are purchased at a price in excess of the nominal. Taking the same example as before, it is assumed that the shares in S Co. Ltd. are bought at a price of 30s. per share. It is necessary to show in the Consolidated Balance Sheet the cost of acquiring control of S Co. Ltd. Since the price paid is in excess of the value of the net assets, the extra amount paid is in the form of a payment for the goodwill of S Co. Ltd.

The Balance Sheets of the two companies will now appear as follows:

H CO. LTD.

	£		£
Capital .	12,500	Investment in S Co.	
Creditors	2,000	Ltd., 5,000 shares	
		at cost . .	7,500
		Sundry assets .	7,000
	£14,500		£14,500

S CO. LTD.

	£		£
Capital .	5,000	Sundry assets	6,000
Creditors	1,000		
	£6,000		£6,000

The Consolidated Balance Sheet is compiled in the same manner as before, but with the addition of 'Goodwill' to show the cost of acquiring control of S Co. Ltd.

CONSOLIDATED BALANCE SHEET OF
S CO. LTD. and H CO. LTD.

	£	£		£	£
Capital . . .		12,500	Goodwill:		
Creditors:			Investment in S		
H Co. Ltd. . .	2,000		Co. Ltd. at cost	7,500	
S Co. Ltd. . .	1,000		Less Nominal Value	5,000	
		3,000			2,500
			Sundry assets:		
			H Co. Ltd. . .	7,000	
			S Co. Ltd. . .	6,000	
					13,000
		£15,500			£15,500

Example III—Minority interests in share capital

It was explained earlier in this chapter that it was not necessary for H. Co. Ltd. to buy all the shares in S Co. Ltd. in order to acquire control. In the following example it is assumed that H Co. Ltd. has in fact purchased 3,000 shares at 30s. each. One method of preparing a Consolidated Balance Sheet is to include only a proportion (in this case three-fifths) of S Co. Ltd's assets and liabilities. In most cases, however, as the capital structure of companies is complex and includes various classes of shares with differing rights, it is more appropriate to include the whole of S Co. Ltd. assets and liabilities, as before, and show the shares held by outside shareholders in S Co. Ltd. as a liability of the group. The Balance Sheets will be taken as follows:

H CO. LTD.

	£		£
Capital .	10,000	Investment in S Co.	
Creditors	1,500	Ltd., 3,000 shares	
		at cost . .	4,500
		Sundry assets .	7,000
	£11,500		£11,500

S CO. LTD.

	£		£
Capital .	5,000	Sundry assets	6,000
Creditors	1,000		
	£6,000		£6,000

The Consolidated Balance Sheet will now appear:

CONSOLIDATED BALANCE SHEET OF
H CO. LTD. and S CO. LTD.

	£	£		£	£
Capital . . .		10,000	Goodwill:		
Creditors:			Investment in S		
H Co. Ltd. . .	1,500		Co. Ltd. at cost	4,500	
S Co. Ltd. . .	1,000		*Less* Nominal value	3,000	
		2,500			1,500
Minority Interest in			Sundry assets:		
S Co. Ltd.:			H Co. Ltd. . .	7,000	
Capital . .		2,000	S Co. Ltd. . .	6,000	
					13,000
		£14,500			£14,500

Example IV—Minority interest in capital profits and reserves

In the following example the Balance Sheets of the two companies include the usual items of capital, reserves and profit and loss account balances. The outside shareholders in S Co. Ltd. are interested in a proportion of the net worth of their company, and thus it is necessary to show this interest as a liability of the group. The Balance Sheets are now as follows:

H CO. LTD.

	£		£
Capital .	10,000	Investment in	
Reserves .	3,000	S Co. Ltd.,	
Profit and		3,000 shares	
Loss Account	1,000	cost 30s. .	4,500
Creditors .	1,500	Sundry assets	11,000
	£15,500		£15,500

S CO. LTD.

	£		£
Capital . .	5,000	Sundry	
Reserves .	1,000	assets	7,500
Profit and			
Loss Account	500		
Creditors .	1,000		
	£7,500		£7,500

In consolidating S Co. Ltd. Balance Sheet it is now necessary to apportion capital, reserves and Profit and Loss Account balance

CONSOLIDATED BALANCE SHEET OF
H CO. LTD. and S CO. LTD.

	£	£	£		£	£
Capital . . .			10,000	Goodwill:		
Reserves:				Investment in S Co.		
H Co. Ltd.. .		3,000		Ltd. at cost .	4,500	
S Co. Ltd. . .	1,000			Less Nominal value .	3,000	
Minority int. (⅖) .	400					1,500
		600		Sundry assets:		
			3,600	H Co. Ltd.. . .	11,000	
Profit and Loss Account:				S Co. Ltd. . . .	7,500	
H Co. Ltd.. .		1,000				18,500
S. Co. Ltd.. .	500					
Minority int. (⅖) .	200					
		300				
			1,300			
Creditors:						
H Co. Ltd.. .		1,500				
S Co. Ltd. . .		1,000				
			2,500			
Minority interest in S Co. Ltd.:						
Capital . .		2,000				
Reserves . .		400				
Profit and Loss Account . .		200				
			2,600			
			£20,000			£20,000

in the proportions of capital held by H Co. Ltd. and that held by S Co. Ltd. Thus three-fifths of these balances can be held as accruing to H Co. Ltd. whilst the remaining two-fifths accrue to the outside shareholders in S Co. Ltd. and are shown in total as a liability of the group. In the Consolidated Balance Sheet, which appears above, an additional column has been added to show the calculations required.

Example V—Pre-acquisition profits

Where at the date of acquisition of control the subsidiary company has existing balances in Profit and Loss and Reserve Accounts, such balances are not available for distribution to the shareholders of the acquiring company. They must be shown in the Consolidated Balance Sheet as capital reserves. It is inappropriate, however, to show such a capital reserve on the liabilities side of the Balance Sheet and goodwill on the assets side, the two balances are therefore set off against each other. In this case the Balance Sheets will be taken as follows:

H CO. LTD. 31/12/......

	£		£
Capital . .	15,000	Investment in	
Profit and		S Co. Ltd.,	
Loss Account	3,000	5,000 shares	
Creditors .	3,500	at cost	6,500
		Fixed assets .	10,000
		Current assets	5,000
	£21,500		£21,500

S CO. LTD. 31/12/......

	£		£
Capital . .	5,000	Fixed	
Reserve . .	250	assets	6,000
Profit and		Current	
Loss Account	500	assets	1,750
Creditors .	2,000		
	£7,750		£7,750

It is assumed that H Co. Ltd. acquired its shares in S Co. Ltd. on 1st January 19—, when S Co. Ltd. reserve stood at £250, and its Profit and Loss Account at £300. (There are, therefore, pre-acquisition reserves of £250 and profit of £300.)

The method is to transfer the pre-acquisition profits to capital reserve, and then deduct the total capital reserve from goodwill. Profits which have accrued subsequent to acquisition are available to the members of the controlling company and may be added to its profits.

CONSOLIDATED BALANCE SHEET OF
H CO. LTD. and S CO. LTD.
at 31 Dec. 19......

	£	£	£		£	£	£
Capital . . .			15,000	Goodwill:			
Capital reserves:				Investments in S			
→Reserves S Co. Ltd.		250		Co. Ltd. at cost		6,500	
→Profit and Loss Account S Co. Ltd. . .		300		Less Nominal value	5,000		
Deducted from goodwill—contra .		550		Less Capital reserve—contra .		550	
Revenue reserves:						5,550	
S Co. Ltd. . .		250					950
Less Transfer to capital reserve .		250		Fixed Assets:			
		—		H Co. Ltd. . .		10,000	
				S Co. Ltd. . .		6,000	
Profit and Loss Account:							16,000
H Co. Ltd. . .		3,000		Current assets:			
S Co. Ltd. . .	500			H Co. Ltd. . .		5,000	
Less Transfer to capital reserve .	300			S Co. Ltd. . .		1,750	
		200					6,750
			3,200				
Current liabilities:							
Creditors—							
H Co. Ltd. .		3,500					
S Co. Ltd. .		2,000					
			5,500				
			£23,700				£23,700

Example VI—Inter-company balances and general example

The last point which is considered in this brief survey of group accounts is the situation where there are transactions between the two companies. It is quite probable that the companies will trade with each other, and these transactions are dealt with in the ordinary manner in the books of account. When the Consolidated Balance Sheet is being drawn up, care will have to be taken in eliminating any inter-company balances by offsetting a liability in one company's Balance Sheet against the corresponding asset in the other company's Balance Sheet.

If one company holds stock which has been purchased from the other, the price at which the transaction will have taken place will be cost plus profit, but as the goods have not been sold outside the companies, when considering the group aspect it cannot be said that the profit has been realised. Any such unrealised profit is, therefore, deducted from the value of the stock of the one company, and the same amount deducted from the Profit and Loss Account of the other company. If there is a minority interest in the subsidiary company it is only the proportion of profit which accrues to the group which must be eliminated.

The following example is a general one to illustrate all the matters which have been under discussion:

H CO. LTD. 31/12/...

	£		£
Capital . .	30,000	Investment in	
Reserve . .	10,000	S Co. at cost	
Profit and		20,000 shares	
Loss Account	5,000	cost . .	32,000
Creditors .	15,000	Fixed assets .	12,000
Bills payable .	1,000	Stock . .	6,000
Owing to S Co.		Debtors . .	8,000
Ltd. . .	1,500	Cash . .	4,500
	£62,500		£62,500

S CO LTD. 31/12/...

	£		£
Capital Ord.		Fixed	
Shares .	30,000	assets .	20,000
5% Pref. Shares	10,000	Stock .	10,000
Creditors .	5,000	Debtors .	10,000
Reserve . .	9,000	Owing by	
Profit and		H Co.	
Loss Account	3,000	Ltd. .	1,500
		Bills receivable	
		.	1,500
		Cash .	14,000
	£57,000		£57,000

The above Balance Sheets are drawn up one year after acquisition, at which date S Co. Ltd'.s reserve stood at £6,000 and its Profit and Loss Account at £1,500. Stock held by S Co. Ltd. includes goods valued at £2,100 purchased from H Co. Ltd. (cost to H Co. Ltd. £1,800).

The method to be followed in compiling the Consolidated Balance Sheet is to transfer the minority interest first, and then all other adjustments are made in proportion to the Ordinary Share

F

capital held by H Co. Ltd. The Preference Shares of S Co. Ltd. carry no voting rights, and are considered as a liability of the group to the Preference Shareholders.

CONSOLIDATED BALANCE SHEET OF
H CO. LTD. and S CO. LTD.
at 31st December 19...

	£	£	£		£	£	£
Capital . . .			30,000	Goodwill:			
Capital reserves:				Investment in S Co. Ltd. at cost .		32,000	
Reserve S Co. Ltd.	4,000			Less:			
Profit and Loss Account S Co. Ltd.	1,000			Nominal value	20,000		
				Capital reserve— contra .	5,000		
Deducted good-will —contra .		5,000				25,000	
							7,000
Revenue reserves and surpluses:				Fixed assets:			
Reserve Account—				H Co. Ltd. . .		12,000	
H Co. Ltd.		10,000		S Co. Ltd. . .		20,000	
S Co. Ltd.	9,000						32,000
Less Minority interest ⅓ .	3,000			Current assets:			
	6,000			Stock—			
Less Transfer to capital reserve (⅔ × £6,000) .	4,000			H Co. Ltd. . .		6,000	
		2,000		S Co. Ltd. .	10,000		
			12,000	Less adjustment (⅔ of £300) .	200		
Profit and Loss Account:						9,800	
H Co. Ltd.	5,000			Debtors—			
Less Stock adjustment .	200			H Co. Ltd. .	8,000		
		4,800		S Co. Ltd. .	10,000		
S Co. Ltd. .	3,000					18,000	
Less Minority interest ⅓ .	1,000			Bills receivable—			
	2,000			S Co. Ltd. .		1,500	
Less Transfer to capital reserve (⅔ × £1,500) .	1,000			Cash—			
		1,000		H Co. Ltd. .	4,500		
			5,800	S Co. Ltd. .	14,000		
Current liabilities:						18,500	
Creditors—							53,800
H Co. Ltd. .	15,000						
S Co. Ltd. .	5,000						
Bills payable H Co. Ltd. .	1,000						
			21,000				
Minority interest in S Co. Ltd.:							
Ordinary Share capital	10,000						
Preference Share capital	10,000						
Reserves .	3,000						
Profit and Loss Account .	1,000						
			24,000				
			£92,800				£92,800

PART 3—THE ACCOUNTANT AND MANAGEMENT

A. General Considerations

When considering the relation between the accountant and management it is well to think about what is meant by the term "management". In books on the subject of management in general much discussion is given to the terminology, and there seems to be some doubt whether an exact definition of management can be agreed upon. For the purposes of this section, however, management is considered from two points of view. The first is the Board of Directors, that body appointed by the shareholders to decide the broad lines of policy on which the company will operate. The second consideration is the executive or salaried managers, who are appointed by the board to put the policy into operation. Thus under the first heading there are the chairman of the board and his co-directors, whilst under the second there are the top executive of the company, the General Manager, and the managers of the functional divisions of the business, such as the sales manager, the production manager, the chief accountant, the personnel officer and so on.

In large companies it often happens that the board consists of full-time directors who are also executive officers in charge of specific functions so that there is such nomenclature as Managing Director, Sales Director, Production Director, etc. In this case the persons filling these offices have a dual capacity, that of director and that of executive. There must be no confusion between the two functions. A board of directors is a body having a corporate responsibility through a majority decision being recorded in the minutes and being conveyed to the chief executive officer by the secretary. Once the board meeting has finished, the director has no authority unless it be for specific purposes given to him by the board, such as to sign contracts on behalf of the company. If he is an "executive director", then he assumes responsibility for this function under the authority of the chief executive. It seems that American practice is much more definite on this point. The Productivity Report of the Anglo-American Council on Productivity, entitled *Management Accounting*, has the following paragraphs:

"Two features in the normal construction of an American company are of particular interest:

"(a) The clear distinction between the function of director and that of an officer of the company. An officer is always called in his daily work by his title as an officer. The fact that he may also be a director does not add any authority to his executive position.

"(b) The clear distinction drawn between the officers and the rest of management."

B. The Accountant as a Director

Consideration will first be given to the position of an accountant who is a member of a board of directors, and is not an officer of the company but an outside accountant, perhaps a member of a firm of professional accountants. In some quarters this development is condemned on the grounds that accountants as a class are too prudent and too conservative in their outlook, whilst what is needed in modern business and industry is a go-ahead, enterprising spirit.

Is this argument valid? It may have some validity so far as concerns accountants who are too steeped in the "historical accounting" attitude. It may arise from the fact that the accountant in his professional capacity as an auditor is the "watchdog" of the shareholders. But this is not the aspect of the accountant's work which is under consideration. The work of the board of directors is interwoven with financial considerations; financial control is inevitable if a business is going to move forward firmly on the basis of facts. Financial information and reports are constantly on the agenda of the board meeting. A board of directors should ideally be composed of a wide cross-section of persons experienced in technical, productive, distributive and other functions of the business, but it is also essential that at least one of their number should appreciate the financial implications of policy. The deliberations of the board will be on a surer footing if one of the members is an accountant who can interpret the financial information.

C. The Accountant as an Executive

Attention will now be focused on the position of an accountant who is an officer of the company, perhaps "the chief accountant". Much has already been said, and will be said, in these pages of the necessity of a modern approach to accounting in industrial undertakings, the necessity for integrating the financial and the cost accounts, and on the application of budgetary techniques. All this demands specialised knowledge and skill on the part of the accountant and in addition an understanding of productive, distributive and managerial techniques.

There are other spheres of activity in which the accountant's special training is of particular service. In business there are increasing demands on the office for more information, and for this purpose new and more specialised equipment is constantly being made available. As a result, office costs tend to increase. Accountants who have played a large part in reducing operation costs must also concentrate on clerical cost reduction, and to this end need to take a wide view of the administration and paper work of an organisation. In connection with the increasing application of electronics to office methods, the electronics engineer can invent and adapt the technical equipment, but it is the accountant who must harness the technique to serve management, the organisation and the community.

D. The Accountant as Controller

It will be apparent from the foregoing that in a large organisation the duties of the accountant have progressed far beyond those of supervising the book-keeping processes and preparing the final accounts and Balance Sheet. There arises the need for someone to control the entire accounting techniques of the organisation. These techniques should be considered in their widest sense, and the accountant should be an executive in charge of a separate technical division of the business. Because of the historical associations of the word "accountant", it is preferable that he be given some other title to indicate his wider sphere of responsibility, and it is in this sense that the title of "controller" is used. The term "controller" reflects the changed outlook of accounting, the emphasis being on control of current and future activities rather than on the recording of past events.

In organising his division the controller has departments dealing with the following sections of the work:

1. *Financial accounting*—this section covers the normal book-keeping and accounting procedures leading to the compilation of the final accounts. There are subdivisions dealing with taxation, preparation of the payroll and the details of purchases and sales routines.

2. *Cost accounting*—cost ascertainment, estimates, standard costing and variance procedure, stores control and inventory preparation.

3. *Budget accounting*—the control of the budget procedures outlined in later chapters.

4. *Organisation and methods and internal audit*—this section specialises in office management and co-operates with all divisions of the organisation in working out office procedures, design of forms, etc. An important part of this section's work is to deal with the introduction of new machines and equipment and to ensure their fullest utilisation.

The controller is responsible for the integration of the work of all sections of his department, and his special tasks are the interpretation and presentation of financial information to management. The controller can have the necessary authority only if he has a place in top management, reporting directly to the chief executive.

CHAPTER VIII

FINANCIAL ACCOUNTING AS AN AID TO MANAGEMENT

A. GENERAL. THE NECESSITY FOR SHOWING A DYNAMIC PICTURE

So far this book has surveyed the normal accounting routine which, modified where necessary, must be carried out in any form or size of business. The later chapters will deal with the detailed analysis of the figures and developments of the accounting function which provide management with a closer control over the work for which it is responsible.

Complex and expensive systems of costing or other means of control may not be justified in small enterprises, and in such businesses the owner or manager will rely on the normal Trading and Profit and Loss Account and the Balance Sheet for financial information. Even in a large concern final accounts, imaginatively constructed and presented promptly, can provide an invaluable source of information to top management so far as the broad trends of the work and the financial position are concerned. But for such purposes the final accounts must be prepared with a more comprehensive end in view than the mere satisfaction of legal requirements or submission to the tax inspector. These two factors, necessary as they are, tend to restrict the usefulness of periodic revenue accounts and Balance Sheets. It is suggested that the accounting system should be primarily designed to provide information to management; statements prepared from the accounts may be suitably adapted for other purposes, *e.g.* the tax computation and the "legal" Profit and Loss Account and Balance Sheet.

The elemental purpose of the final revenue account is to show the profit for the period, and the purpose of the Balance Sheet is to show the financial position at the end of the period. But the influences which affect a modern business, whether it be a small retail shop or an international group of companies, are so complex that management cannot be content merely to be told that a certain profit has been made or that the business is now worth a certain sum.

Management is continually planning for the future and taking steps to avert the future hazards which may come in such forms as greater competition, the closure of markets, higher costs, and scarcity of labour, materials and funds—to mention at random a few of the recurrent risks of enterprise.

A manager regards a business or a department of a business as a continuing centre of work, and it is this dynamic aspect which must be presented by any form of accounts.

B. THE NECESSITY FOR TOPICALITY

1. Up-to-date accounting

The first essential for the presentation of a dynamic picture of events is that final accounts must be presented to management soon after the period or point of time to which they relate.

To be more precise it may be fairly said that final accounts presented three months after the date to which they are made up are of historical interest only. Within that period, for example, even the most assured market may have ceased to exist, as a result of, say, a more powerful competitor or of an adverse foreign-exchange rate.

Some methods of ensuring prompt accounting were suggested in Chapter III. Generally speaking, the problem depends on the way in which the accounting system is organised and the routine carried out. The usual difficulties in presenting up-to-date accounts are: (a) outstanding charges and income not entered in the books, and (b) valuations of stocks and work in progress.

2. Interim accounts

For similar reasons final accounts prepared at only yearly intervals are insufficient guides to management in the immediate control of the affairs of the business. A year's revenue account is affected by the costs, buying, selling, manufacturing and financial situation, by the labour market and the general economic state of affairs during the previous twelve months. It can only be compared with the plans formed over twelve months ago or results dating back a further twelve months.

Even for the smallest business some form of interim account, preferably monthly, possibly quarterly, is essential if the business is to be controlled efficiently. The time is past when guesswork or intuition commanded success. Monthly accounts are a matter of routine for efficient large concerns, and in many cases are available within fourteen days after the last day of the month concerned.

Interim accounts drawn up so promptly and for such short periods must of necessity contain approximations. But approximation based on sound and consistently applied principles need not detract from the accuracy of the trends shown or the general impression conveyed as to the financial stability of the business.

It is, perhaps, not generally appreciated that even annual accounts to which an auditor's report is attached, in almost all cases contain items of which the precise value is a matter of opinion. Different methods for charging depreciation have already been examined; stocks are entered at valuations which can only represent someone's opinion; there is no inflexible rule as to the rate and amount of overheads to be applied to work in progress; allowances for taxation and provision for doubtful debts have to be estimated.

C. Methods of Ensuring Up-to-date Accounts

1. Outstandings and accruals

Prompt payment and an efficient system of checking can prevent the accumulation of an unwieldy volume of outstanding invoices at any time. Similarly, an efficient routine for "chasing" outstanding debtors balances can prevent an accumulation of unpaid debts. Some of the accounting aids which assist in preventing abnormal outstandings were described in Chapter V. Prepayments and accruals need not cause any delay at balancing time if the amount of the accrued charge or credit is entered in the accounts via a suspense account at monthly intervals by the method shown in the following examples:

CAPITAL ACCOUNT
Rent suspense

	£				£
		Jan. 31	Rent payable 1 month at £1,200 p/a .	.	100
		Feb. 28	Rent payable .	.	100
		Mar. 31	Rent payable .	.	100
		,, 31	Balance c/d (prepaid		
Mar. 31	Cash . . . 600		rent) . .	.	300
	£600				£600
Apr. 1	Balance c/d (prepaid rent) . . £300				

Revenue account

Rent payable

		£				£
Jan. 31	Rent suspense	100				
Feb. 28	Rent suspense	100				
Mar. 31	Rent suspense	100	Mar. 31	Profit and Loss Account		300
		£300				£300

PROFIT AND LOSS ACCOUNT

		£
Mar. 31	Rent	300

In the above example rent is paid half-yearly, one quarter in advance. By means of a regular monthly entry of the sum accrued in the accounts the necessary balances are available (*a*) for the Balance Sheet, viz. the £300 prepayment to be shown as an asset, and (*b*) for the Profit and Loss Account, viz. £300 rent accrued due.

A similar procedure should be adopted for every recurrent item of income or expenditure.

In many cases, such as rates, electricity and water, the exact amount payable or receivable may not be known in advance, but a reasonable estimate based on experience will suffice for the presentation to management of a picture of the trend of events by means of an interim account.

The method shown can be extended to overheads of an irregular nature, especially where the concern operates with the aid of a system of preconceived budgets. An interim account covering the first month or the first three months of the year would present a misleading picture if it omitted any proportion of, say, staff bonuses payable at Christmas or heavy charges for advertising normally incurred only in summer months. For such overheads a twelfth of the annual estimated charge should be debited to the revenue accounts and credited to a suspense account at monthly intervals.

To the extent that an eventual payment of the estimated charges or credits so entered in the books were found to be different from the actual figure an adjusting entry would be made and the estimate for ensuing periods also similarly amended.

It may be remarked at this point that for the purpose of drawing up trustworthy interim accounts a form of budgeting may be regarded as essential. This aspect of accounting in advance of the event is discussed more fully in a later chapter.

2. Provisions and reserves

It has been noted that a provision is a charge against profits of which the precise amount cannot be ascertained with reasonable accuracy. Provisions must therefore be brought into interim accounts. They may be considered under two headings: those which are of regular occurrence, such as provisions for bad and doubtful debts; and those which arise from some unforeseeable contingency, such as the need to provide for a loss on exchange, a fall in stock values or a liability under a guarantee or in consequence of a pending legal action.

The solution to the problem of dealing with provisions in interim accounts is, like all accounting problems, a question of organisation and routine. Whether accounts are drawn up at monthly or quarterly intervals the manager of a small business or the accountant of a large one should set aside a certain time each month for the purpose of assessing the provisions (and reserves) which will be required at the end of the month.

The current provisions for doubtful debts can, for the purpose of interim accounts, be estimated by applying a percentage to debtors balances. The adequacy of such a provision can be tested by seeing whether the total of actual bad debts written off over a sufficient period to a separate Bad Debts Account is covered by the provisions made during that period. In a small business the manager should have sufficient knowledge of his customers to be able to assess the prospects of obtaining full payment of each account. In a larger business it will be the responsibility of the clerk in charge of the debtors accounts to report on any slow-moving balances by means of a monthly list with his comments attached.

Provisions for non-recurring items should be passed through the books as soon as the estimated liability occurs. Such matters as legal actions or compensation for loss of office are outside the normal routine of business but within the knowledge of the chief executive, whose responsibility it is to see that proper provision is made in the accounts for possible liability. This is one of the many instances demonstrating the need for management to understand the accounting function. In too many cases it is assumed that the accountant will become aware of some new liability which has been incurred, apparently by a process of clairvoyance.

Reserves are divisible into capital reserves and revenue reserves, the latter in turn being subdivided into the general and specific headings.

All allocations to reserve are within the discretion of management, although the accountant is certainly entitled and expected to advise on the matter. The allocations normally require to be authorised by a board meeting or similar authority. There is, however, no reason why, for the purpose of interim accounts, the accountant should not, in the absence of a board meeting, make a provisional appropriation to a specific reserve, in accordance with normal policy. The amount to be allocated to a general reserve is usually decided by top management on the basis of the year's profit, and may therefore be left out of interim accounts.

Allocations to or from capital reserves, such as profits or losses on the sale of fixed assets, or share premiums reserved, will be so obvious as to cause little difficulty. It is, however, necessary that the entries are made as and when the transaction occurs.

Allocations to a tax fund are variously described as reserves or provisions or are not included in either of these headings. Since taxation limits the amount available for the proprietors or for appropriation to reserve, it is essential that an estimate of the sum required be included in interim accounts.

3. Valuations

(a) *Stocktaking unnecessary for interim accounts*

Probably the greatest impediment to the regular and prompt production of interim accounts is the difficulty of valuing stocks and work in progress. In view, however, of the number of approximations necessary to interim accounts the difficulty of valuing stocks seems to have been over-emphasised. It is unnecessary, for example, to undertake a complete stocktaking every time accounts are prepared.

In a large business selling a wide variety of articles the valuation of stocks depends largely on the efficiency of the costing system, or more precisely of the stock records by value. A system of stock records can be regarded as indispensable in even the smallest enterprise, not only for accounting and costing purposes but also to maintain operating efficiency. The subject is examined in more detail later. Even without any system of stores or stock accounts, it should be quite practicable to obtain a reasonable valuation of stock for interim accounting purposes.

(b) *Valuation from stock records*

The expression "stock" is usually applied to finished goods available for sale. "Stores" refers either to raw material awaiting incorporation in the manufactured article or indirect materials, such as oils, cleaning materials and chemicals, which assist in the operations of production, selling or providing a service. "Work in progress" should be shown separately in accounts, and refers to partly made manufactures or contracts in course of completion.

Provided that there is an efficiently organised and regularly maintained system of records for each main item or group of stock, the balances shown on these records may be used for the purpose of preparing interim accounts without further checking. These records show, as a basis, receipts, issues and balances of stock held, with prices for conversion into value.

In this connection the principle of internal check and internal audit should be applied to stock records. The store-keeper should be responsible for checking a portion of the stock against the records at regular intervals so that by this means the whole of the stock is checked at least twice a year, probably more often, dependent on such factors as the rate of deterioration and usage. The internal audit consists of an independent test of samples of stock at irregular periods either by an internal audit section in a substantial business or by the manager himself in a small one. Such checking and auditing routines enforce accuracy of stock records and save expensive overtime at the end of accounting periods.

Where no stock records exist the direct cost of goods sold can be estimated on the basis of known gross profit percentages on sales. Little difficulty should be experienced in making a reasonably accurate calculation of this nature in the case of a small business concerned only with buying and selling goods and not with manufacture. It is in all cases necessary to make a few sample tests of cost and profit percentages applicable to individual sales, and it is desirable for sales to be analysed broadly by gross profit ratios so that costs can be estimated with sufficient accuracy.

By this means a monthly revenue account for a shop can be drawn up on the following lines:

TRADING AND PROFIT AND LOSS ACCOUNT
of "X" Confectioner and Tobacconist.
For the month of January 19............

	£	£
Sales of confectionery for the month		1,000
Less Direct cost of confectionery (assuming average gross profit of 20 per cent of sales)		800
Gross surplus on confectionery		200
Sales of cigarettes, tobacco, etc.	500	
Less Direct cost of cigarettes, tobacco, etc. (assuming average gross profit of 10 per cent of sales)	450	
Gross surplus on tobacco, etc.		50
Total surplus		250
Deduct overheads:		
Salaries and national insurance	90	
Advertising	5	
Maintenance of shop	10	
Electricity and other services	8	
Premises, including rent and rates	50	
Depreciation of furniture, fittings and equipment . .	15	
Sundry expenses	22	
		200
Net surplus for the month subject to taxation		£50

For a manufacturing business such a method of compiling interim accounts involves a wider degree of approximation in estimating profit percentages, because direct cost, in such a business, includes various ingredients of labour, material and other expenses. The method suggested may be used, however, pending the installation of an efficient system of costing and stock records.

In any case where an account is drawn up on the basis of estimating direct costs of sales there is considerable danger of error unless the most careful sample checks are made from time to time as to actual costs. In short, the above is a stop-gap method, and stock records are essential in any business both for the purpose of accurate accounting and for the tight control of work and expenditure.

D. THE PRINCIPLE OF COMPARISON
1. Comparison with the past

The financial position is represented by the Balance Sheet (or a similar document) which lists the assets and liabilities of the concern as obtained from the "capital accounts" in the Ledger.

The financial position is shown as at a point of time and has been likened to a snapshot photograph of a business. But management is more interested in something like a moving picture, and it is insufficient for assets and liabilities to be shown at one point in time only.

Each main group in the Balance Sheet should therefore be compared with the values which existed at one or more previous points of time not too remote from the date under consideration.

A Balance Sheet prepared in vertical form as in the example on page 86 may be easily compared with the situation as it existed at the end of the previous month and at the end of the previous year or such other date as may seem apposite according to the rapidity with which the business is developing or contracting.

A far more effective method of judging the rightness of Balance Sheet totals is to compare them with a scientifically compiled budget of the capital situation. The subject is considered more fully in Chapter XI, but at this point it may be said that a budget of capital items should be assessed not only on the basis of the past but also on future intentions and expectations. It is therefore in theory sufficient to compare current figures with budgeted totals only, and no other comparisons, such as with results of previous periods, need cloud the picture.

2. Comparisons between inter-related figures in the account

The dynamic and true picture produced by showing comparative figures either of the past or of a budget may be extended by presenting assets and liabilities as ratios one to another and also by relating them to appropriate totals in the revenue accounts. In fact, it may be said that the principle of comparison should be applied to every accounting statement produced for the guidance of management.

The most important relationships between figures in the same issue of accounts may be summarised as follows:

(a) *The availability of funds*

    (i) Ratio of current assets to current liabilities.

    (ii) Ratio of liquid assets to current liabilities.

(b) *The adequacy of stocks*

    (i) Ratio of stocks of finished goods to sales (or more accurately to sales orders outstanding).

    (ii) Ratio of stores of raw materials to output (or more accurately to orders outstanding on the works).

(c) *The control of debtors and creditors balances*

    (i) Ratio of debtors to sales (in this case the recent trend of sales should be used).

    (ii) Ratio of creditors to purchases: again using recent trends of purchases.

(d) *The make-up of capital or net assets*

    (i) Ratio of fixed and net current assets, subdivided as required, to total assets.

    (ii) Ratio of fixed capital funds, *i.e.* proprietors fixed capital, plus long term-loans and capital reserves, to fixed capital assets, thus showing the ultimate security of investors' money.

(e) *The adequacy of profits*

    (i) Ratio of net profits (after tax) to total net assets.

    (ii) Ratio of net profits (after tax) to fixed assets.

In all cases these ratios (which are best expressed in the form of percentages) should be again related either to past figures or, better still, to a budget or forecast of the position intended at the date concerned. It is, for example, hardly informative to tell a manager that stocks represent 10 per cent of orders outstanding. If, however, the additional information is supplied that the percentage has been steadily declining from, say, 20 to 10 per cent over the past six months, there is a clear implication that stock levels may be falling to a dangerous level, and management should take action to restore them. It is a waste of time both to the accountant and to management for any figures to be produced which are not calculated to induce action by management.

E. Profit as a Sign of Efficiency

1. The nature of profit

At this point it is desirable to consider the nature of profit and its use as an indication of efficiency. As may have appeared from the preceding pages, the ascertainment of profit for accounting purposes is by no means a simple matter, nor is the meaning of the term free from ambiguity. Profit from the point of view of the Inland Revenue, or from the point of view of a government department negotiating a contract with industry, is often quite a different figure from that understood by the manager or owner of a business. Indeed, the accounting view of profit, which is governed largely by law and by the established conventions of the profession, does not necessarily represent the sum which the owner or manager of a business considers free for withdrawal. The necessity for making appropriations from conventional profit to cover taxation dues, specific reserves for future contingencies, general reserves to maintain the capital in face of inflation, competition, external developments and so forth, tends to qualify the interpretation of profit as the sum which can be distributed to the proprietors of a business.

If, therefore, the nature of profit is a matter of opinion or depends on a point of view, the question arises as to whether profit can be effectively used as an overall sign of the efficiency of an enterprise.

The purpose of this section is to suggest means by which the difficulties inherent in the use of profit for such a purpose can be resolved.

2. Profit related to capital

(a) Methods of calculating the relationship

It is hardly informative to say that a business is prospering because it has made, say, £100,000 profit in a year. The bare statement would be equally meaningless if only £1,000 were quoted as the profit. When an investor hears that the profit of a concern is a certain amount he automatically tries to relate that figure to some comparable standard. The comparable standard may be last year's profit, the share capital, the profit made by a similar concern or the net capital or capital employed in the business in question.

It is suggested that the last-mentioned basis of relationship is the only trustworthy guide. The share capital may not represent anything like the real capital owned by shareholders owing to "ploughing back" of profits or even losses of capital. Nor, for similar reasons, is it necessarily comparable with the real worth of share capital last year. Comparisons with the profit of a similar concern may be misleading because the capital structure of the two businesses (*e.g.* the proportion of capital financed by equity as opposed to loan capital) may be quite dissimilar, and so might policies as regards allocations to reserve, depreciation rates, employee remuneration or even the desire to show the greatest possible profit on sales.

Nationalised undertakings cannot be said to exist for the purpose of making the maximum profit out of their operations. The primary motive behind such bodies is, presumably to provide the best service to the State, subject to meeting a fixed rate of interest on their capital. A like policy may be attributed to many large companies and groups of national importance. Directors of private enterprise frequently refrain from increasing sales prices, and sometimes lower them, in order to maintain customer good-will.

In spite of these considerations the profit motive remains one of the mainsprings of enterprise and a spur to efficiency. It is clearly the desire to make profits which inspires the search for more effective methods, reduced unit costs, better organisation and greater turnover. Profit represents, therefore, a basic indication of efficiency, particularly if it is related to capital employed.

(b) *The interpretation of profit for this purpose*

There remains the problem of interpreting both profit and capital employed. It has been noted that opinions differ about the precise meaning of both these terms. Nevertheless, if the interpretation is consistent year by year in any one concern the trend shown by the relationship will be significant.

Thus it may be assumed that a company which showed a profit of, say, 7·5 per cent on capital employed last year compared with 7·4 per cent the year before and 7·3 per cent the year before that, is doing well and, *prima facie*, improving in efficiency. It may be dangerous to draw any further conclusion from the profit figure, and indeed the improvement in profitability *may* be due more to external economics than to internal good management.

The profit to be related to capital employed may be: (*a*) profit before taxation allocations; (*b*) profit after taxation allocations; (*c*) profit after deducting specific reserves; (*d*) profit before or after deducting interest on long-term loans; or finally (*e*) profit entirely free for distribution to the proprietors, *i.e.* the "divisible surplus".

Since specific reserves and allowances for tax on the current year's profits ought to be reserved before distribution to the proprietors (although legally the directors may not be bound to reserve such amounts), it appears that profit can be effectively related to capital employed only after allowance has been made for these amounts. A similar argument, with perhaps less force, might also be applied to allocations to a general reserve, leaving the figure of divisible surplus as the proper amount to be related to capital employed.

Many companies are financed to a large extent by long-term debentures or loan capital. Since such capital may constitute a major source from which profits ensue (whether or not such profits are sufficient to cover the interest payable on the debentures), it may be considered that long-term loan interest forms part of the surplus to be related to capital employed. A comparison of rates of return on capital with other concerns will be misleading unless debenture interest is treated as part of the surplus. A similar argument applies to fixed interest payable on Preference Shares.

Concluding this examination of the nature of profit, it may be suggested that the surplus to be used for any calculation of true profitability should ignore fixed returns payable as a result of particular arrangements of the subscribed capital structure but should include specific appropriations which prudent businessmen would make before distributing the surplus.

(c) *The interpretation of capital employed*

Capital employed can be assessed by two methods: one by listing the capital funds such as debentures, issued share capital, plus reserves; and secondly, on the basis of the real assets less liabilities.

The following is a summarised version of a Balance Sheet showing both methods:

X.Y.Z. Ltd. and its subsidiary companies
CONSOLIDATED BALANCE SHEET
27th March 19............

Capital employed

	£	£
Authorised and issued capital:		
Preference Shares	3,500,000	
Ordinary Shares	3,000,000	
		6,500,000
Share premium Account		125,000
		£6,625,000
Revenue reserves:		
General reserve	1,127,000	
Contingency reserve	41,000	
Profit and Loss Account	222,000	
		1,390,000
Income tax:		
On current year's profits . . .		927,000
Debenture stock and mortgages . . .		2,250,000
Total (represented by net assets) . . .		£11,192,000

Net Assets

	£	£	£
Fixed assets			6,625,000
Current assets:			
Stock and work in progress . .		2,110,000	
Debtors and deferred charges . .		3,456,000	
Tax reserve certificates . . .		480,000	
Investment (market value £468,825) .		565,000	
Balances at bankers and cash in hand		987,000	
		£7,598,000	
Deduct			
Current liabilities and provisions:			
Creditors and accrued liabilities	2,624,000		
Bank loans	15,000		
Provision for taxation . . .	244,000		
Proposed final dividend . . .	148,000		
		3,031,000	
Net current assets			4,567,000
			£11,192,000

It will be noted that in the above example the total of capital employed includes long-term loans in the form of debentures and mortgages but not the short-term bank loan. Reserves are also included as part of capital, although if a specific reserve existed for the purpose of meeting an impending liability, it might be considered reasonable to deduct it from gross assets for the purpose of arriving at the total of capital employed. The fund to meet income tax on the current year's profits might also be excluded from capital employed for the purpose of assessing rates of profitability, even though such tax would not become payable until the end of the following year.

In this case it will be noted that the issued share capital amounts to only approximately 60 per cent of the capital employed, and the sum attributable to shareholders after adding reserves is over £8,000,000 compared with £6,500,000 of normal share capital. Any conclusions drawn from the rate of dividend expressed as a percentage of issued capital would therefore be misleading as representing the profit-earning capacity of the group as a whole. Similarly, the exclusion of debentures and mortgages from capital employed would tend to confuse the picture of profitability, since the money subscribed by debenture holders may in fact be earning for the group a greater or lesser return than the rate (in this case 4½ per cent) payable on the debentures.

The only firm conclusion, which it seems, can be drawn from the circumstances discussed above is that both the absolute amount of profit and of capital may represent matters of opinion. Yet the relationship between the two (provided they are consistently assessed on the same basis) will be truly comparable period by period.

The percentage of profitability between different companies is frequently made the subject of comparison, but clearly the conclusion to be drawn from such comparisons should be treated with considerable reserve.

(d) Profit related to fixed capital

Fixed assets are held for the purpose of providing a source of income. The rate of profitability earned by fixed assets can be a useful indication to management as to whether the utmost advantage is being gained from the possession of those assets. Nevertheless, any change noted in the percentage of profit on the value of fixed assets will need careful interpretation if the change is due to the purchase or sale of fixed assets acquired when money values were quite different from those existing at the point of time under consideration.

The purchase of new fixed assets at prices considerably higher than those given for the old assets will transfer a large sum from current assets (cash) to fixed assets without necessarily affecting immediate profit-earning capacity. The profit expressed as a percentage of fixed assets will then tend to fall, although the percentage on capital employed may remain constant.

In such a case it may be more significant to express profit as a percentage of fixed capital funds, *i.e.* issued shares and debentures plus capital reserves. Again, however, the relationship may be unsound if there is a large general reserve maintained year by year and so effectively constituting part of fixed capital funds. The capitalisation of reserves by the issue of bonus shares implies that many so-called reserves are, in effect, part of the permanent capital of the business.

Movements in the percentage of profit on fixed capital or fixed assets may, however, be worthy of note if there has been no significant change in the valuation or constitution of these totals. In such a case a substantial fall in the profit percentage on fixed assets may indicate unused facilities, such as buildings and machinery.

3. Profit as a guide to functional management

(a) *The different viewpoints of profit*

So far profit has been considered in relation to some aspect of capital, and such a viewpoint is largely the concern of top management. Profit calculated as a percentage of capital employed represents a broad guide to top management as to the overall efficiency of the business; and calculated as a percentage of investors' fixed capital forms a basis for dividend policy and allocations to reserves.

Functional management is concerned with profitability to the extent that it gives an indication of the efficiency of each function of the business. For this purpose functional management represents the direction of the purchasing, producing or operating, and selling functions (the administrative and research or experimental sides of a business being treated for this purpose as ancillary to the main functions mentioned).

Profit must be interpreted for functional management in relation to the particular side of the business concerned. Thus the relationship of profit to capital employed or shareholders' funds might be of little more than academic or general interest to a production manager or sales manager.

The work of the production manager is represented in monetary terms by factory cost, and it is thus the gross profit before deducting general or establishment overheads which interests works management.

Assuming there is complete co-ordination between purchasing, producing and selling policy, the works management can influence profit by reducing unit costs in the factory and thus increasing gross profit before deducting general overheads. To this extent, then gross profit will constitute a *prima facie* guide to the efficiency of the works departments.

(b) *Profit and sales management*

Sales management can influence profit in two ways: one, by altering prices, and the other, by increasing or curtailing sales. In a competitive market or one sensitive to price, sales management often has little latitude in matters of price. Probably the first consideration of sales management working in any field is the maintenance and, if possible, the extension of sales turnover. Within limits an increase in sales produces an immediate rise both in overall profits of the business and in the percentage profitability of a particular unit of manufacture or service sold. These effects are, of course, largely due to the fact that an expansion in sales does not normally increase fixed costs, and increases semi-variable costs by a smaller ratio than the percentage increase in income.

The selling departments can therefore receive useful guidance from statements of profit expressed as percentages of sales turnover.

A sales manager also needs information as to the effect on profitability of changes in price and of changes in turnover. He requires analyses of sales and profitability by particular lines or groups of sales, by sales divisions within the organisation, and by markets or areas of sales. Only by such analyses received promptly and regularly will the sales manager be able to judge where his efforts are best concentrated.

A constant concern of sales management is to produce the maximum profit by maintaining the balance between price and turnover. In order to assist sales management in this vital matter clear information must be provided (and understood by the sales departments) as to the method of applying overheads to unit costs. A statement that the cost of selling a particular article is, say, five shillings, can be quite misleading in connection with the problem of attaining the utmost profit by adjusting the pattern of the selling effort. Costs presented to sales management—as, indeed, to any kind or strata of management—must be shown divided into the variable and fixed elements.

If a business is selling 10,000 of product "A" a year at a cost of £0·25 each and for a price of £0·37½, the profit resulting from such sales would be:

$$10,000 \times (£0·375 - £0·25 = £0·125) = £1,250$$

Assume the sales manager concerned estimates that he can add 50 per cent to sales only if the price is reduced to £0·32½ each. A false conclusion would be drawn if the resulting profit were assessed as:

$$15,000 \times (£0·325 - £0·25 = £0·075) = £1,125$$

If such is the case the project is not justified. In fact, a proportion of the cost of £0·25 would consist of an apportionment of fixed overheads (leaving out of consideration, for the sake of simplicity, semi-variable costs) and the proposal should be expressed by the accountant in some such calculation as follows:

PRESENT POSITION

	£
Annual sales turnover:	
10,000 articles at 37½p	3,750
Deduct (a) variable cost, 10,000 20p	2,000
Gross profit (i.e. approx. 46 per cent of sales)	1,750
(b) overheads	500
Net profit (i.e. 33⅓ per cent of sales)	£1,250

PROPOSAL

	£
Annual sales turnover:	
15,000 articles at 32½p	4,875
Deduct (a) variable costs, 15,000 at 20p	3,000
Gross profit (i.e. 38 per cent approx. of sales)	1,875
(b) overheads (allowing a small increase to cover semi-variable overheads)	550
Net profit (i.e. 27 per cent of sales, approx.)	£1,325

The conclusion to be drawn from the above statement is that the proposal is likely to increase overall profits by £75 a year as compared with a reduction in profitability shown by the preceding calculation. However, the benefit of the proposed rearrangement of sales in this product must be qualified by the lower percentage profitability ensuing. It would not be justified if it resulted in a reduction in the selling effort applied in other directions where a higher percentage profitability is obtainable.

(c) *The responsibility of the accountant*

Many other factors affecting profitability may have to be taken into account in connection with a projected expansion in sales. If the expansion proposed in any particular line is considerable the production and purchasing programme, the organisation of the factory, the adequacy of tools and space, and financial considerations may be affected.

Thus a proposed increase in the sales of a particular article might involve the purchasing department having to pay higher prices for the raw material required, owing to the increased demand; further output may increase fixed overheads as a result of greater requirements in factory space, machines and supervision; lastly, the financing of increased output may involve the payment of interest on money borrowed for the purpose or even a larger total of dividends payable on any increased share capital which may be necessary. The extent to which turnover may be increased without increasing so-called "fixed overheads" is limited in any organisation.

All these matters are best expressed by the management concerned in monetary terms. The services of the accountant will be called for whenever any change in the sales or production programme is contemplated. The accountant will be unable to give the necessary information to management unless his technique and organisation are sufficiently flexible to present clear and concise pictures of future probabilities as well as commentaries on past results. It is equally essential for functional management in other sides of a business to have at least a broad knowledge in accounting terms of the possible monetary implications of their work. Without such knowledge, purchasing, production and sales managers would be unable to state their requirements from the accounting departments, or to understand the information which is produced as a result.

F. The Funds Flow Statement

An important management accounting statement is known as the Funds Flow Statement. This statement is derived from an analysis of the changes which have taken place in the various Balance Sheet items between two accounting dates. The Funds Flow Statement shows the sources and uses of funds during an accounting period. Funds are provided by outsiders (increases in liabilities or loans) or owners (increases in capital or reserves) or by the release of amounts previously tied up in assets (decreases in assets). Funds are used to add to assets (increases in assets) or to reduce indebtedness to outsiders (decreases in liabilities or loans) or to pay dividends or repay capital to the owners (decreases in capital or reserves).

Such changes in items on a balance sheet as between one accounting date and the next are related in two ways:

(i) The net change in assets = the net change in liabilities and owners' equity (*i.e.* capital and reserves).

(ii) Increases in assets + Decreases in liabilities and equity = Decreases in assets + Increases in liabilities and equity.

The second relationship is basis for preparing a Funds Flow Statement.

A useful preliminary to the preparation of the statement is the compilation of a Comparative Balance Sheet, of which the following is an example:

MANUFACTURERS LIMITED
Comparative Balance Sheets for 1964 and 1965

	December 31st 1964 £	December 31st 1965 £	Increase or decrease £
Share capital	400,000	400,000	—
Revenue reserves . . .	235,000	243,000	8,000
Owners' equity . . .	635,000	643,000	8,000
6% Debenture stock . . .	—	175,000	175,000
Current liabilities:			
Trade creditors . . .	32,000	76,000	44,000
Bank overdraft . . .	—	26,000	26,000
Taxation	2,000	1,000	(1,000)
Total current liabilities . .	34,000	103,000	69,000
Total equity and liabilities .	£669,000	£921,000	£252,000

MANUFACTURERS LIMITED (contd.)

Comparative Balance Sheet for 1964 and 1965

	December 31st 1964 £	December 31st 1965 £	Increase or decrease £
Fixed assets:			
Land and buildings . .	75,000	75,000	—
Plant and equipment . .	246,000	378,000	132,000
Fixtures and fittings . .	88,000	101,000	13,000
Vehicles	1,000	3,000	2,000
	410,000	557,000	147,000
Less Accumulated depreciation .	105,000	28,000	(77,000)
Fixed assets, net . . .	305,000	529,000	224,000
Current assets:			
Cash	14,000	11,000	(3,000)
Debtors	55,000	123,000	68,000
Stocks	187,000	249,000	62,000
Investments . . .	100,000	—	(100,000)
Prepaid expenses. . .	8,000	9,000	1,000
Total current assets . .	364,000	392,000	28,000
Total assets. . . .	£669,000	£921,000	£252,000

From this Comparative Balance Sheet statement a Funds Flow Statement can now be prepared.

MANUFACTURERS LIMITED

Funds Flow Statement for the year ended 31st December 1965

Sources of funds	£	Uses of funds	£
Decreases in assets:		Increases in assets:	
Cash . . .	3,000	Fixed assets, net . .	224,000
Investments . .	100,000	Debtors . . .	68,000
		Stocks . . .	62,000
	103,000	Prepaid expenses .	1,000
			355,000
Increase in liabilities:			
Creditors . .	44,000	Decreases in liabilities:	
Overdraft . .	26,000	Taxation . . .	1,000
Debentures . .	175,000		
	245,000		
Increases in reserves .	8,000		
	£356,000		£356,000

It can be seen that the Funds Flow Statement provides a clear indication of the changes which have taken place in the financial position of the company, particularly for those who are not versed in reading Balance Sheets. For management purposes such a statement provides a starting-point for further investigation of the causes of fund movements. In the preceding example, for instance, more information regarding the changes in fixed assets would be required.

G. INVESTMENT IN ASSETS

1. The importance of the subject

To a large extent the manager's principal responsibility is to make decisions, and a decision in business is usually a choice between several alternatives. Most of the problems which face management from time to time involve the investment of money. When a business is established the immediate problem is to invest the owners' or shareholders' funds in the most productive manner within the objects for which the business is set up. A similar situation arises in an existing business when further funds are obtained for the purposes of development. But, in a smaller compass, the daily activities of business involve a series of investments in such things as fixed assets, stock, personnel and various works, selling and administrative services. These day-to-day activities may necessitate the transfer of funds from one investment to another, such as when funds are withdrawn from stock exchange securities to buy plant; or the borrowing of further funds, such as when a bank overdraft is drawn on to pay for purchases of stock.

In all such operations it is the responsibility of the management to ensure that the funds are applied in a manner which will produce an adequate return to the owners. The owners may be the partners in a firm, the members of an incorporated body or, in the case of nationalised industry, the general public. An adequate return means, it is suggested, not only a basic rate of interest on the capital employed (such as the return obtainable without appreciable risk on a long-dated government security) but also profit sufficient to compensate for the risk inherent in the whole enterprise. Even though the ultimate responsibility must rest with the management, it is the accountant's function and duty to give advice on the economics of the investment.

In formulating his advice the accountant should consider some or all of the following factors which are likely to be present in any investment problem:

(a) the present return being obtained on the funds to be used; or

(b) the cost of borrowing the funds;

(c) the minimum rate of return required, usually calculated as a percentage of the capital employed in the venture; and

(d) the comparative returns which are likely to be obtained on the alternative methods of investing the money.

One of the most frequent examples of the general problem is the acquisition of plant, *e.g.* machinery, instruments, vehicles, land and buildings. On a larger scale are investments in subsidiary companies, take-over bids and substantial projects of development or diversification.

Three methods of approach are to be considered for measuring the likely return from a proposed investment. The first is the cash-flow method, the second the marginal approach and the third the more conventional assessment of profitability, after allocating to the project equitable apportionments of overheads. These methods are not stated in any particular order of importance or merit, and they are not mutually exclusive. It is a matter for the manager and the accountant to give each method its due emphasis according to the nature of the particular problem which has arisen and the circumstances in which it arises.

2. The cash-flow approach

This approach may be said to be based on the idea that an investment of money is made primarily to extract from it further money to spend or invest elsewhere. Thus, for the purposes of the cash-flow approach the determining factor in the choice between two or more alternative investments is the relative cash which will issue from them. A development of this method is to discount the cash flow, and this aspect of the subject will be considered later. Meanwhile, however, it is considered desirable to emphasise the fact that cash flow is not the same as profit. The nature of the difference between the two concepts of the "return" is worthy of detailed examination because the measurement of a project of investment on the basis of cash flow may give a different picture of its merit than if the profit approach were made. Cash flow and profit will only be equated when a business or a particular venture is finally wound up and all the assets are liquidated and the liabilities paid off. This situation is not, of course, contemplated with a continuing business.

With the object of comparing cash flow and profit the following example is submitted for consideration.

Assume that a merchandising business is established with a capital in cash of £100,000. During the first year's operations sales of £200,000 are made; purchases amount to £150,000; administrative and selling expenses, all paid in cash, are £20,000; fixed assets are bought for £60,000 in cash; customers pay £190,000; payments are made to creditors of £120,000; at the end of the year the fixed assets are valued at £48,000 and the stock at £10,000.

The cash flow from the enterprise will be:

	£	£
Receipts from debtors		190,000
Less Paid for fixed assets . . .	60,000	
Paid for creditors	120,000	
Paid for expenses	20,000	
Total payments		200,000
Cash flow—deficit		£(10,000)

The profit from the enterprise will be:

	£	£
Sales		200,000
Less Cost of sales—		
Purchases	150,000	
Deduct Stock at end . . .	10,000	
		140,000
Gross profit		60,000
Less Expenses	20,000	
Depreciation	12,000	
		32,000
Net profit		£28,000

The profit shown above can also be calculated by subtracting the net assets, or capital employed, at the beginning of the year from the total at the end of the year, assuming that no capital is withdrawn by way of dividends or otherwise, and no additional capital is brought into the business.

	£	£	£
Net assets at the end of the year			
Fixed assets, at cost		60,000	
Less Depreciation		12,000	
			48,000
Current assets:			
Cash at beginning		100,000	
Less Net outgoings		10,000	
		90,000	
Debtors:			
Sales	200,000		
Less Receipts	190,000		
		10,000	
Stock		10,000	
Total current assets		110,000	
Less Creditors—			
Purchases	150,000		
Payments	120,000		
		30,000	
Net Current Assets . . .			80,000
Net assets at end of year . . .			128,000
Deduct Opening capital . . .			100,000
Profit, as above			£28,000

In the above example it will be seen that the profit exceeds the cash flow, but this will not always be the case. Consider the results of a further year's operations. Assume, for this purpose, that the transactions in the second year were the same, with the following exceptions: no further fixed assets were acquired; £200,000 was received from debtors; purchases were reduced to £140,000 so as to maintain the stocks at £10,000; payments to creditors were also £140,000. The results will then be as follows:

SECOND YEAR

	£	£
Cash flow		
Receipts from debtors . . .		200,000
Less Payments to suppliers . .	140,000	
Expenses	20,000	
		160,000
Cash flow—increase . .		£40,000

SECOND YEAR (contd.)

		£	£
Profits			
Sales			200,000
Less Cost of sales—			
Stock at beginning . . .		10,000	
Purchases		140,000	
		150,000	
Stock at end		10,000	
			140,000
Gross profit			60,000
Less Expenses		20,000	
Depreciation		12,000	
			32,000
Net profit			£28,000

Once again, the profit figure above can be checked by deducting the capital employed at the beginning of the year (£128,000) from that at the end of the year (£156,000). The calculations are as follows:

	£	£	£
Net assets at end of year			
Fixed assets, at cost		60,000	
Less 2 years' depreciation . . .		24,000	
			36,000
Current Assets			
Cash at beginning	90,000		
Cash flow	40,000		
		130,000	
Debtors at start	10,000		
Sales	200,000		
	210,000		
Receipts	200,000		
		10,000	
Stock		10,000	
		150,000	
Deduct Creditors—			
At beginning	30,000		
Purchases	140,000		
	170,000		
Payments	140,000		
		30,000	
Net current assets . . .			120,000
Capital employed at end of year . .			156,000
Deduct Capital at beginning of year . .			128,000
Net profit, as above			£28,000

It is sometimes assumed that cash flow is equivalent to profits plus depreciation, but this would only be true if the investment in the fixed and current assets, and the amount of the creditors, remained unaltered. The fact that, in the above example, profits plus depreciation equals cash flow is due to the figures having been adjusted so as to leave the investment in fixed assets (at cost), stock and debtors, less the credit received, the same at the end of the year as it was at the beginning of the year. In fact, due to the inevitable fluctuations which occur in business activity, this would never exactly occur; but profits plus depreciation might give a rough guide to cash flow in a stable business and one where no significant investment in stocks or plant were made. It may therefore be instructive to continue the process of comparing cash flow with profits.

In the third year assume that sales are increased by 10% and the relevant figures become:

THIRD YEAR

		£	£
Cash flow			
Receipts from debtors	. . .		210,000
Less Payments to suppliers	. .	175,000	
Payments for expenses	. .	22,000	
			197,000
Cash flow	. . . .		£13,000
Profit			
Sales	. . . . .		220,000
Less Cost of sales—			
Stock at beginning .	. .	10,000	
Purchases	. . .	160,000	
		170,000	
Stock at end .	. . .	16,000	
			154,000
Gross profit	. . .		66,000
Less Expenses .	. . .	22,000	
Depreciation	. . .	12,000	
			34,000
Net profit	. . . .		£32,000

In this year it will be observed that profit plus depreciation (£44,000) is considerably different from cash flow. This because there is a higher investment in stock and debtors and greater payments to creditors. It will be good practice for the reader to draw

G

up the statement of net assets at the end of this year, and thus
confirm the figure of profit given above.

In the fourth year a further increase in activity occurs, and the
results are shown below.

FOURTH YEAR

		£	£
Cash flow			
Receipts from debtors	. . .		240,000
Payments to suppliers	. .	170,000	
Expenses	. . .	23,000	
			193,000
Cash flow	. . .		47,000
Profit			
Sales	. . .		250,000
Less Cost of sales	. . .		175,000
Gross profits	. . .		75,000
Less Expenses .	. . .	23,000	
Depreciation	. . .	12,000	
			35,000
Net profit	. . .		£40,000

In the fifth year activity is reduced because the plant is wearing
out, and at the end of the year it is sold for £5,000. The results
are as follows:

FIFTH YEAR

		£	£	£
Cash flow				
Receipts from debtors .	. . .			210,000
Receipts from sale of plant	. .			5,000
Total receipts	. . .			215,000
Less Payments to suppliers	. . .		150,000	
Expenses .	. . .		22,000	
				172,000
Cash flow .	. . .			£43,000
Profit				
Sales .	. . .			200,000
Cost of sales.	. . .			140,000
Gross profit	. . .			60,000
Less Expenses .	. . .		22,000	
Depreciation .	. .	12,000		
Deduct Capital profit	. .	5,000		
			7,000	
				29,000
Net profit .	. . .			£31,000

The reader should calculate the net assets at the end of the fifth year, and the figures should result in the following financial position:

	£	£
Fixed assets		Nil
Current assets		
Cash	233,000	
Debtors	20,000	
Stock	16,000	
	269,000	
Less Creditors	10,000	
Capital employed . . .		£259,000

The five years' results may now be summarised as follows:

Year	Profit £	Cash flow £
1	28,000	(10,000)
2	28,000	40,000
3	32,000	13,000
4	40,000	47,000
5	31,000	43,000
	£159,000	£133,000

The difference between the two sets of figures is represented by the remaining investment in stocks and debtors, less the sum owing to creditors. Over the five years the profit represents an average return of £31,800 or 31·8% on capital, and the cash flow represents 26·6% on capital. It is interesting to note that the original investment will be "paid back" in terms of cash in a little over four years.

3. Discounting the cash flow

Money due in the future is not worth so much as the same amount of money now. Apart from the fact that there must always be some risk of not receiving money expected in the future, immediate money can be invested and thus yield a return. If a trader were offered the choice of receiving payment of a debt of, say, £1,050 in a year's time or of receiving £1,000 immediately, and he knew that he could invest the money at $7\frac{1}{2}$ per cent, he would opt to receive the immediate payment, because in a year's time it would have grown, with interest, to £1,075. If the choice was between receiving £1,100 in two years' time and £1,000 now, the latter option would be taken because, by re-investing the first year's interest of £75 the original sum would have grown to about £1,156 in two years' time.

Thus, a refinement of the cash-flow method of assessing the economics of capital investment is to discount the successive expected increments of cash at a suitable rate of interest; in other words, to arrive at the present value of the increments of cash flow. When these present values are added together the total will represent the value of the project in terms of present cash.

The two major problems associated with this device are: (a) to decide on the period over which the calculations are to be made, and (b) to assess the appropriate rate of interest or discount to be used. The former problem must probably be decided in relation to the foreseeable future of the project concerned, or the period over which reliable estimates can be made. Perhaps up to ten years is a feasible period for most projects and, in any event, the remoter the period so the present value of the increment of cash diminishes. So far as the rate of interest is concerned, the minimum rate must, it is suggested, be the rate payable on money to be borrowed for the purpose of the project. If, however, there is a reasonable expectation of exceeding the rate on borrowed money by investing the cash flow externally or in the business the higher rate should be used. If the money will be retained in the business, then a practical approach is to use the rate of return normally achieved on capital employed in the business.

The present value of the successive increments of cash flow can be calculated from factors, obtainable from Present Value Tables, applied to the cash-flow figures, as in the following example. In this case a rate of interest of 5 per cent has been used.

Year	Cash flow £	Factor	Present value £
1	(10,000)	0·9524	(9,524)
2	40,000	0·9070	36,280
3	13,000	0·8638	11,229
4	47,000	0·8227	38,669
5	43,000	0·7835	33,691
Totals	£133,000		£110,345

Thus the present value of the cash flow from the investment, discounted at 5 per cent, over 5 years, gives a figure of £10,345 in excess of the money originally laid out, and even for this short period the investment would appear to be worth while. Perhaps one of the more important uses of this device is to compare the respective merits of two alternative investments. It will be appreciated that a comparison of the respective discounted cash flows from the alternative projects may show quite a different picture from a comparison of the cash-flow figures themselves.

4. The contribution

The contribution is the surplus after deducting from expected revenue the marginal costs likely to be incurred by the project. The marginal costs are for most practical purposes the variable costs, *i.e.* costs which exclude all fixed overheads, such as depreciation, costs of space and fixed administrative and supervisory expenses. The true marginal cost would include such fixed costs as are directly due to the existence of the project.

The justification for this means of measuring an investment, or of comparing one or more alternative investments, is that the only costs which should be taken into account are those outgoings which the investment incurs or, conversely, the calculations must exclude all expenses which will continue whether the investment is made or not. Further, it is claimed that the inclusion of depreciation in the figures is counting the capital cost of any fixed assets twice, for, on this argument, depreciation is simply the spreading forward of the capital cost over future periods of account.

It will be observed that the measurement of an investment by means of the contribution is likely to produce figures close to the cash flow, since most variable costs are paid in roughly the same period as they are incurred. There will, however, be differences in respect, for example, of the investment in stocks of materials and delays in receiving payment from sales.

5. The profit approach

This heading is intended to refer to the assessment of an investment by means of estimating the profit to be derived after making normal apportionments of expenses, including fixed expenses and depreciation. This approach is likely to produce a lower return on the investment than by using the "contribution" and one which, in the initial years, is higher than the cash flow, although in later periods profit may fall below cash flow because of the inclusion of depreciation.

The basis of the "profit approach" is that it sets out to measure the losses and gains of value resulting from the investment, whether or not these values are represented by cash inflow and outflow. A true picture of the profit arising out of an investment should take account of any interest which can be earned on the net cash receipts, and of any payment of interest on borrowed money which can be saved. Depreciation of fixed assets is charged in the computation because it is an attempt to assess the loss of value which is occurring through use and time. The apportionment of fixed expenses is justified on the grounds that if the space, administrative facilities, etc., were not applied to the investment concerned they would help to earn income in other directions, or they could be dispensed with in the long run.

6. Conclusion

The general subject discussed in this section is a matter of considerable controversy, but it is unwise to be dogmatic about the merits or demerits of any particular approach. As mentioned earlier, the method to be applied to a given problem will depend largely on the circumstances of the business. It could well be that a decision to invest might have to be considered after considering all of the methods of approach outlined above. If the situation is that the generation of cash is important for a business, perhaps because of further impending projects of development, the cash-flow approach may be decisive. If the cash-flow approach is used in considering alternative projects there can be little doubt that discounted cash flow will give a sounder basis for comparison than the actual net cash receipts.

Subject to the foregoing consideration, and without detracting from the undeniable simplicity of the cash-flow approach, it remains true that most businesses exist for the purpose of making profits. In the long run it is the net profit which will constitute the final measure of a successful business, although the possession of sufficient liquid resources is also an essential. Thus, whatever may be the cash flow derivable from an investment, the profitability of that investment cannot be ignored. An important problem is whether profit should be assessed after apportioning fixed expenses or after charging merely variable or marginal costs. Once again, it is suggested that both viewpoints must be considered; but it may be said that marginal costing is essentially a short-term approach, and for an investment of an enduring character the cost of the fixed facilities which it will use must represent a factor in the assessment.

H. The Replacement of Fixed Assets

1. When to replace

Related to the problems associated with capital investment are those concerning the replacement of fixed assets, particularly machinery. The reader will probably call to mind a number of businesses and, indeed, whole industries which have declined largely owing to a reluctance to modernise capital equipment. But the question as to whether a particular machine should be replaced cannot be decided solely on the basis that another machine is available which will do the job quicker or more efficiently. That factor will probably initiate consideration of the problem and, although it will be of undoubted importance, it may not be decisive. The real test, as in all business problems, is whether the business profits will be greater after the machine is replaced.

This, therefore, is again a problem of anticipated income and anticipated cost. Past figures will be significant only to the extent that they may give a guide to the future. One common misapprehension in dealing with the problem of replacing a fixed asset is to be influenced by the balance standing on the books in respect of the old machine, *i.e.* cost less depreciation. The machine has been paid for, the depreciation has been charged in the accounts; these are things of the past, the real question is: what are the income and outgoings likely to be in the future, compared with the situation if the old machine were sold and another obtained in its place.

Theoretical problems of this nature often predicate that a machine earns a certain income. This may indeed be true, but a machine is only one factor in the complex process of producing a product or service, and it is extremely difficult in practice, if not impossible, to define in terms of money how much the machine has contributed to the income. The only satisfactory way to assess what change in profits will occur by replacing a machine is to re-budget the whole of the Profit and Loss Account of the organisation in which the machine is installed.

It is, however, possible to assess the comparative running costs of the old machine compared with the situation if it is replaced. The difference between these running costs, probably expressed as an hourly rate, will indicate the cost saving which will be derived from replacement. The first question is: What are the items of cost involved? Provided that the replacement will not involve greater or less usage of the standing facilities of the business, *e.g.* space, administration and supervision, fixed costs can be ignored in making the comparison.

The variable costs involved include the maintenance and running costs of the respective machines, such as power, greases, oils, repairs, small tools and the wages of the operatives. All these items should be expressed as a rate per hour, or possibly as a rate per unit produced if the units are homogeneous.

An important factor will be depreciation. This must be estimated on the most realistic basis available in respect of the new machine. For comparative purposes the depreciation on the old machine will not be the figure currently being charged in the accounts. The true loss of value which will be incurred in continuing to run the old machine will be the value foregone; that is to say, the amount for which it could be sold now less the amount for which it could be sold at some point in the future. For this purpose it is usually convenient to assess the saleable value in a year's time. There is no point in going further, because there is a reasonable assumption that the running costs, productivity and maintenance of the old machine will steadily worsen in later years.

Interest payable or foregone on the capital involved in either situation should be added to the costs for the purpose of calculating the hourly rates. The question as to what rate shall be used for the purpose follows the same lines as discussed in the preceding section dealing with the general problems of investment in assets. In the case of the old machine the interest should be calculated on the capital foregone, *i.e.* the saleable value of the asset; not, it should be noted, the balance of value not yet written off in the books. In the case of the new machine the capital involved in its acquisition will be the cost of that machine less the sum recovered by sale of the old machine.

With these calculations the respective running costs of (a) retaining the old machine, or (b) replacing it with another machine, can be compared. If the running costs per hour or per unit of the new machine are less than that of the old machine, then replacement is clearly indicated. The fact that replacement of the old machine involves taking a book loss in the accounts for the year of replacement is immaterial for the purpose of these calculations, for that loss will really refer to previous periods and means that the depreciation charged in the accounts in the past was inadequate. The existence of a heavy capital loss in the accounts will be material to the extent that it will invite comment!

There will, however, be a number of situations where a calculation of the kind indicated above shows that the running costs of a new machine exceed that of the old machine. There must be many cases where an old machine is operating quite efficiently but, because its scrap value is small, real depreciation is insignificant. In such a situation the relative productivity of the alternatives must be considered. If it is possible to put a price on the output of the two machines, then comparative Profit and Loss Accounts can be drawn up for the next year and the anticipated profit from each related to the capital investments. But, as mentioned above, it is not always feasible to produce such a statement, especially where a machine will be used on a variety of work. The exercise of preparing a new budget for the complete operation of which the machine may constitute a small part is, perhaps, the most logical approach, but again not very practicable in the majority of situations.

A possible solution to this difficulty is to prepare notional Profit and Loss Accounts for the old and the new machine, assuming that they will be applied wholly to a particular kind of work of a standard nature. One or two exercises of this kind could be carried out on sample products or operations. For this aspect of the exercise it would be desirable to include fixed costs, such as the cost of space and works administrative services, by means of rational apportionments. The machine with the greater productivity would then absorb a smaller proportion of the fixed costs per unit of output, and its costs would to this extent be lower than the other.

I. Statistical Aids in the Interpretation of Accounts

1. Additional statistics

The figures recorded in the accounts which form part of the double-entry system refer to past activities of a business and, in view of the necessary economy required in the accounting function, the information is, or should be, summarised. The double-entry system does not therefore by any means contain the whole of the facts which may be required for detailed investigations as to past results or for controlling and foreseeing future operations.

Certain additional statistics not contained in the accounts will be required in even the smallest business. In large concerns a scientifically designed service of statistical data will be maintained, probably in a separate section of the financial department, so as to keep all levels of management informed on matters affecting efficiency.

The basic statistics required in any business are considered in relation to the three operating functions of purchasing, producing and selling.

2. Purchase statistics

(a) *Analyses of goods bought*

The essential need to analyse purchases is so that some form of analysed revenue accounts may be prepared with a view to finding the relative profitability of the various sales or services. The need to analyse profit and loss to its source is obviously derived from the elemental motive of finding ways of increasing profitability, or where profits are adequate, to improve the service provided by the organisation, of which one of the means will be the reduction of cost. The analysis should have a definite object in view, such as one mentioned above. There are too many instances in business of purposeless analyses made for no other reason than "because it has always been done like this" or "because this is a big total".

Analysis of purchases may, in a small business, be dealt with by a subsidiary ledger system reconciling to the "purchases account" in the control ledger. In a large concern the analysis may be so detailed as to require a more involved record, probably best obtainable by the aid of punched cards. In all cases, however, the analysis must agree in total with the accounts.

In a large concern in addition to the analysis of purchases by groups or kinds of material, additional breakdowns will be required by stock code numbers, and by divisions or branches. In all cases purchases of fixed assets or capital items will be separated from revenue items.

(b) *Analysis of orders issued and outstanding*

The necessity for planning ahead means that at any point of time there is in most businesses a substantial total of material or goods ordered but not yet delivered or entered in the accounts.

No planning of sales or production can be effective unless statistics are readily available to show the extent of material on order and the probable dates of delivery. The purchasing officer requires such information so that he can take the necessary action to ensure that plans are not upset or facilities left idle for want of material. On the other hand, it is equally essential that capital should not be tied up and interest on capital payable as a result of material purchased long before it is required or of the purchase of unwanted stores.

Another important advantage to be derived from the analyses of purchase orders is that such statistics are useful in guiding certain purely financial aspects of a concern.

Plans for the provision of future funds will depend to a large extent on the volume of payments which are to be expected to meet future purchases.

The relationship between current trends of purchase orders expressed in value and the total of creditors forms a useful guide in controlling the latter total. In a period of development the total of creditors tends to rise and in a period of contraction the total should fall. The difficulty is in finding a yardstick for assessing the correctness of the movement. The relationship between creditors and liquid funds may indicate either that action is required to increase liquid funds or to reduce creditors. The total of trade creditors can, however, be appraised by relating it as a percentage to the current trend of purchase orders.

A record of purchases of capital assets (or fixed assets) is essential for compliance with the Companies Act, which provides that capital commitments shall be noted on the published accounts.

3. Sales statistics

(a) *Analysis of sales made*

Reference has already been made to the necessity for analysing sales by: (*a*) groups or kinds of sale; (*b*) divisions or branches of the organisation; and (*c*) markets or areas (including the very necessary division between home and overseas sales). In order to achieve the objects of controlling costs, income and profit, and tracing these factors to their sources, the various analyses for all items of income and expenditure must, where applicable, follow the same pattern.

For a cinema, for example, cost, sales and profitability need analysing, as a minimum, between that derived from: (*a*) ticket office takings, and (*b*) restaurant income. Expenditure, including purchases and labour charges as well as sales, should therefore be shown under these two minimum headings.

The close relation between the accounting and the statistical service suggests the desirability of placing both under common control, *i.e.* under the head of the financial department, whether such person is called accountant, secretary or controller.

(b) *Analysis of orders received and outstanding*

For much the same reasons that it is necessary to watch purchase orders, so sales orders must in all sizes and kinds of business be carefully recorded and analysed in order to control future operations of the whole business in the most efficient manner.

In the majority of enterprises, except possibly where a seller's market prevails, it is the volume of sales orders which, within the limits of available facilities, influences all the other activities of a business. The expression "sales orders" in this connection may be extended to enquiries received for the provision of services, such as are supplied by financial institutions, *e.g.* banks, building societies, insurance companies, and by transport undertakings, educational establishments and so forth.

4. Analysis of works orders

For a business which resells articles without any further process other than, perhaps, packaging, and for a business providing services, the orders received from customers also represent the orders to be placed on the operating departments.

In a manufacturing business, however, it is usually necessary for the orders received from customers to be converted into a form suitable for passing on to the works. For a repetitive process having a normally steady basis of sales, the orders issued to the works are orders for the manufacture of stock. Such orders are initiated by the stock-keeper at the point when stock in any article has fallen to the ordering level. The ordering levels are amended from time to time according to the volume of customers' orders being received and anticipated (subject, of course, to any limitations of manufacturing capacity).

Orders from customers for special work, or work of a non-repetitive nature, are passed on to the works department more or less as they are received.

The fact that this further procedure has to be carried out in respect of customers' orders entails the recording of a further body of statistics covering works orders received and outstanding. Such a record is an essential aid to the works manager in planning future activity, and in assessing the adequacy of his stocks of raw material. In carrying out these duties works management will probably be more concerned with quantities than monetary values. Nevertheless, a further useful financial ratio may be obtained by relating the value of works orders outstanding to the value of raw material stores.

It will certainly be very difficult to assess the cost value of works orders outstanding without a system of standard costing, or unless the works orders cover items for which past costs are available and still reliable.

5. Labour statistics

(a) *The purpose of labour statistics*

As occurs in varying degree with all statistical records, the kind and volume of labour statistics required for the guidance of management differs widely in different businesses and different functions. In particular, the detailed labour statistics for executive, administrative, selling and factory, or direct hourly paid, workers follow quite dissimilar forms.

Certain principles may, however, be applied to the organisation of labour statistics of any nature and for any organisation. The underlying objective of all such information should be to demonstrate the efficiency of management and of subordinate personnel.

In a modern business labour statistics should be prepared for the information and guidance of two spheres of management, that is: (*a*) personnel management, responsible for implementing and advising on personnel policy covering all employees, and (*b*) functional management, whether in the sales, administrative or works departments. Where in a small business there is no separate personnel manager, that function may be ascribed to the chief executive, *e.g.* the general manager or managing director.

(b) *Statistics for personnel management*

The personnel manager needs the following basic information from the financial department:

   (i) Labour turnover: by departments, expressed also as percentages of total employees, and showing trends.
  (ii) Average earnings: by departments, trades and grades of labour, showing trends.
 (iii) Absenteeism: analysed as above, lateness, sickness.
 (iv) Overtime: hours, analysed as above.

All these statistics are more readily available from the financial department because of its responsibilities for the recording of times and the payment of wages and salaries. The figures help to demonstrate the effectiveness of personnel policy and point to the action required to remedy any defects in that policy.

(c) *Statistics for functional management*

   (i) *The objects of such information.* Since functional management has a large responsibility—if not the sole responsibility—for putting into effect the personnel policy of a business, such management needs copies of the information mentioned above, so far as it relates to the function or department concerned.

Apart from questions of personnel policy, works managers, sales managers and heads of the administrative departments are responsible for the efficiency of the work carried out in their departments, and this largely refers to the efficiency of the labour in those departments. One broad guide to the efficiency of labour, but by no means an exclusive guide, is represented by the cost of labour in relation to the work carried out. Some methods of presenting such relationships are indicated below, but the figures are always subject to the qualification that increasing mechanisation or other devices substituting some other cost for labour may reduce the relative labour cost per unit of work but provide no indication of increasing labour efficiency.

(ii) *Labour statistics for works departments.*

1. The cost of labour, analysed by departments divided by the units of work done.

For this purpose the units as representing the work carried out in a period may, according to the nature of the operations, be represented by such measures as numbers of articles produced (if uniform), ton-miles, passenger-miles, flying-hours, machine-hours, weight or measurement of material manufactured or direct man-hours.

2. Bonus and piece-work earnings.
3. Relationships between direct and indirect workers, by numbers and cost.
4. Relationships between numbers of supervisors and workers.
5. Idle time and reasons therefor.

6. Further points on business statistics

The scope and nature of a statistical service varies widely according to the needs of the management concerned, the type of business and the peculiarities of that business. The foregoing consideration of statistics has deliberately set out to indicate only the broad lines on which such a service should be planned. Before initiating clerical procedures those responsible must be satisfied that the information to be prepared will be such as some level of management is demanding or ought to know. The question "Is this information likely to induce action to improve efficiency?" must be answered in the affirmative, or the work should be not undertaken.

The basic statistics mentioned in the preceding paragraphs are only such as are related to or derived from the accounting system. In any large concern a great deal of further statistical information, quite independent of the accounting system, will be required by functional and general management. But such information falls more properly within the study of production, sales and personnel management.

J. The Presentation of Statistics

1. The object of graphical presentation

Information can be communicated to management in three ways, in words, by figures or in graphical form. Graphical form in this sense is intended to signify the use of charts, diagrams, graphs or other pictorial devices. Quite often it is found that a combination of all the three is helpful.

Generally speaking, the purpose of graphical presentation is to show some fact "at a glance". A chart or graph is designed to clarify the meaning of figures and to save the time of the reader.

Some of the essential principles to be observed when presenting information in graphical form may be expressed as follows:

(a) A brief title should indicate precisely and simply the object of the chart or graph.

(b) Absolute impartiality is essential. The curves of a graph can, for instance, easily be adjusted to "prove a point".

(c) Simplicity and lucidity are the key words in graphical presentation.

(d) Fact must be clearly distinguished from assumption. Thus, the continuance of a curve to cover as yet unrecorded data should be indicated by some such device as dotted lines.

2. The presentation of trends

(a) *Arithmetic scale graphs*

A simple graph is probably unequalled for the presentation of trends, and its message can be understood by people who find difficulty in interpreting tabulated statistics. This type of graph is illustrated in Fig. 8, page 165.

Two points are of particular importance in drawing arithmetic scale graphs. One is that the horizontal line is best used for the time scale, *e.g.* months, days and so forth. The second point is that the vertical scale must commence at zero, that is, at the point where it intersects the horizontal scale.

(b) *Logarithmic scale graph*

The logarithmic or ratio scale graph is possibly somewhat more difficult to comprehend, but it is admirable for the presentation of rates of change.

The illustration shows two changes in prices, in one case the price has risen from £20 to £30, an increase of £10, and in the other the price has risen from £60 to £90, an increase of £30; but in both cases prices have increased by one-half, *i.e.* the rate of change is 50 per cent.

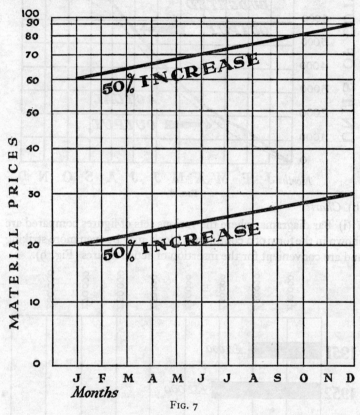

Fig. 7

3. The presentation of comparisons

(a) *Graphs*

A simple graph containing two curves or lines will indicate comparisons for most practical purposes, such as comparisons with past results, budgeted results or with related figures.

Owing to the frequent fluctuations in output, purchase or sales figures, comparisons are often best shown by means of cumulative graphs as in the illustration.

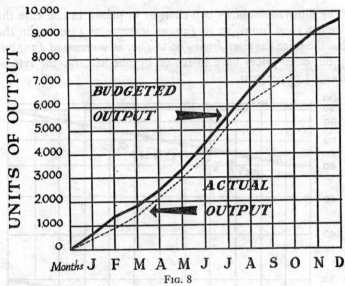

FIG. 8

(b) *Charts*

(i) Bar diagrams, where the various sets of figures compared are shown in the form of a continuous block, may be even more striking and are convenient for the insertion of actual figures (Fig. 9).

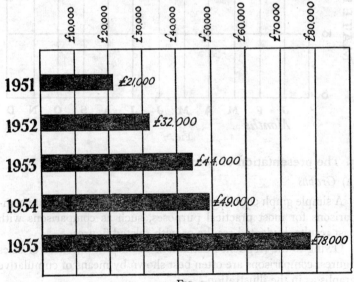

FIG. 9

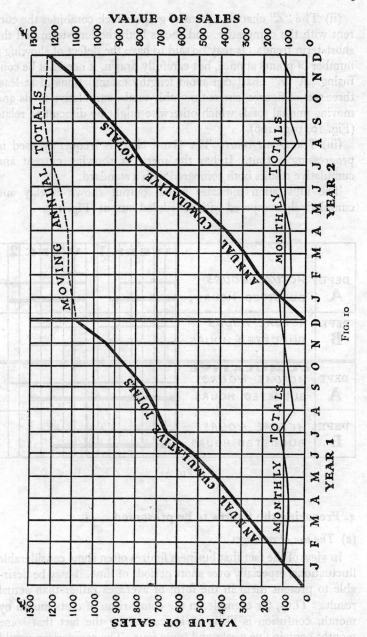

FIG. 10

(ii) The "Z" chart is a form of graph which combines the current with the cumulative, and shows both the long-term and the short-term trends. It may be said to have the defect of showing a number of points at once, but carefully drawn, it need not be confusing. A "Z" chart can avoid lengthy examinations of at least three sets of figures, current monthly totals, cumulative totals and moving annual totals which otherwise might be difficult to relate (Fig. 10, page 166).

(iii) *The Gantt chart.* The Gantt chart is frequently used in progressing output. It has the merit of showing current and cumulative results both compared with a standard.

The illustration indicates actual output shown weekly and cumulatively compared with scheduled output (Fig. 11).

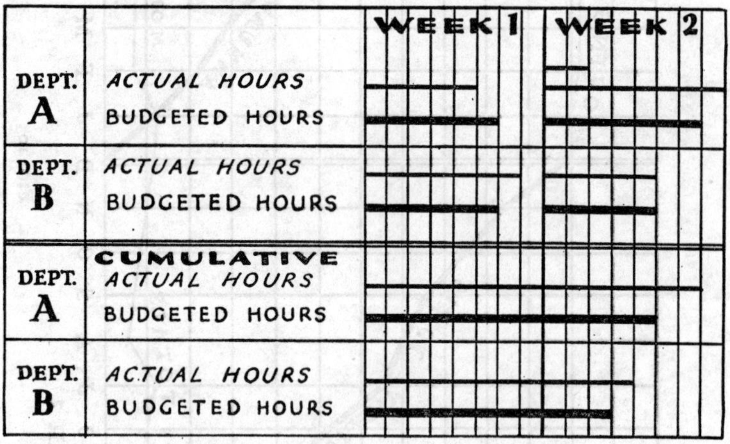

		WEEK 1	WEEK 2
DEPT. A	ACTUAL HOURS		
	BUDGETED HOURS		
DEPT. B	ACTUAL HOURS		
	BUDGETED HOURS		
DEPT. A	CUMULATIVE ACTUAL HOURS		
	BUDGETED HOURS		
DEPT. B	ACTUAL HOURS		
	BUDGETED HOURS		

FIG. 11

4. Preparing the figures to be presented

(a) *The use of averages*

In view of the fact that business figures often show considerable fluctuations, especially over short periods of time, it may be desirable to present them in the form of averages rather than actual results. Thus, for example, in the comparison of costs month by month, confusion is likely to be caused by the fact that some months contain five weeks and some four. The comparison would be clearer if average weekly totals were presented or, better still, by the average cost per working day in each month.

Exceptional divergences from normal in a list of figures may tend to distort the trend or falsify a comparison. Thus, if the hours taken in machining successive batches of a certain uniform job were: 20, 21, 40, 24, 20, the arithmetical average of such times would be $125/5 = 25$ for each batch. This average is plainly inflated by the exceptional 40 hours. A geometric average would produce a more reliable impression of the average time to be expected in future, and would be calculated thus:

$$\sqrt[5]{20 \times 21 \times 40 \times 24 \times 20} = 24 \text{ hours approx.}$$

A useful aid in depicting trends of fluctuating results is the moving average. The sales of a shop, the orders taken by a particular salesman or branch may, for example, fluctuate fairly considerably week by week. End-of-the-month salary payments affect deposits in banks and building societies. The effect of such fluctuations or trends can be eliminated by the use of a five-weekly moving average, calculated as follows:

Week ended				Weekly takings £	Cumulative £	Five weeks moving average £
Jan.	1	.	.	.	1,000	1,000	
,,	8	.	.	.	950	1,950	
,,	15	.	.	.	900	2,850	890
,,	22	.	.	.	800	3,650	930
,,	29	.	.	.	800	4,450	940
Feb.	5	.	.	.	1,200	5,650	940
,,	12	.	.	.	1,000	6,650	970
,,	19	.	.	.	900	7,550	
,,	26	.	.	.	950	8,500	

A moving annual total is useful for the purpose of watching and checking the trend of figures extending over twelve months. This device eliminates the effect of the various holidays and other seasonal influences.

The moving averages calculated above were found by dividing by five each successive five-weeks total. The moving annual total is calculated by the same method except that each twelve-months total is not averaged. A moving total without averaging may be calculated for any period, say, quarterly or half-yearly, but it is customary to use this device for twelve-monthly periods.

Moving averages or moving totals are particularly appropriate for translation into graphical form, especially if the "Z" chart method is used. The method of recording figures in the three columns of current, cumulative and moving annual totals can be sufficiently informative without graphical presentation provided wide fluctuations do not occur.

CHAPTER IX

INTRODUCTION TO COSTING

A. MEANING AND PURPOSE OF COSTING

Costing is frequently looked upon as the operation of calculating the cost of an article for sale as a basis upon which the selling price may be fixed. Whilst the ascertainment of cost for the purpose of price-fixing remains of importance, the art or science of costing is in fact able to offer a far wider service to management.

Costing has been defined by the late H. J. Wheldon (*Cost Accounting and Costing Methods*) as "the proper allocation of expenditure". It involves "the collection of costs for every job, process, service or unit, in order that suitably arranged data may be presented . . . as a guide in the control of business. It deals with the cost of production, selling and distribution".

It is important to note that the emphasis in this description is laid on the use of costing as a guide in the control of business. Such guidance, as will be indicated, covers a far wider field than price fixing. Prices are usually more directly influenced by supply and demand than by costs. Moreover, it has often been suggested that one of the primary duties of management is to control costs so that the desired profit shall be gained on the price obtainable; this is a different exercise from that of using costs to control prices.

Costs are, however, widely used as a basis for price fixing, particularly in connection with government contracts and other transactions where prices are subject to government control. Nevertheless, the use of costing to guide managers in achieving efficiency may be said to constitute its primary function.

B. INTEGRATION OF COST AND FINANCIAL ACCOUNTING

Whether related to jobs, processes, articles for sale, departments or to some measurement of work, unit costs should be regarded as breakdowns or analyses of the figures appearing in the expenditure accounts of the double-entry system. In a modern system of industrial accounting there is no independent cost ledger or financial ledger, but the complete accounting system is amalgamated into one set of double-entry accounts. In other cases the figures posted to the cost ledger are reconciled at regular intervals, probably monthly, with the figures shown in the revenue accounts of the financial ledger.

Whichever system is adopted, the expenditure accounts and the cost accounts are interdependent. The application of financial and cost accounting to the service of management should be planned as one co-ordinated service, and for this purpose should be under common control. Integration does not therefore imply only the amalgamation of two systems of accounts but it also entails the amalgamation of the accounting sections, including the cost office, into one unified department. It is, furthermore, desirable in the interests of the efficiency of the financial division that clerks shall be given the opportunity of obtaining experience in both financial accounting and cost accounting, in other words, in records of total-expense headings and of breakdowns or analyses.

C. THE UNIT OF COST

In planning a costing service the first matter to be decided is the unit for which a cost is to be ascertained. The basic unit will not necessarily be the article to be sold nor any measurement of that article. It should be a factor which is best capable of measuring all work carried out in a business or in a department of a business, but consideration must also be given to the practicability and expense of using the unit which best fulfils this principle.

In a jobbing or repairing works where jobs undertaken are of a wide variety, the man-hour may well represent the most convenient unit for costing purposes. In a machine shop or other works largely dependent on the usage of machines the machine-hour is appropriate; in processing material the unit cost may be the process-hour. In some cases costs will depend upon some measurement of output, for example, in the gas industry, where costs are related to cubic feet of gas produced. In others it is often informative to assess costs in relation to a measurement of a fixed asset—in agriculture costs are often related to the acreage of the land. It is a popular misconception that costing is an operation peculiar to a producing unit. The costs per mile, per ton-mile, per flying-hour and so forth are of vital concern to transport undertakings; hospital management is interested in costs in relation to beds; and schools in the cost per pupil.

The conception of costing as an exercise in assessing and

controlling unit costs means that it is applicable to any kind of enterprise and is beneficial to all. In all kinds of work it is possible to establish a unit on which all costs depend or should depend. The cost of such a unit will then represent the focal point of cost control.

The calculation of unit costs in the sense outlined above does not by any means preclude the ascertainment of the cost of units of sales for price-fixing purposes. Only where the article or service provided is consistently uniform will it be convenient to base the costing system on the unit of sale. Where costs are required in connection with price fixing it is usually necessary for an estimating department to assess the number of units, *e.g.* man-hours, machine-hours, passenger-miles, etc., entailed by the sale and for the unit cost to be applied to that figure.

A further adjustment to the estimate may be required where the unit costs, as prepared primarily for control purposes, omit some ingredient of costs. Thus, costing by man-hours in an engineering works may exclude bought-out parts or work sub-contracted; in many cases unit costs are compiled in the first place exclusive of fixed overheads, which may be subsequently applied on a percentage basis.

D. An Elementary Exercise in Costing

Because the allocation to units of variable, semi-variable and fixed charges largely depends on turnover, it is essential that unit costs be expressed in these three stages or, at least, in the two stages of variable and fixed costs.

The analysis of the expenditure accounts in the double-entry system should therefore begin by segregating the expenditure into groups corresponding to these headings.

In a simple organisation where the direct work is concentrated on a standard product or service, the ascertainment of past costs per unit merely entails dividing the totals recorded in the revenue accounts by the number of units produced or supplied over the period used.

Example

The annual costs of operating a passenger ferry service across a river are as follows:

Cost per journey £	Cost per passenger £	Variable Costs	£	£
0·50	0·05	Direct wages of boatmen	1,500	
0·13	0·01	Fuel for boats	400	
0·03	0·00½	Other direct expenses	100	
£0·66	£0·06½	Total variable costs		2,000
		Semi-variable costs		
0·25	0·02½	{ Indirect hourly wages, e.g. maintenance engineers and watchmen . . .	750	
0·05	0·00½	{ Indirect material, including paint, grease and repair expenses . . .	150	
0·03	0·00½	Other semi-variable expenses . . .	100	
£0·33	£0·03½	Total semi-variable costs . . .		1,000
		Fixed costs		
0·66	0·06	Staff salaries	2,000	
0·17	0·02	Rent of premises	500	
0·10	0·01	Depreciation	300	
0·07	0·01	Other administrative expenses . .	200	
1·00	0·10	Total fixed costs		3,000
£2·00	£0·20	GRAND TOTAL COSTS FOR THE YEAR .		£6,000

Number of journeys 3,000
Number of passengers carried – – 30,000

The foregoing statement would, for the undertaking concerned, provide the management with a useful basis for the control of expenditure if it is prepared for, say, monthly periods.

It should be borne in mind, however, that the value of these figures is qualified by the following considerations:

1. The picture shown refers to the past. It would be dangerous to assume, even in such a simple case, either that the turn-over (in terms of trips or passengers) will remain constant in the future or that individual items of expense will be unchanged. Wage-rates may rise, depreciation may rise or fall, and so may the cost of material and office expenses.

2. The costs are average costs over the period, in this case a year. During slack times many of the expenses, particularly fixed costs, will continue. So that if such a statement were drawn up for a period less than a year but which included a slack time, the total cost per passenger or journey would appear much greater.

Subject to these qualifications, however, the form of the statement does provide a clearer guide to the manager in controlling his business than would be shown by the bare statement that the cost per journey was £2·00 and that the cost per passenger was 20p. From the detailed statement shown it is comparatively easy to estimate the effect on overall costs and costs per unit of a change in turnover. A succession of such statements will show the trend of each broad heading of cost in relation to turnover, and thus the costs may be controlled on this basis. Movements in the figure of boatmen's wages are, for example, meaningless unless they are related to trips or passengers.

It is possible from such a method of showing unit costs to calculate the minimum price at which additional passengers may be carried without incurring a loss on the journey. Such price must cover the variable costs and a proportion of the semi-variable costs, but need not cover the fixed costs. Assume, for example, the normal charge is 25p for each passenger and a further 1,000 passengers could be induced to undertake the journey by reducing the price to, say, 12½p in a slack period. Then it would be worth while to accept the additional passengers at a price below the overall cost of 20p as may be seen from the following calculation:

	£	£	£
30,000 at 25p		7,500	
Less Costs of 30,000 at 20p		6,000	
Surplus on carrying 30,000 passengers at normal prices and after absorbing all fixed costs . . .			1,500
1,000 at 12½p	125		
Less Additional expenditure involved, i.e. variable plus semi-variable costs (probably only a proportion of the latter would be involved), 1,000 at 10p . . .	100		
Surplus on 1,000			25
Total profit on carrying 31,000 passengers . . .			£1,525

The above exercise in costing indicates that only a very limited use can be made of a unit cost expressed as a total figure covering all headings of direct and overhead expenditure. Such overall costs may alter according to the period covered, the output or turnover to which they are related and the purpose for which they are calculated.

A booklet produced by a Committee of the Institute of Chartered Accountants in England and Wales, entitled *Developments in Cost Accounting*, states: "A cost can only be a convention; and the expression 'an accurate cost' can have meaning only within the particular convention chosen as appropriate to the purpose for which the cost is required."

E. COSTING FOR A COMPLEX BUSINESS

1. Preliminary analysis

Most businesses are complex in that the output produced or the services provided are not uniform and are the outcome of the work of a number of dissimilar departments each engaged on a different process or operation. The goal of cost analysis is the ascertainment of unit costs, but essential information for management is produced at stages in this process of analysis.

The first stage in the analysis is to allocate the expenditure to the broad divisions of the undertaking. In a manufacturing business these divisions will normally comprise: Administration, Operational or Manufacturing, Research and Experimental, and Selling. The Purchasing Department may, especially in a non-manufacturing concern, be treated as a separate division, and in a large business a further division, often called "Headquarters", may exist for the overall control of a number of separate operating or selling units. The fixed expenses which cannot be directly ascribed to departments, such as rent, rates, taxes, audit and legal fees, may be allocated to a further heading under some such title as "General Overheads" or included under "Administration".

The second stage of analysis is the allocation of expenditure to the departments within the broad divisions. The departmental cost accounts thus produced are invaluable for the purpose of assisting departmental managers to plan and control their operations and expenditure, especially if a system of budgetary control is in operation.

2. The apportionment of expenses

It is necessary to distinguish between the expressions "allocation" and "apportionment". In the sense used here "allocation" means placing expenditure at the source where it is known to arise. Thus, wages paid to fitters may be allocated to the fitting shop by means of analysis of the pay-roll. The rent of accounting machines may be attributed to the accounts department. For the purpose of the departmental control of expenditure it is essential that no costs shall be attributed to a departmental manager unless it is certain that they arise in that department and are (at least to some extent) within his control.

The apportionment of expenditure means the division of a cost on an arbitrary basis where more exact analysis cannot be made. Thus, the rent of a factory may be apportioned to departments on the basis of floor space, lighting on light points and welfare costs on numbers of employees.

In order to calculate a unit cost of a particular process or operation so that such costs may be comparable one with another some apportionment of expenses will be necessary and will constitute the third stage of analysis. It is widely held that misleading impressions of the real incidence of cost may be given if the apportionment of expense is carried too far. It seems, nevertheless, to be generally agreed that an attempt should be made to find the total cost attributable to each operating or works department, and for this purpose certain reasonable apportionments of such items as rent, electricity, water, fuel, depreciation, welfare charges and ancillary factory services, such as maintenance, security, progress and planning, should be made. The object should be to apply to a works department as great a quantum of expense as possible without entering into the realm of guesswork or controversy.

3. The use of cost centres

A further development of the analysis of expense is to apportion expenses to cost centres which represent the focal point of particular processes. Thus, in a press shop the cost centres are each heavy press, in a machine shop each large machine tool or perhaps a group of small tools. The costs which have been allocated to the works department so far are apportioned in turn to each cost centre so that the cost per machine-hour may be calculated and controlled.

The principle of costing by cost centres may be applied to almost any form of industry or commerce. Thus, in a store the cost of selling may be segregated into cost centres represented by particular counters; in a restaurant the cost centre may be the table; in a hotel the room or suite; in a mine the working face.

4. The apportionment of administrative costs

On the principles enunciated above a great deal of the costs of an undertaking can be directly applied to the operating or works departments or to cost centres within those departments. The costs so apportioned or allocated will include variable, semi-variable and fixed elements of cost, and should be so distinguished. There remains a large sum of expense which cannot be said to have arisen within the operating departments. These charges include the costs of the administrative departments, including the financial sections, the selling and buying departments, the experimental or research division, headquarters and general expenses. These expenses are often loosely described as "overheads".

If it is desired to obtain an overall cost per unit overhead costs must be applied on some reasonable basis to the direct factory or operating centre. Where the unit of cost is centred in the selling departments, as in a store (or possibly in the buying department, where the buying function governs all other costs), it is to such departments that the remaining costs or overheads must be applied.

Methods of applying overheads vary widely, and any method must, by its nature, be arbitrary. All methods of applying overheads rest on an estimate of: (a) the overhead expense, and (b) the output likely to be achieved during a convenient future period. Thus, where the unit of cost is a man-hour and the period selected is a year, it is necessary to estimate the number of man-hours likely to be achieved in the year and to divide this number into the estimated overheads in order to arrive at a rate of overheads to be applied to each man-hour.

In other cases overheads are apportioned to works departments on some broad basis as a percentage of direct wages, as a rate per man-hour or machine-hour, or of some quantitative measurement of output (e.g. tons, feet, numbers of articles), and thence included in a machine-hour rate or other unit of costing.

Past costs may, of course, be indicated by merely dividing the actual overheads for a period by the number of units of output or service produced. But apart from the fact that the information may well be out of date before it is presented, the overall costs so calculated vary widely from period to period owing to the incidence of holidays and the fact that the precise amount of many overheads will not be known until the end of a year.

The application of overheads to unit costs constitutes one of the most difficult problems in the preparation and the interpretation of costs.

F. OTHER APPLICATIONS OF COSTING

The broad principle of analysing expenditure so as to calculate the cost of a unit of work is, or should be, the basis of any costing system, particularly where the cost system is operated for the principal purpose of controlling expenditure.

Considerable modifications of the methods outlined above are found in particular industries and individual businesses, particularly where the prime interest in costing is as a aid in fixing prices.

The methods in use may be generally classified under the following headings:

1. Job costing

Job costing is used in engineering works for the purpose of finding the cost of each particular order placed in the works. For the purpose of job costing the direct labour element of a job is found by apportioning each workman's wages according to the time he spends on each job, as recorded on time sheets or job cards. Direct material is costed by priced requisitions on the stores. Bought-out parts and work sub-contracted is directly allocated to each job by the costing section of the accounts department on the authority of the order placed with the supplier or sub-contractor. Overheads may be allocated as a simple percentage of labour cost or hours, as a machine-hour rate, as a percentage of material cost or by some such other method as is appropriate and practicable for the organisation concerned.

2. Batch costs

Batch costs are job costs amalgamated into convenient batches of similar work. Usually batch costing is carried out where the jobs are too small to justify individual costing and where there would be difficulty in deciding the exact allocation of material or labour to particular jobs.

3. Contract costs

Contract costs are a further development of job costing where it is desired to find the cost of carrying out a complete contract for a customer probably involving numerous jobs and batches of jobs. Contract costing is carried out in heavy engineering such as shipbuilding, bridge-making, and in the erection of buildings or blocks of buildings. In many cases a self-contained accounting system is maintained at the site where the work is taking place, and returns are compiled for transmission to the head office, where the figures are incorporated in the main double-entry system.

4. Process costs

Whereas any form of job costing is intended primarily to find the cost of completing customers' present or future orders, process costs are carried out largely with a view to controlling work by financial means. Process costs are usually applied in a works where the final product has passed through a number of stages or processes. The term might be applied to any searching costing system operating in an engineering works where "processes", such as machining, pressing and treatment, are undertaken. Process costing is, however, usually applied to such industries as textile manufacture, where wool, cotton, asbestos, rayon and so forth undergo such processes as carding, dyeing, spinning and weaving; or to gas, chemicals and paper-making. An important objective in process costing is the evaluation of wastage.

5. Operating costs

The term operating costs may be used to cover any costing system designed to measure the unit costs of providing services as opposed to products. In particular, the term is applied to transport undertakings, where costs are expressed in such units as passenger-miles, ton-miles or flying-hours.

6. Multiple costs

Multiple costing describes costing systems where a combination of the methods outlined above are used. A business producing a variety of dissimilar goods and services of a non-repetitive nature will need a multiple costing system.

7. Single or output costs

As distinguished from multiple costing, the term single or output costing is used to describe costing systems dealing with the production of a uniform product when it is only necessary to find the cost of a quantitative measure of the product produced.

The dividing line between these conventional classifications is rarely precise. In some cases too much emphasis is laid on the ascertainment of the cost of a particular sale, *i.e.* of a product or service, rather than on the use of costing to control expenditure. In concentrating on finding the cost of an article to be sold the effectiveness of the system as a means of valuing the work or effort involved in producing the article may be reduced. The cost of a particular sale can never be stated with precision, if only because such cost will largely depend on the particular convention used in applying overheads. The comparative profitability of different groups of sales can, however, be demonstrated by converting unit costs into costs of particular products or services. A well-planned business will set out to reduce its unit costs to the figure calculated to produce the desired profit on the planned turnover.

H

CHAPTER X

THE ELEMENTS OF COST

A. The Basic Element

For practical purposes costs are best considered under the three headings of labour, material and other expenses, the last being a useful collective title referring to all charges other than those incurred as a direct result of employing people or obtaining material. Essentially all costs are due to the use of labour and material, and certainly every cost contains at least a proportion of labour charges, that is, the cost of work performed by some person or persons, possibly incurred by some remote supplier. Material such as coal has no value until it is extracted from the earth and distributed by man's labour. Land itself requires some expenditure of labour before it becomes useful or has a value.

Because labour charges enter into all costs the control of the labour element of cost is of great importance, not only for an individual business but also for national, and indeed international, prosperity.

The purpose of this chapter is to review the techniques used for recording, analysing, presenting and controlling costs under the three headings of labour, material and other expenses.

B. Labour Costing

1. Time recording

Labour costs consist of the remuneration paid for people's work, plus, in some cases, certain other charges directly related to the employment of people, such as national insurance (employers' contributions), pensions costs and welfare expenses. It is more common, and certainly more simple, to restrict labour costing to wages and salaries, leaving the remaining charges incurred by labour within the heading of "other expenses".

Labour charges are either direct or indirect. Direct labour represents work directly applied to the product or a service to be sold. It may be apportioned to the unit of cost or job either on the basis of the time spent by a workman on the job or (in the case of pure piece-work) as a price for some physical measurement of the product. In many cases a combination of these two principles is used. Whatever method of apportioning wages is in force time is always an important factor.

The time taken by a workman on a unit of output (*e.g.* a job) is recorded on a weekly or daily time sheet, or in more advanced systems on a card prepared for each job by the works office. The time spent on each job is best recorded on the card by means of a time clock, and whatever system is used the record should be checked and approved by a member of the supervisory staff in the works, such as a foreman or charge hand or a section leader in a drawing office.

The use of time clocks for job booking purposes should not be confused with the recording of the time of entering and leaving the factory on gate cards. The recording of time at the gate or entrance to the works is essential for disciplinary purposes and for reconciling the job times with total time spent in the factory or other centre of work.

For obvious reasons the recording of times on job cards by means of a clock is preferable to a hand-written time sheet or ticket. In all cases it must be borne in mind that the mere recording of times gives no indication of efficiency, and except with the tightest supervision, provides many opportunities for inaccurate bookings. There will, for example, be a natural reluctance to book on idle time where a higher rate of pay may be obtained by continuing to book on a job. Even though, however, the cost of direct labour incurred on each job or operation may be represented only approximately on the basis of the recorded time, such time records are invaluable aids in the allocation of overheads and are essential for the calculation of hourly wages where bonus systems are in operation. It has already been emphasised that a unit cost cannot be expressed with absolute precision and that it depends on the convention applied and the methods of allocation and apportionment in use. Because, however, the adage "time is money" is and will always remain true, the time recorded by direct workers is one of the best factors for the apportionment of overheads. For this reason times should always be recorded even where payment is made on a pure piece-work basis.

2. The analysis of wages

The payment due to each worker at the end of a week is calculated by the aid of gate cards and the records of times occupied on each job, or the output records of a piece-work system. The calculation takes account of basic pay for the hours of attendance, bonuses for speedy work on individual jobs, and also overtime rates and higher rates for night and week-end work.

The calculation of basic pay, overtime and higher rates for night and week-end work depends largely on the gate-card records. Bonuses for speedy work are calculated on the information provided by the job records, bonus hours or rates being indicated by the time clerk. In addition, of course, deductions, such as for national insurance, P.A.Y.E., pension contributions, club subscriptions and group insurances, are taken into account in calculating the net sum due to the employee. Weekly totals of the gross pay due to the employees and totals of each deduction must be obtained for posting to the revenue accounts of the double-entry system.

Considerable clerical work by time clerks and wages clerks cannot be avoided, but many labour-saving methods are available for reducing this indirect labour to a minimum. For a large concern accuracy and speed can be obtained by the use of calculating machines, and punched-card systems or an electronic computer are invaluable for the preparation of extensive pay-rolls, the analysis of labour by unit costs and departments, and the compilation of totals for posting to the control accounts.

3. Incentive schemes

(a) *The broad categories of remuneration*

Payments for the use of labour fall within the following categories:

(i) Fees, representing an agreed price for the work done or to be done, such as director's fees and consultants' fees. Normally, fees, particularly those payable to solicitors, accountants and so forth for professional services, are excluded from the category of "labour costing" and are treated as "other expenses".

(ii) Monthly salaries, usually calculated on the basis of annual sums, of which one-twelfth, or a more precise apportionment by days, is paid each month. Monthly salaries are normally paid for supervisory work, and whilst such charges can be allocated to departments, it is often unwise to attempt any further apportionment to jobs or unit costs except on the same basis as other departmental overheads are apportioned. In some cases, however, a skilled technician paid on a monthly basis may be solely engaged on a specific job or customer's order, and his salary can therefore be applied to that unit without difficulty.

(iii) Weekly salaries, normally payable to administrative staff or for supervision in the works. Except for draughtsmen or technicians working on specific jobs or projects, such salaries must be included in the appropriate overhead classification for apportionment to unit costs.

(iv) Hourly wages. Whilst various incentive schemes are in force for some monthly and weekly paid staff, such schemes are particularly applicable to hourly paid personnel directly engaged on the supply of the product or article for sale.

(b) *Incentives for hourly paid workers*

Some manufacturers believe that efficiency in direct departments can be best achieved by the payment of high wages at a flat rate per hour or day, by avoiding overtime and ensuring by a high level of leadership and supervision that work is performed to the standards required. The incentives in such a case may be broadly summarised as including the workers' desire to retain a well-paid and otherwise attractive job, a natural pride in personal skill and workmanship and the realisation that the prosperity of the employer will redound to his own and his fellow workers' benefit.

The payment of a flat rate simplifies accounting routine. Complex wage structures and incentive schemes are, however, in operation in many industries and undertakings, and these schemes create correspondingly complex accounting routines.

Wide use is made of monetary incentives normally involving higher rates of pay for satisfactory work carried out at a speed greater than certain assessed standards. The object of increasing rates of pay for a higher turnover is largely to reduce the incidence of fixed overheads on unit costs. The principal methods in operation are examined below.

(i) *Straight piece-work.* The term "piece-work" is applicable strictly to wages paid exclusively on the basis of numbers of units produced or some quantitative measurement of output, such as payments which are made to out-workers in the hosiery industry based on a price for each article. Whilst this method has the advantage of simplicity both for the employer and the employee, it has a limited incentive effect owing to the fact that: (a) the worker places a higher value on additional work above normal, and (b) the additional payment at standard rates may result in a smaller net rate for the worker after income tax has been paid. For these and other reasons many modifications to straight piecework are in operation and are designed to provide monetary incentives for additional effort.

(ii) *Premium bonus.* Premium-bonus schemes combine plain time rates with payment based on results, and provide bonus rates for output above normal.

All such schemes entail the assessment of a standard of normal output generally intended to be the output of an average man of normal ability for a standard working week, say forty-four hours.

The factors which are used to assess the standard output must obviously vary with the kind of work and the particular industry involved.

In a simple application the standard of output in a box-assembling factory may be a certain number of assemblies completed in an hour. In a jobbing engineering works the standard may have to be assessed anew for each particular job or operation, whether such work be, for example, the machining of bar metal, the fitting of components into a main assembly, riveting, painting or any of the wide variety of occupations to be found in an industrial concern. The assessment of the standard is made by rate-fixers, preferably in combination with work-study experts and usually in consultation with the operatives concerned and their supervisor. Trade-union representatives take a close interest in the assessment of standards which are to be used as a basis for workers' remuneration.

On the basis of the assessed standard of output the worker is paid bonus rates on output in excess of the standard.

Two main systems of bonus are in operation. The first and probably most widely used is called the 'Halsey' system, which entails paying the basic hourly rate for the actual hours occupied on a job plus the same rate per hour on half the time saved above the time allowed. The rate-fixed time is widely known as the "price for the job".

Example

Time allowed	10 hours
Basic rate per hour	15p
Time taken	6 hours
Time saved	4 hours

Pay for the job:	£
6 hours at 15p	0·90
$\frac{4}{2} = 2$ at 15p	0·30

Pay for 6 hours (actual work), *i.e.* an actual rate of 20p per hour. £1·20

Another method of operating a premium bonus scheme is known as the "Rowan" system, which provides for the payment of the basic rate per hour for the actual time taken on a job, plus the basic rate on that proportion of the time saved which the time taken bears to the time allowed.

Example

Time allowed	10 hours
Basic rate per hour	15p
Time taken	6 hours
Time saved	4 hours
Bonus hours $\frac{6}{10} \times 4$	2·4 hours

Pay:	£
Basic, 6 hours at 15p	0·90
Bonus, 2·4 hours at 15p	0·36
Total pay for the job = ...	£1·26

Representing an actual rate per hour of $\frac{£1·26}{6} = 21\text{p}$.

Under both systems the actual rate of payment per hour rises with the saving in time. Up to the point where 50 per cent of the time allowed is saved the actual rate per hour is higher under the Rowan scheme, but thereafter the Halsey scheme gives a rapidly rising bonus, which exceeds that obtainable under the Rowan scheme.

Various other forms of incentive schemes for hourly paid labour have been operated, and the above examples of commonly used methods are noted with the object of indicating the broad lines of these schemes for direct workers.

For many kinds of work neither premium nor piece-work payments can be employed. In such cases incentives may be based on such factors as the bonus earnings in the workshops where premium bonus applies. Such methods are applicable to work carried out in service departments, such as maintenance and treatments, or where the nature of the work is unsuitable for rate-fixing, as in many experimental shops and tool rooms.

(iii) *Other incentive schemes.* Other incentive schemes are briefly summarised below.

The Priestman–Atkinson system involves the payment of a bonus represented by a percentage varying with output above an assessed standard, perhaps the output of a normal period before the introduction of the scheme. The "output" may be measured by weight of completed work; by a points system, weighting individual products where they represent different degrees of effort; by value of output; by value of sales or other measurements.

Under the Scanlon system bonus fluctuates with the ratio of labour costs to the volume of production, or some other relation between the workers' efforts and output.

Many other schemes are in operation in different industries, generally entailing the payment of bonus rates for output above normal, either calculated for the entire works or for teams of workers. In all cases the measurement of output needs to be expressed as a unit (*i.e.* per man, man-hour or machine-hour), owing to the fact that increased production may be obtained by augmenting the labour force or by further mechanisation, without calling for any additional efficiency.

(c) *Incentives for other employees*

(i) *Profit sharing and co-partnership.* Bonus schemes for administrative employees may be classified as: (*a*) those based on profit or cost; (*b*) those based on some measurement of output; and (*c*) those depending on the appraisal of a supervisor.

Various profit-sharing schemes, often combined with a form of co-partnership, have been in operation in many concerns since the beginning of the century and probably before. In many cases a class of administrative employee, say from junior executive upwards, is paid a bonus calculated on the balance of profit remaining after payment of a fixed rate to shareholders. The calculation is often weighted for the various earning levels, and in some cases is applied by means of a percentage which diminishes as profits rise.

Co-partnership schemes normally involve the allocation or issue of shares to employees, generally subject to a minimum length of service. The shares issued to employees do not usually carry voting rights, and the dividend payable on such shares is often subject to the payment of a minimum return to the other shareholders.

Apart from encouraging employees to assist, so far as their particular functions permit, in improving profitability, such schemes help to reduce labour turnover. The ownership by employees of a part of the capital of a company is designed to induce employees to identify their interests with those of their employer, and to promote team work. With or without this financial interest some companies instil an active interest in managerial problems by arranging for employees to act as directors of junior boards or committees responsible, under the direction of the principal board appointed by the shareholders, for policy decisions in respect of some aspect of the work of the undertaking.

A defect of such schemes is that the profitability of a company is sometimes more dependent on external influences, or top management decision, than on the efficiency of junior management or individual employees. Moreover, whilst by virtue of profit-sharing schemes employees are able to share in the prosperity of their employers, they do not share the losses. Furthermore, inefficient employees may share in increased profits which they have done nothing to create, while on the other hand, exceptional effort may go unrewarded. Generally the relation between effort and reward is often too remote for profit-sharing schemes to be inducements for the efficient performance of particular tasks, but the effectiveness of such schemes on the general attitude of employees to their work should not be under-rated.

(ii) *Job incentives for clerical workers.* There is a growing realisation that the principle of paying higher rates or bonuses for exceptional effort is just as capable of being put into effect on certain jobs in offices as it is in the factory.

Whilst bonuses can be paid to supervisors on the basis of departmental cost reductions or other indications of team efficiency, job incentives are naturally more applicable to non-supervisory staff, particularly those doing work of a routine nature. Thus, the punchers and verifiers working on a punched-card installation can be paid bonuses calculated on output above an assessed normal.

Essential pre-requisites to the operation of monetary incentive schemes for clerical workers (as indeed, for any kind of work), are: (*a*) a steady, uninterrupted flow of work, *i.e.* no waiting time: (*b*) work of a uniform nature and requiring a uniform standard of skill: (*c*) the scientific assessment of standards of output giving adequate allowances for fatigue and natural needs.

The principle of incentives for exceptional work can be applied to such routine duties as ledger postings (based on the number of postings), especially with a mechanical installation; invoice and order typing; envelope addressing; wage calculations; and many other routine and uniform tasks of a like nature.

A great deal of administrative work is not of a routine nature, and for such work bonuses must depend on a personal assessment of the individual's work by his or her supervisor. Alternatively, bonus is payable on the output of the entire factory or division compared with a standard, such as the Priestman–Atkinson or Scanlon systems referred to previously.

The assessment of an individual's value by a supervisor is often aided by a points-rating system by means of which points are given for such qualities as punctuality, co-operation, adaptability, progress, intelligence, and general conscientiousness. Many managers, however, find that the appraisal of a subordinate's worth is too complex a matter to be reduced to points given for a necessarily limited number of attributes.

C. MATERIAL COSTS

1. The objectives of material costing

The object of material costing is to find the value of material used on a job, process or unit of cost with a view to controlling expenditure on material in relation to output and to assist in price-fixing and estimating.

Material costs may be divided into the direct and indirect elements, direct material being such as can be precisely allocated to the units of cost. Direct material includes bought-out parts for incorporation, without any further processing of importance, into the finished article. Indirect material includes such consumable stores as cleaning material, greases and oils, and treatment material.

The control and accurate recording of material costs presupposes an efficient organisation for indenting, ordering, storing, requisitioning, issue and accounting. The broad principles of the routine required are examined below.

2. Indenting for material

It is necessary in any size or kind of business organisation for a programme of material requirements to be drawn up, covering a sufficiently long period ahead for economical purchasing and capable of revision as changing circumstances dictate.

On the basis of this programme desirable stock levels are reviewed and future requirements discussed with the purchasing department with a view to ensuring adequate supplies, conserving storage space and finance, and obtaining the financial benefit of bulk purchases or a favourable buying market. The correct balance between these sometimes conflicting considerations is relatively of as great importance to a one-man business as to an international combine.

Except for special requirements which cannot be foreseen, and subject to the general programme of output having been communicated to the purchasing department, indents (or requests on that department to order goods) normally originate from the stores when the level of any particular class of material has fallen to a pre-determined point—the "ordering level". There will be a number of indents passed to the purchasing department other than from the stores, such as those for the purchase of capital assets, articles for the administrative departments and exceptional purchases required by the operating or experimental departments. It is, however, essential that authority to issue such indents should be limited to selected managers and to the stores controller.

3. Ordering and receipt by stores

On the authority of an indent the purchasing department prepares an order on a supplier for the goods required, and a copy of this order is passed to the originator of the indent and to the cost office.

When the goods are received and checked against the delivery note a goods-inwards note is prepared by the goods-inwards section, recording the supplier, description of goods, quantity received and condition. A copy of this note is passed to the buying department for checking against the order.

It is desirable that the goods-inwards section should be under the control of the stores supervisor so that no further documentation is required in order to pass the goods into store forthwith. Particularly with bought-out parts (which should be dealt with in the same manner as material for processing) it may be necessary for the goods to be subjected to tests by the Inspection Department, for which purpose a special routine must be organised.

It is very desirable for all purchases to be recorded by the stores and to be issued to the department requiring the articles on the authority of a requisition. This routine should be followed even in the case of bought-out parts or exceptional purchases which are required immediately by the operating department. If the routine of indent, order, goods-inward note and requisition is not followed, even for bought-out parts required immediately, the value of the items will not be recorded in unit cost records without instituting special procedures and thus hampering orderly routines.

It is the practice in some businesses for such items as maintenance materials not required in connection with any production process to be issued to departments without passing through stores and for the costs to be recorded against a maintenance heading in the general ledger. Such a method prevents the desirable integration of unit costs records with the so-called "financial accounts".

4. Accounting routine

(a) *Reconciling requisitions with purchases*

The accounting routine is best visualised from two points of view. One objective is to record purchases of materials in the expenditure accounts of the General Ledger under such headings as raw material, consumable stores, consumable tools, bought-out parts, factored goods or such other headings as may be convenient for the particular business concerned. The other objective is to ascertain the cost of material used on the various jobs, orders from customers or other units. The cost of material used during an accounting period will not correspond with the cost of purchases during that period owing to the fact that a proportion of the material used will have been drawn from stock existing at the beginning of the period (*i.e.* from purchases made in earlier periods) and, on the other hand, some of the material purchased in the current period will be carried forward as stock for use in a subsequent period. An essential accounting operation in connection with material costs is to reconcile the usage of a particular period with the purchases. This reconciliation, which should be made at the end of each accounting period, takes the following form:

		£
Stock at the beginning .	. . . .	1,000
Add Purchases in the period .	. . . . . .	2,000
		3,000
Less Stock at end .	. . . .	1,500
		1,500
Subtract Stock adjustment (representing gains or losses on stocktaking)		100
Cost of material used during the period as shown by the summary of requisitions from stores	. . . . . .	£1,400

(b) *Recording purchases*

When a supplier's invoice has been passed for payment, after the routine described above has been carried out, it is entered in the Purchase Day Book or Journal. This Journal is analysed, (*a*) by the General Ledger Account, *e.g.* raw material account, bought-out parts account, etc., and (*b*) by the stores account, *e.g.* maintenance material, grease, treatments, bar metal, etc. Where a large number of purchases is made these analyses are most conveniently made by means of punched cards. The procedure in such a case is for a list of invoices approved for payment to be sent to the punched-card section at, say, monthly or more frequent intervals. Cards are punched from the information as to General Ledger and Stores Ledger account numbers which are shown on the copies of the goods-inwards notes relating to the approved invoices.

The Purchase Journal, whether prepared by hand or as a machine tabulation, provides the figures for posting to: (i) the General Ledger material accounts, (ii) the Creditors ("bought") Ledger, and (iii) the Stores or Stock Ledger.

(c) *Stores routine*

Bin cards should be maintained for each class of stores, and these cards should record the description of the stores, and the maximum and minimum limits (plus, possibly, an "ordering limit"). Each main class of stores should be given a distinctive number or alphabetical symbol referring to such items as (in an engineering works) sheet metal, bar metal, treatment material, paint, maintenance materials, consumable stores and so forth.

Suitably broad divisions of purchases should be made in a like manner for other types of industry, and such classifications will be of particular importance for the control of stocks in a distributive business. These broad divisions can then be broken down as required, by means of a subsidiary numbering system for each detailed class of store as recorded on a bin card.

The bin cards bear columns headed "Receipts", "Issues" and "Balance". The receipts column is entered on the basis of a copy of the goods-inwards note or a goods-inwards book from which such notes are compiled. The issues column is entered on the basis of requisitions to be signed by the appropriate supervisor when stores are withdrawn. Credit requisitions will be required for stores returned by the operating departments.

With a planned production programme stores are not issued to the direct works shops merely because a requisition is presented. The works planning officer should issue the store-keeper with a schedule of material requirements for a particular job. The job number, which is noted by the works office on the worker's job card, corresponds with the number quoted on the material schedule. It is the responsibility of the store-keeper to issue for each job no more than the quantity of material stated on the material schedule. It is desirable that excess requirements are issued only under the authority of a responsible supervisor.

5. The valuation of stocks and stores

(a) The effect of the valuation

The accuracy of the profit figure shown by the accounts and of the unit costs shown by the cost statements depends to a considerable extent on the valuation of material used and that which remains in stock at the end of each accounting period. In ascertaining either the cost of sales or the cost of material used in production or operation it is necessary to assess the value of the stores of raw material, bought-out parts, finished goods and work in progress at the beginning and end of the period. In job costing it is necessary to value the material requisitioned for the job.

Thus, correct accounting for profits and costs, correct estimating and effective control are to a considerable extent dependent on the principles under which the various kinds of stocks are valued.

The essential question to be decided in this respect is whether to value at: (i) original cost, (ii) current values, or (iii) the cost of replacement.

The most widely used method is to value stocks at original cost, or market price prevailing at the time of valuation if the latter is lower than original cost. This is the basis regarded as obligatory in the annual published accounts of limited companies and other bodies whose accounts are subject to professional audit. Any higher valuation than at the lower of cost or market price would be anticipating profit on unsold stock. Conversely, too low a valuation would have the effect of creating a secret reserve, which, at least in the case of limited companies, would mislead investors and the general public as to the true profitability and financial resources of the business.

For the purpose of presenting information to the public the present conventions as to the valuation of stock are firmly established. Nevertheless, considerable discussion has arisen in recent years as to: (i) the correct basis of pricing requisitions and thus of charging material to unit costs, and (ii) the desirability of charging to reserve the probable cost of replacing stocks.

The problems which have been debated are largely the result of the rising trend of prices which has occurred, in particular, since the end of the Second World War.

These problems and some of the remedies which have been proposed are examined below.

(b) *The methods of valuation*

If the price or cost of a particular category of stores or stock remains unchanged over a considerable period the only problem which arises is to apply the price or cost, first, to the material used (in order to find the cost of output), and secondly, to the remaining stock (in order to prepare the Balance Sheet or other statement of the financial postion).

Where, however, the price or cost of a category of material frequently changes, the value of remaining stock will depend on the value assigned to the material used. The various methods of valuing material used are set out below:

(i) *First in first out (F.I.F.O.)*

Example. A transport company begins operations with a stock of 2,000 gallons of petrol bought at, say, 20p a gallon. Subsequently a further 1,200 gallons are bought at 20½p a gallon; 2,720 gallons are used, leaving a stock at the end of the period of 480 gallons.

	£	£
Cost of purchases:		
2,000 gallons at 20p		400·00
1,200 gallons at 20½p		246·00
3,200		646·00
Deduct Cost of petrol used:		
2,000 gallons at 20p	400·00	
720 gallons at 20½p	147·60	
2,720		547·60
Value of stock 480 gallons at 20½p		£98·40

Note that if the amount used had been only 1,800 gallons the statement would read as follows:

	£	£
Cost of purchases as above		646·00
Deduct Cost of petrol used 1,800 gallons at 20p		360·00
Value of stock		£286·00
Representing:		
200 gallons at 20p	40·00	
1,200 gallons at 20½p	246·00	
		£286·00

(ii) *Last in first out (L.I.F.O.)*

	£	£
Using the above example:		
Cost of purchases		646·00
Deduct Cost of petrol used:		
1,200 gallons at 20½p	246·00	
1,520 gallons at 20p	304·00	
2,720		550·00
Value of stock 480 gallons at 20p		£96·00

(iii) *Average price.*

The average price of issues, and thus of resultant stock, depends on the various points of time at which purchases and issues are made. The method requires issues to be priced at the average price of the stock which existed at the time of issue.

The entries in a stock card showing transactions based on this system would appear as in the example shown on page 213.

(iv) *Base stock.* Some manufacturers in the post-war years have adopted the principle of valuing, for Balance Sheet purposes, base stock only, which in this sense refers usually to stocks or rather "stores" of raw materials. The interpretation of "base stock" and the precise method of valuation may vary widely with different concerns. The essential principle, however, is to value as part of the capital of the concern only that amount of raw-material stock which is required to maintain normal production. Temporary increases of stock or stores holdings resulting from fluctuations in buying or marketing conditions are not included in the valuation.

The effects of this method are: (*a*) to charge against revenue in the current year those purchases which bring stock above the basic levels and thus insure against falls in the value of the abnormal stocks: (*b*) to assist in maintaining stability of profits; and (*c*) to assist in maintaining a stable and probably conservatively depicted financial position.

The base-stock method of valuation affects only the overall revenue account and the statement of the financial position of a business. The costing of material to jobs, processes and other units is not affected, and the actual value of material stores as shown by the stores accounts needs to be reconciled to the lower figure of base stock shown in the overall financial accounts.

(v) *Valuation at standard cost.* A valuation of issues and stock at a fixed standard price avoids much of the calculations necessary with other methods, although such a method entails the collection of variances between actual and standard cost by means of a "material variance" account. In many standard costing systems, however, material is priced to jobs at actual cost.

Where numerous small fluctuations occur, the pricing of material issues at a standard figure does, however, considerably simplify costing procedure without significantly affecting the picture shown by the costing. It is essential that the standard prices should be continually reviewed, otherwise a continuous downward or upward trend of prices might produce both incorrect unit costing and incorrect stock valuation.

Date	Receipts			Issues			Balance of Stock		
	Units	Unit price	Value	Units	Unit price	Value	Units	Average price	Value
		£	£		£	£		£	£
1st January	2,000	0·200	400				2,000	0·200	400
1st February	1,200	0·204	245				3,200	0·202	645
1st March				1,000	0·202	202	2,200	0·201	443
1st April	600	0·208	125				2,800	0·203	568

(c) *Valuations of manufactured articles*

(i) *The guiding principles.* Stocks of raw material, bought-out parts or stocks of goods for re-sale without further processing cannot be valued at a price higher than their cost price, whatever the methods used to determine that figure.

The value of a manufactured article is in the long run dependent on the cost of labour, material and other expenses which have been incurred in making it. Of these ingredients of cost the material element may in some instances be quite small. One of the objects of costing is to determine or estimate the cost of the finished article, but it does not necessarily follow that such cost is to be treated as the value to be entered in the revenue account and capital statement.

Two guiding principles govern the valuation of finished stock. In the first place, the valuation must not exceed the known or estimated selling price, and secondly, the valuation must not include profit. It is also pertinent to observe that an excessively low valuation has the effect of creating a secret reserve and of understating profits, both contrary to good accounting precepts.

From the above principles it follows that the cost of finished stock represents the maximum valuation, but such figure must be reduced to the extent that it is estimated to exceed the selling price which will eventually be obtained by the manufacturers. The amount of such "writing down" of stock will have to be charged against revenue of the current period.

Partly finished work should also be valued on the basis of cost, provided that any future costs which will be necessary to complete the work do not bring the total above the selling price. The valuation of partly finished work or "work in progress" entails, therefore, the reasonable assessment of future costs on that work. This is only one example of the fact that sound accounting is not only a question of recording past events but also involves a large degree of reasoned estimate and knowledgeable forecast.

The valuation of either finished goods or work in progress is therefore predominantly a question of determining costs. The direct or variable cost of manufacture can be applied to product costs with a high degree of accuracy by means of the labour and material costing systems described above. Other direct expenses incurred in manufacture, such as sub-contracted work, may also be incorporated in product costs without great difficulty. The remaining expenses of business, termed "overheads", can be apportioned only on some arbitrary basis which, in essence, represents at best a matter of opinion. Overheads are tending to increase in relation to direct costs, partly because of increased mechanisation, and often form the largest ingredient of overall costs. The allocation of overheads is described in the next section.

(ii) *The application of overheads*

Overheads as an element of value. In valuing stocks of manufactured articles or work in progress a point of vital importance is the extent to which overheads shall be added to the known direct costs.

The question does not arise in a retail selling business, where the valuation of stock is normally made at the lower of cost (*i.e.* purchase price) or market value of the goods bought for resale. Whilst in theory the same principle applies to the valuation of stocks of manufactured goods or work in progress, the real problem is in the meaning of the word "cost" in this connection.

Does the word "cost" merely cover the purchase price of material and bought-out parts included in the finished or partly finished goods plus the wages of workmen whose labour is directly applied to the produce? If so, the value of the same product would differ according to whether, for example, it was produced largely by manual labour or by machinery, and to the extent that overhead expenditure in the form, say, of a methods and organisation department, had economised in direct material and labour costs.

For such reasons it is generally agreed that at least a proportion of overheads should be included in the valuation, provided, of course, that the resultant figure of costs does not exceed the known probable sales price for the completed article or the appropriate proportion of partly completed work.

The effect of allocating overheads to manufactured stocks. Overheads will include a large element of fixed costs or those which do not vary in relation to output. If, for the purpose of valuing manufactured stocks, total overheads are spread over the output the resulting value of the stock will be shown as high in periods of low output and low in periods of high output.

In the first place it is questionable whether the asset of stock should be valued at a higher figure than normal in the Balance Sheet merely because output is reduced. Is the capital of the business worth more on that account? Secondly, the effect on profits of including full overheads in valuations will be to anticipate that a portion of the fixed costs will be recovered out of the sales of a future period. When the business is slack the amount of fixed overheads carried forward into the future will be greater than in periods of full production and high level of sales.

The effect of including fixed overheads in valuations is demonstrated by the following example:

FIRST YEAR

		£	£
Sales 500 articles at £4)	. . . .		2,000
Less Cost of sales:			
Variable costs (1,000 articles at £1)	. . . .	1,000	
Fixed costs (£2 per article)	. . . . .	2,000	
Cost of output (£3 per article)	. . . .	3,000	
Deduct Stock at end (500 articles at £3)	. .	1,500	
Cost of sales (£3 per article)	. . . .		1,500
Profit (£1 per article sold)	. . . . .		£500

SECOND YEAR

		£	£
Sales (250 articles at £4)	. . . .		1,000
Less Cost of sales:			
Variable costs (500 articles at £1)	. . . .	500	
Fixed costs (£4 per article)	. . . . .	2,000	
Cost of output (£5 per article)	. . . .	2,500	
Add Opening stock, as above	. . . .	1,500	
		4,000	
Deduct Closing stock:			
250 articles at £3	. . . . .	750	
500 articles at £5	. . . .	2,500	
(750 articles at an average of approx. £4·33½ each)	.	3,250	
Cost of sales (£3 per article)	. . . .		750
Profit (£1 per article sold)	. . . . .		£250

	£	£
Sales (1,000 articles at £4)		4,000
Less Cost of sales:		
Variable cost (250 articles at £1)	250	
Fixed costs (£8 per article)	2,000	
Cost of output (£9 per article)	2,250	
Add Opening stock, as above	3,250	
Cost of sales (£5·50 per article)		5,500
Loss (£1·50 per article sold)		£1,500

Three solutions to the problems involved in stock valuations have been put into practice.

One solution is to value stock so as to include variable costs only. Such variable costs may or may not include an element of variable overheads in addition to direct costs. An approximation to this method is the practice of valuing manufactured stock on the basis of factory cost only, leaving out of account other overheads, whether variable or not. This practice appears to contain certain defects in that "factory cost" may include fixed elements, *e.g.* depreciation of idle equipment, and the overheads omitted will almost certainly contain variable items. A further defect of this method lies in the fact that stocks, and hence the capital employed in the company, may thereby be undervalued.

A second solution is to value stock at standard costs. The precise meaning of standard costing is discussed in the next section, but broadly this means a valuation on the basis of normal costs. Fixed overheads may or may not be included in the standard cost, but generally the proportion allocated to the product will be that arrived at on the basis of normal output. The standard cost may therefore be high during periods of low output, and will require adjustment.

Probably the best solution which has appeared so far is the method of valuing only base stock, particularly where base stock itself is valued on standard costing principles. It might be objected in this case that actual stocks will usually exceed base stocks, and the capital of the concern will thereby be undervalued. Whilst the base-stock method has the effect of helping to present a truer trend of profitability, it may result in the creation of something like a secret reserve. There seems to be no reason why in appropriate cases stock valuations as shown in Balance Sheets should not be written up to totals more representative of reality by means of the adjustment of reserve accounts. The revenue accounts need not be affected.

D. OTHER EXPENSES

1. Other direct expenses

In addition to direct labour and direct material there will be other direct expenses of a miscellaneous nature which can be charged direct to jobs or units of cost. Depending on the trade and business concerned, other direct expenses will include, for example, travelling and subsistence allowances payable to employees working away from the factory, sub-contractors' charges, costs of special tools bought or manufactured for specific orders and such sundry expenses as can be charged directly and without great accounting difficulty to the jobs. These other direct expenses will be debited to the cost accounts concerned as a result of charging instructions entered on invoices, expense sheets and cash vouchers, the amounts being then analysed on the appropriate abstracts.

2. Other indirect expenses or overheads

(a) *The basis for applying overheads to cost units*

Probably in any business the largest amount of other expenses will be those of an indirect nature, *i.e.* those which cannot be directly attributed to the productive work in the workshops or operating departments except by a process of more or less arbitrary apportionment. It is not, for example, possible to say with precision what proportion of rent or the administrative departments salaries is applicable to a particular job carried out in the works. Where, however, as is usually the case, the accountant is required to present unit costs bearing an appropriate share of full overheads, then a logical system must be devised for applying such overheads to the cost units. In particular, the presentation of costs, including an apportionment of full overheads of the business, is essential if such costs are to be used as a basis for price fixing, estimating and the submission of claims under cost plus contracts. In some concerns it is considered sufficient to apply administrative overheads as a simple percentage on works cost, whilst in others a more elaborate process of apportionment is undertaken on the grounds that the administrative and selling effort varies considerably between the different products. In most cases it is desirable to apply at least works overheads to cost units.

The conventional bases for apportioning overheads are listed below:

> A percentage on direct labour cost.
> An amount per direct labour hour.
> A percentage on direct material costs.
> A percentage on total direct costs.
> An amount per machine hour.
> An amount per process or operating hour.

Various composite calculations for particular operations, *e.g.* amounts per passenger-mile, per ton-mile, per flying-hour, per capacity ton mile.

Amounts per unit of cost, *e.g.* per customer, enquiry, restaurant table, hotel room, school student, hospital bed, etc.

(b) Labour and machine rates

If overheads in a workshop tend to vary closely in relation to man-hours, then the most appropriate factor for applying shop overheads is a rate per man-hour; if overheads move in relation to machine-hours, then the machine-hour rate is the most appropriate. The application of overheads as a percentage on direct wages, or compounded in an hourly rate for the job, is frequently adopted for reasons of convenience although it is often open to objection in that overheads are not usually increased where rates of pay for a particular job happen to be high.

A man-hour rate or percentage on direct wages is usually applicable to an assembly or fitting shop, where the numbers of hours worked influence such overheads as floor space used by the labour, supervision and indirect labour costs, etc. The calculation of the appropriate amount to be included in hourly rates depends, in the first instance, on a budget or estimate of the direct labour cost or the total man-hours to be worked in a given period and, secondly, on a budget of the overheads which are to be recovered in the same period. The following example shows the calculation of both a percentage on direct wages and a rate of overheads per man-hour:

CALCULATION OF OVERHEAD RATES

Last year actual		This year estimate
£80,000	Estimated overheads for the year	£120,000
£160,000 640,000 hours	Estimated direct labour fo the year, based on the work scheduled . . .	£360,000 1,440,000 hours
50% 12½p	Overhead percentage on direct labour . Overhead cost per man-hour . . .	33⅓% 8p

In a machine shop the appropriate basis is likely to be a cost per machine-hour for incorporation in a machine-hour rate. The calculation is on similar lines to that shown above for the man-hour rate, except that an estimate of the scheduled working hours of the machines is substituted for man-hours. An important element of cost to be included in a machine-hour rate is depreciation of the machines. Where it is considered adequate to use the depreciation charged in the financial accounts, probably a fixed amount per annum calculated on cost or the reducing balance, such depreciation will be spread over estimated machine-hours in the same way as rent of the space occupied by the machines and other overheads of the machine shop, including time of the operators, setters and supervision, are allocated. It may, however, be considered more logical to assess a rate of depreciation according to the usage of the machines and, additionally, to calculate such rate on the basis of the replacement value of the machines rather than on the book value as recorded in the financial accounts. The amount of depreciation thus recovered in the machine-hour rates will not be in agreement with the total depreciation on machinery charged in the financial accounts, so that the variance between the two systems must be reconciled.

In a complex business the greatest precision in the costing of overheads is obtained by calculating rates for individual machines or related groups of machines. For such purposes the applicable overheads of the factory as a whole must first be estimated and apportionments then made on logical bases (e.g. floor space, numbers of personnel, metering of power, etc.) to the individual machines or groups of machines. A simplified example of the calculation is shown below:

CALCULATION OF MACHINE-HOUR RATES

1. Estimated overheads of the business . . . £120,000

2. Overheads applicable to operating departments . £80,000

3. Overheads applicable to machine shop . . . £60,000

4. Apportionment of overheads to cost centres in the machine shop, being individual machine tools or groups of related machines:

		£
Cost centre A		10,000
,, B		25,000
,, C		15,000
,, D		10,000
Total as in 3 above		£60,000

5. Estimating machine-hours and cost per machine-hour in each cost centre:

	Hours	Rate per hour £
Cost centre A	2,000	5
,, B	2,500	10
,, C	3,000	5
,, D	1,000	10

(d) *Complex systems of overhead recovery*

In a simple system of costing, such as might be in operation in a small manufacturer consisting largely of a fitting and assembly shop, job costs are often expressed in the following form:

JOB No. 1001

DIRECT COSTS:	£
Labour (2,010 hours)	400
Material	150
Bought-out parts	125
Total direct costs	£675
OVERHEADS:	
At 100% on direct labour . . .	400
Grand Total	£1,075

A statement in such a form may suffice for a small business where all operations are within the direct control of the proprietor or manager. Where, even in a small business, a substantial proportion of the costs consist of administrative, financial and selling expenses it will be desirable to separate the factory overheads from the selling, administrative and financial overheads, so as to preserve in the unit costs the sharp distinction which in fact exists between the costs of making or processing a product, the costs of selling it and the administrative and financial expenses incurred in running the business as a complete unit of operations. Broadly speaking, the larger and more complex the business, the greater will be the necessity for presenting unit costs showing at least these classifications of expense.

The selling, administrative and financial expenses are frequently applied to unit costs as a percentage on total direct costs, although in a complex business a more involved method may be adopted so as to weight this oncost by the effort involved in the administrative departments in respect of each kind of product or service. In such a business the job-cost statement might appear in the following form:

JOB NO. 1001

		£	£
1. FACTORY COST:			
Raw material	. . . . . .		150·00
Bought-out parts	. . . . .		125·00
Machining time: 2 hours at £5 an hour	. .		10·00
Fitting shop:			
100 hours	. . . . . .	25·00	
Shop overheads at 50%	. . . .	12·50	
			37·50
Assembly shop:			
1,500 hours	. . . . . .	300·00	
Shop overheads at 130%	. . .	390·00	
			690·00
Total factory cost	. . . . .		£1,012·50
2. ADMINISTRATIVE AND SELLING OVERHEADS:			
At 10% of factory cost	. . . .		101·25
TOTAL COST	. . . . . .		£1,113·75

The percentage to be applied to factory costs to cover the appropriate share of the remaining overheads of the business will be based on a budget or estimates of these expenses to the extent that they are applicable to the product line concerned. For example, the 10 per cent oncost used in the preceding example might have been derived from a statement prepared by the accountant on the following lines:

PRODUCT LINE ....
(Jobs Series 1,000–15,000)

Estimated Revenue Account for the Six Months Ending 31st December

	£	£	Percentage of factory cost %	Percentage of sales %
SALES		100,000	143	100
FACTORY COST		70,000	100	70
Gross profit . . .		£30,000	43	30
Less OVERHEADS:				
Administrative . . .	4,000			
Selling	2,000			
Distribution . . .	750			
Financial . . .	250			
Total overheads . .		7,000	10	7
NET PROFIT . . .		£23,000	33	23

It will be appreciated that, however intricate and carefully calculated a system of costing may be, the final result must of necessity contain conventionally spread expenses which are not directly incurred because a particular job is undertaken in the works. In the preceding example the general overheads may contain an element of rent which it cannot be said was incurred because that particular job was carried out. The rent and much of the administrative expenses of the business would continue to be incurred if that job had not been undertaken and even if no other job had replaced it. Thus when the accountant submits a statement showing the "cost" of a product, job or process, including an apportionment of full overheads, he is not suggesting that the total of that cost has been incurred because that product, job or process has been carried out, but he is endeavouring to indicate the amount of money which must be recovered out of the sale of the eventual product under existing conditions.

The "existing conditions" referred to in the preceding paragraph mean the estimated rate of turnover and the estimated cost of overheads which the accountant has used in making his assessment of the overhead percentages to be applied. A rise in turnover will, if the overhead percentage is not amended, give rise to an over-recovery of overheads in the amounts applied to unit costs; and will in fact mean that the jobs are costing less to carry out than before that rise occurred.

The question as to whether overheads rates should be adjusted with every significant change in the cost of overheads or the rate of turnover is a matter of continual difficulty with a costing system based purely on so-called "historical costs". If a necessary change in overhead rates is unduly delayed, perhaps in the hope that an expected rise in turnover will remedy the situation, the change when it is made will not normally counteract the past under-recoveries, so that the costs of the recent past will be to that extent false; or, if the overhead rate is raised sufficiently high to take into account past under-recoveries, then the cost of jobs then completed will be too low and the cost of jobs not then completed will be too high. Furthermore, frequent changes of overhead rates are likely to confuse the price fixers, possibly damage customer goodwill and might mislead the management as to the real efficiency of the business.

The difficulties indicated in the previous paragraph can probably be resolved only by a combination of careful long-term and short-term budgeting of future activities and rigid control by the management to ensure that the budgets are achieved. Given these two requisites, overhead rates can be established for sufficiently long periods to account for any temporary fluctuations in activity or costs, and thus give stability and comparability to the cost returns. If the budgets of cost and activity are in relation to the efficient usage of all available facilities any over- or under-recovery of overheads will represent an additional guide to the efficiency of the management at the various levels concerned. The use of standard costing rates on these lines is further discussed in a subsequent section.

(e) *The treatment of under- and over-recovered overheads in the accounts*

At the end of any period to which accounts are balanced and financial statements prepared there will be an amount of overheads either over-recovered or under-recovered in the costing rates, as shown by the following simple illustration:

	£
Actual company overheads for the year as shown by the financial accounts	250,000
Overheads have been applied to unit costs by applying 80% on direct labour, which for the year amounted to £235,000.	
Therefore, overheads recovered in unit costs = 80% of £235,000 or	188,000
Under-recovery	£62,000

The situation briefly set out above is a serious one, for it means either: (*a*) that the unit costs have not included a sufficient amount of overheads, or (*b*) that the overheads of the business were excessive in relation to the turnover. The under-recovery should not, of course, have been allowed to continue for a year and would undoubtedly have resulted in a loss of profit.

The accountant's responsibility is to bring the situation to the notice of the management promptly and at frequent intervals so that the necessary corrective action can be taken. For this purpose a periodical cost statement is required for each cost centre, workshop or department, and a specimen form is set out below.

OVERHEAD STATEMENT

WORKS DEPARTMENT ....

Month of January—4 weeks

	£	£
Direct Labour		10,000
Shop Overheads:		
Variable—		
Indirect labour	2,045	
Consumable stores	110	
Sundry expenses	120	
		2,275
Semi-variable—		
Electricity	190	
Supervision	8,550	
Consumable tools	135	
		8,875
Fixed—		
Building expenses	1,100	
Maintenance of equipment	120	
Depreciation	50	
Personnel and welfare	235	
		1,505
Total Overheads		£12,655
Less Recovery at 110% of direct labour . . .		11,000
Under-recovery		£1,655

For the company as a whole, or for a division of a company, it is important to show the effect of the under- or over-recovery on profits, as in the following example:

COMPANY OVERHEAD RECOVERY
Month of January—4 weeks

		£
SALES	. . . .	1,000,000
Less Direct cost of sales	. . . .	750,000
GROSS PROFIT	. . . .	£250,000
Less General overheads—		
Selling costs	 100,000	
Distribution costs	 15,000	
Administration costs	 20,000	
Financial costs	 10,000	
		145,000
Profit before adjusting for overhead recovery	. .	£105,000
Under-recoveries:		
Assembly shop	 1,655	
Machine shop	 345	
Inspection shop	 590	
Total under-recovery	. . . 2,590	
Over-recovery:		
Engineering dept.	 1,090	
Net under-recovery	. . . . . .	1,500
NET PROFIT	. . . .	£103,500

In order to clarify the points being made, the foregoing statements have been drawn up in a simple form. It should, however, be borne in mind that, according to the requirements of the managers concerned, such statements would, in practice, contain many further details of the expenses and sales. Furthermore, additional columns would be required showing the cumulative figures for the current financial year (or, possibly, a moving average or moving annual total), each column of figures being compared with the budget for the period concerned. It is sometimes held that if a budget is shown it is unnecessary to refer to the results of a previous period, but managers frequently find it useful to compare results with those of the same period in the previous year or, perhaps, those of the last complete financial year.

E. STANDARD COSTS*

1. The meaning of standard costs

Standard costs have been defined as the value of work which it is estimated should be produced in a given period of time. Some

---

* For a complete treatise on this important subject see *Flexible Budgetary Control and Standard Costs*, by D. F. Evans-Hemming (Macdonald and Evans Ltd., price 45s.).

variations as to the precise meaning of standard costing may, however, be noted in text-books and in practice.

Some accountants refer to budgetary control and standard costing as though they were synonymous terms. Budgetary control is considered in the next chapter of this book; the term is there used in its widest sense as denoting a system for planning, co-ordinating and controlling the whole operations and every function of a business. Standard costing as used in the present context refers to a method of accounting for unit costs so that such costs may be controlled with reference to standards of what they should be. Whatever may be the precise meaning ascribed to the two terms, it is undoubtedly true that they are closely related; the broad control of business operations depends to a considerable extent on the control of unit costs.

The standards which are applied to unit costs refer to all the elements of cost—labour, material and other expenses, including "overheads", although in some cases it is found expedient to assess standards for only one or two of these elements, the others being costed on an "actual" basis.

A factor of vital importance in assessing standards is to postulate the level of activity to which they relate. Wide variations may occur in unit costs according to whether a business is working to, say, 90 or 75 per cent of potential capacity. The general standard of efficiency expected in a workshop, office or sales counter will also be of great importance. In some cases the standards are based on maximum efficiency of labour, and the most economical usage of material and other services, and assume the business is working at maximum capacity. In other words, such standards represent the ideal; and actual efficiency is measured by the extent to which it falls short of that ideal. This method is often said to carry the disadvantage that workers are thereby discouraged because they become aware that they can never hope to attain, let alone exceed, the standards set. More usually, and probably more effectively, the standards are based on a level of practicable achievement and a normal level of activity.

A standard is initially an amount of work to be carried out in a certain period of time. The standards are converted into monetary figures of unit costs in order that the labour, time, material and other expenses involved may be expressed in the common denominator of money, and so that the costs so obtained may fulfil the other purposes of costing, *i.e.* price fixing and control.

Standard costing is not limited to manufacturing concerns or to those producing a uniform product or operating a uniform service. The principle can be applied with success to any enterprise where it is practicable to define the unit cost. Standard costs may be applied to individual works orders, to batches, to contracts, to numbers, weight or other measurements of production or service. They are particularly useful when expressed in the form of the volume of work per man-hour, machine-hour or process-hour. They may be applied to ascertaining costs per sale, customer or enquiry, to ton-miles, passenger-miles, flying-hours and similar measures of activity.

Where standards are based on normal efficiency and output they form better guides to price fixing than do so-called "actual" costs, which may fluctuate with every temporary change of circumstance or level of activity. They are particularly effective in valuing stocks, for a valuation at standard avoids the anomalies discussed in a previous section, especially those relating to the allocation of overheads.

Probably the greatest benefit to be derived from the introduction of standard costing lies in its use to management in controlling unit costs so that the desired level of efficiency and profitability is attained.

Standard costing should simplify the accounting routine, for with an efficient system there is no need to operate an intricate and expensive procedure for the collection of innumerable "actual" job costs.

The economic and efficient performance of the work of a business will depend to a great extent on the proper co-ordination of all the functions so that they are all contributing their shares to the common objective. Budgetary control assists management to achieve that co-ordination and thus to reduce unit costs. The budgetary control of overheads is essential to a standard costing system which aims to apply overheads to the direct-cost standards.

2. The assessment of the standards

(a) *Direct costs*

The initial assessment of the standards in terms of effort or quantities is not normally an accounting responsibility, although

I

the advice of an accountant experienced in such matters may well be found useful. The initial standards consist of measurements of output or service to be supplied or produced within a given period of time, and are assessed in those terms by experts in the operations concerned. Monetary values will probably not be involved in the beginning.

Thus the responsibility for assessing the amount of work which can be performed by a man of average ability within an hour may be assigned to work-study personnel. Where such a service is not available the assessment may be carried out by rate-fixers, although it should be borne in mind that the standard times set up for the purpose of calculating premium bonus may need considerable adjustment before they can be used as standards of efficiency. Where neither work study nor rate-fixers are used the initial assessment of the standards may be carried out by junior management subject to the approval of the executive in charge of the operation in question, and, in suitable cases, with the guidance of production engineers.

In this connection it is worth noting that the resistance to standard costing often found amongst the owners of small businesses is probably largely due to a supposed inability to assess the standards required. In fact, the foreman or manager of, say, a small engineering works is often in a better position to assess and control the time which should be spent on the jobs than is his counterpart in a large concern. The "hit-and-miss" costing of many small workshops could, it is suggested, be revolutionised into an effective instrument, at little if any additional cost, by the intelligent use of standard costing principles.

Obviously the function and status of the persons responsible for assessing the original standards of performance will vary widely with different kinds of enterprises. It is always desirable that the standards should, so far as possible, be agreed as representing practicable targets by the people who will do the work or their immediate managers.

The standard usage of material is likewise a matter for assessment by experts, and should initially be expressed in terms of volume or some other suitable physical measure.

The output of a factory per man-hour, machine-hour or process-hour is not by any means solely dependent on the efficiency of the operatives, but is also considerably influenced by such matters as factory organisation, the type of machines and equipment used, the availability of tools and stores, the jigging, the standardisation of jobs, the flow of work and similar items of industrial efficiency. The process of assessing standards is likely to reveal improvements which can be made in such matters, and with this end in view production engineers or the production planning staff should always be consulted when standards are being discussed for a factory.

Once the quantitative standards have been decided, the next operation is to express them in terms of money, *i.e.* cost. This operation is primarily a matter for the accountant, but he must for the purpose take into account any imminent changes in probable cost due to fluctuations in material prices, wage-rates, the prospective use of different kinds of materials or grades of labour. The conversion of quantitative standards of direct work into costs will be immensely facilitated if the broad programme of output, purchasing and personnel requirements has been first established by a budgetary system.

(b) *Indirect costs*

Whilst in the beginning the assessment of standards is primarily concerned with direct costs, the principle can be applied with advantage to many ancillary operations. An air-line will be interested not only in the direct cost per passenger or ton-mile or flying-hour, but will also establish standards for maintenance work, such as engine changing and the periodic overhaul of aircraft.

The allocation of semi-variable and fixed costs, or overheads generally, to direct costs is primarily an exercise in cost accounting. In applying overheads to direct standards the accountant will need to maintain the closest liaison with functional management so that the effect on overheads of future departmental plans may be taken into account. In particular, overheads will be affected by the type and number of indirect workers, salesmen and office staff to be employed, by changes in transport arrangements and packaging, by the programme of research, and by depreciation on equipment, machinery and other fixed assets. Again, it may be emphasised, all these matters are best arranged and set out in the form of departmental budgets. The effect on unit costs of the volume of output will, of course, be a vital consideration at this stage.

It is necessary for a decision to be made as to the period of time to which the standards are expected to apply. Thus, where trade is suffering a temporary recession, it would be unwise to spread the overheads over an abnormally low level of output. Whilst the standards must be regarded as essentially flexible and subject to constant review, it is usually found impracticable to alter them at too frequent intervals. Temporary fluctuations in trade may explain variances from standards. It is usual to relate at least the overhead element in standard costs to a period sufficiently long to "even out" temporary fluctuations in output.

(c) *Profit control through standard costs*

When the standard costs are first produced and considered by management, they may be too high in relation to sale prices. Top management will thus have the opportunity of insisting that measures be taken for reducing costs so that they shall yield the desired profit on sales. Broadly speaking, three lines of approach to the problem of increasing profitability are open to management: to raise prices, to increase turnover or to reduce costs.

In a competitive market prices are dictated more by the influence of supply and demand than by the level of costs in a particular business, so that profits cannot normally be enhanced merely by raising prices. The pattern of sales may well bear careful investigation so as to ascertain whether the turnover of the more profitable lines can be increased. Consideration may also be given to the relative advantages of factoring instead of making certain articles and to the benefits which may be derived from selling products ancillary to the main production. Nevertheless, an essential line of attack when profits are threatened is to concentrate on the reduction of unit costs rather than the increase of unit prices.

Unit costs may be reduced by increasing turnover, thus effecting a greater "spread" of fixed and semi-variable overheads. The attention of the management will certainly be directed also to possible reductions in direct costs by improvements in organisation, mechanisation, methods and labour incentives, but in many cases economies can be effected in the cost of indirect departments, works, selling and financial, in relation to output.

3. Reporting the performance

Whilst the exercise of assessing standards for all kinds of work is likely to have a salutary effect on the efficiency of an organisation, the principal instrument of control is represented by reports from the accountant comparing actual performance with the standards. The control will be exercised by the various ranks of management, but the effectiveness of that control will depend to a considerable degree on the quality of the information provided. The reports must be up to date and clearly expressed, and one of the most important responsibilities of the accounting function in this matter is the analysis of variances between standards and actual costs.

The variances should be divided into those over which the manager to whom the statement is addressed has some measure of control, and those over which his efforts can have no influence. Thus a variance due to rises in material prices, higher basic wage-rates or the spread of overheads will not be within the control of a works foreman, but the usage of tools, material, labour and machines will fall within his responsibility.

Variances may be further classified as follows:

A. VARIABLE COSTS
    1. Labour variances—
        (a) wage-rates;
        (b) labour effectiveness, *e.g.* operating times.
    2. Material variances—
        (a) price;
        (b) usage.

B. OVERHEADS (suitably subdivided as appropriate)
    1. Effect of output.
    2. Effect of individual costs of overheads.

The variances are usefully expressed as ratios as follows:

1. Wage rate ratio: $\dfrac{\text{Actual hours at actual rate}}{\text{Actual hours at standard rate}}$

2. Labour effectiveness: $\dfrac{\text{Actual hours at standard rate}}{\text{Standard hours at standard rate}}$

3. Material price: $\dfrac{\text{Actual price at actual usage}}{\text{Standard price at actual usage}}$

4. Material usage: $\dfrac{\text{Actual usage at standard price}}{\text{Standard usage at standard price}}$

In addition to finding the precise category of cost which has caused the variance, the accounting service will be immensely enhanced if, in reporting to senior management, notes are appended as to the root causes of the variances and of any measures being taken or proposed to improve the performance. This additional service entails a good knowledge of all aspects of the work of a business and the ability to obtain the necessary co-operation from all kinds of personnel, some of whom may be indifferent to financial matters.

In some applications of standard costing, "actual" job costs continue to be recorded, and in the cost returns each "actual" job cost is compared with the assessed standard for that job. For this purpose the basic documents, *e.g.* job cards and material requisitions, contain separate columns for "actual" and standard costs. The efficiency of such a system depends upon whether the additional clerical work involved is justified by the usefulness of the information provided.

It is, however, quite practicable to introduce standard costing and at the same time to reduce the routine work in the costing department. In many applications of standard costing the process of accumulating "actual" job costs becomes unnecessary, as the standard costs are used for estimating, price-fixing and planning, and the variance analysis is used for control purposes.

In the case of a workshop producing a uniform product, to take a simple illustration, the actual costs are obtainable in total from the normal departmentalised financial records and an operating statement can be compiled on the following lines:

CABINET ASSEMBLY SHOP

Costs for Week Ending .... Output: 625 units

Cost element	W.i.p. at beginning	Costs for the period	W.i.p. at end	Cost of finished output	Cost per unit
	£	£	£	£	£
Labour . .	650	640	880	410	0·65½
Material . .	1,350	1,360	1,590	1,120	1·79
Overheads .	1,000	768	798	970	1·55½
Total . .	£3 000	2,768	3,268	2,500	4·00

The actual unit costs may then be compared with the standards in the following manner:

	Standard cost per unit £	Actual cost per unit £	Variance + or − on standard £
Labour	0·62	0·65½	+ 0·03½
Material	1·93	1·79	− 0·14
Overheads . . .	1·25	1·55½	+ 0·30½
Total	£3·80	£4·00	+ £0·20

The foregoing is intended to show, in a simple form, how actual costs can be compared with standards even though the laborious and costly process of compiling "actual" costs for each job is no longer carried out. Where, as is the case with many businesses, the production is not uniform, it will still be necessary for the cost section to price each job card and material requisition and to list the totals for each class of work in order to arrive at the actual value of labour and material expended on each product group. The essential economy achieved by standard costing is, however, in that analysis of expense is required only in product groups, subdivided as necessary, rather than in individual jobs.

Statements in the form illustrated above would rarely provide sufficient information for a manager to decide precisely where the source of inefficiency lies. In the first place the variances should be classified, so far as it is practicable to do so, as controllable and non-controllable, according to the responsibilities of the manager to whom the statement is addressed. Secondly, a further analysis of the variances, at least under the "price" and "usage" headings, would be required. Using the figures shown above, the variances in total for the period may be further analysed as on page 219.

Notes on the variance analysis on next page

1. *Labour*

   (a) £2 excess costs was due to the use of skilled labour on a job which called for the use of semi-skilled labour only.

   (b) £3 excess costs was due to operating times above the assessed standard.

   (c) £10 excess costs was due to a general rise in rates of pay and was not considered to be within the control of the shop superintendent.

CABINET ASSEMBLY SHOP

Variance Analysis for the Week Ending ....

Output: *Budgeted—650 units; actual—625 units*

Cost element	Actual cost	Standard cost	Total variance	Controllable Rate or price	Controllable Hours or usage	Controllable Others	Non-controllable Rate or price	Non-controllable Hours or usage	Non-controllable Others
	£	£							
Labour	410	391	+ 19	+2	+ 3		+10		+ 4
Material	1,120	1,203	− 83		− 12		−97		+ 26
Overheads	970	781	+189			+59			+130
TOTAL	£2,500	2,375	+125	+2	− 9	+59	−87	—	+160

(d) £4 excess costs was due to rectification work as a result of the use of faulty material. This was not considered controllable by the shop, as material supplies were not ordered or inspected within the shop.

2. *Material*

(a) The £12 favourable variance was due to material usage within the shop being below the assessed standard.

(b) The £97 favourable variance was due to a reduction in the cost of material arranged by the buying department, and this saving was not therefore attributable to the work in the shop.

(c) The £26 excess costs represented the cost of unsuitable material which could not be recovered from the suppliers, and was not the fault of the shop.

3. *Overheads*

(a) The £59 excess costs was due to idle time of operators above the standard allowed.

(b) The £130 excess costs was due to a rise in "fixed" overheads applied to the shop, *e.g.* rent and building maintenance, and was not controllable by the shop superintendent.

The control of departmental overheads would be dealt with by separate statements sent to the managers responsible (including the executive in charge of building maintenance) and more properly fall within the budgetary system.

In theory at least it can be maintained that all variances are controllable at some point in the organisation, and the variances listed above as being outside the control of the assembly shop manager would be reported to other managers responsible. Thus the cost of rectifying the faulty material would be attributed either to the buying department or the inspection department or both.

Certainly responsibility for the rise in labour rates cannot be attributed to any inefficiency within the business, but it could be maintained that it is the responsibility of overall works management to endeavour to counteract such increases by improving methods. The sharp rise in overhead costs is controllable in some measure by top management, if only by achieving greater absorption by increasing turnover. In some businesses the control of overheads is of greater importance than the control of direct costs within the operating departments. There is a growing tendency for administrative costs to be controlled in relation to predetermined standards or budgets based on detailed studies of organisation and methods.

In order that effective action can be taken to remedy controllable variances in the works, it is necessary for the managers concerned to receive variance statements at weekly intervals immediately after the end of each period concerned. In some businesses daily statements are issued. The rapid collation and analysis of costs normally entails the use of mechanised systems in the accounts department, and the growing use of electronic computers will undoubtedly give a much-needed impetus to the submission of up-to-date cost returns, and hence to the control of costs. The installation of a full system of mechanised accounting does involve considerable expense, which should be looked upon by management as an investment capable of producing a considerable return in the form of lower costs.

As pointed out above, the control of expense is not confined to the works departments and the cost variances need reporting to other functions and other levels of management where remedial action is required. Material price variances must be drawn to the attention of the buyers and overhead variances to the department managers concerned. For such purposes it may be unnecessary to institute a regular system of weekly reports, and *ad hoc* statements drawing attention to controllable variances of significance may be sufficient. Departmental overheads are normally dealt with by monthly budget statements as discussed in the next chapter.

Sales managers are concerned with the profitability of the products or services which they are responsible for selling, and their selling policy may be affected by the variances which are occurring on such products. The product profit and loss statements issued to sales managers should therefore contain summaries of the cost variances which are being recorded. The chief executives of the business, *e.g.* general manager, commercial manager, production manager, etc., who are particularly concerned with the co-ordination of their various functions, also require product profit and loss statements showing the major variances. Monthly or weekly statements on the lines shown below should be submitted to the top management, the sales managers receiving only statements dealing with the products with which they are concerned.

With regard to this statement it is necessary to point out that the precise form in which such a statement is prepared, and the variances or cost headings which it contains, vary widely according to the nature of the business and the needs of the various managers to whom the statement is addressed. The essentials are that the important variances from pre-determined budgets and standards shall be clearly shown, and that the statement be submitted promptly after the period to which it refers.

ANALYSED PROFIT AND LOSS ACCOUNT

	Total		Product Group A		Product Group B		Product Group C	
	Budget	Actual	Budget	Actual	Budget	Actual	Budget	Actual
SALES . . .								
Direct costs (standard)								
GROSS MARGIN (STANDARD) . .								
Less Variances:								
Labour time . .								
Labour rates . .								
Material usage .								
Material price .								
Rectification .								
Works overhead								
Totals . . .								
GROSS MARGIN (ACTUAL)								
Less General overheads:								
Selling . .								
Distribution .								
Administration .								
Financial .								
Totals .								
NET PROFIT . .								

4. The arithmetic of variances

Labour and material variances may be calculated as follows:

Labour Rate: actual hours at actual rate minus actual hours at standard rate.

Labour Efficiency: actual hours at standard rate minus standard hours at standard rate.

Material Price: actual quantity at actual price minus actual quantity at standard price.

Material Usage: actual quantity at standard price minus standard quantity at standard price.

It is important that managers shall understand the arithmetic by means of which standard cost variances are calculated, and with this object in view some examples of the principal calculations involved are set out below. The subject has, however, now become somewhat complex, and the reader is referred to text-books on standard costing for more advanced treatment.

(a) *Direct Cost Variances*

Basically the main variances consist of a price and a usage aspect, and for the purpose of illustrating the various methods by which these variances may be calculated direct material is considered first.

Assume the standard material cost of a job was:

		£
10 lb. at 25p	=	2·50
and the actual cost was:		
12 lb. at 30p	=	3·60
Giving a variance in total of		£1·10 adverse

The problem is to break this variance down into the part due to the price difference and the part due to the excess usage. There are two possible sets of calculations of which the first is the usual method and the second is gaining some support among accountants.

First method		£
Price variance: 12 lb. at 5p	=	0·60 adverse
Usage variance: 25p for 2 lb.	=	0·50 adverse
Total		£1·10 adverse

The above example is the normal calculation and follows the formula set out above. It will be observed that the usage variance is valued at standard price, but the price variance is calculated at actual usage. One reason for the latter treatment is that if the price variance is taken at the earliest point, *i.e.* on the invoice for the goods, the actual usage will not then be known. The buyer may, however, object that he is not responsible for the quantity of the material used, but if the price variance is calculated on standard usage, then the usage variance must be increased to make the total right. The calculation would then become:

Price variance: 10 lb. at 5p   =   £ 0·50 adverse
Usage variance: 30p for 2 lb   =   0·60 adverse

  Total   £1·10 adverse

It should be emphasised that the example shown immediately above is NOT used, but is included to illustrate the argument. In order to overcome this difficulty the suggestion has been made that a three-part variance is the more logical, and such a variance would be calculated as follows:

Second method
Price variance: 10 lb. at 5p   =   £ 0·50 adverse
Usage variance: 25p for 2 lb.   =   0·50 adverse
Joint variance: 2 lb. at 5p   =   0·10 adverse

  Total   £1·10 adverse

Some readers may visualise these calculations more easily from the following figure:

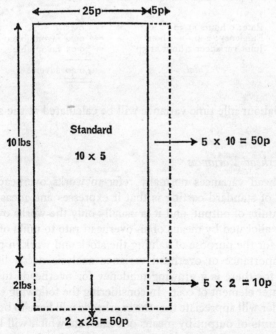

Fig. 12

Direct labour variances also include differences due to the price and the usage of the labour, but in this case they are called rate and efficiency variances.

Assume the standard labour cost of a job was:

		£	
9 hours at 20p	=	1·80	
and the actual cost was:			
8 hours at 25p	=	2·00	
giving a total variance of		£0·20	adverse

By the normal method the variances would be analysed as follows:

		£	
Rate: 8 hours at 5p	=	0·40	adverse
Efficiency: 20p for 1 hour	=	0·20	favourable
Total		£0·20	adverse

The three-part variance would be as follows:

		£	
Rate: 9 hours at 5p	=	0·45	
Efficiency: 20p for 1 hour	=	0·20	favourable
Joint variance: 1 hour at 5p	=	0·05	favourable
Total		£0·20	adverse

The labour idle time variance will be calculated at the standard rate.

(b) *Overhead Variances*

Overhead variances normally refer to works overheads. The essence of standard costing is that it expresses and measures the cost of units of output, and it is usually only the works overheads that are allocated by means of an overhead rate to units of output, at least for the purpose of valuing the stock and work in progress. The importance of overhead variance analysis needs little emphasis, for there is a growing tendency for overheads to become the greater element of cost. In considering the following examples the reader will appreciate that the overheads will have to be applied to the units of output by means of some rate which will be based on a measure of the output. Thus the overhead rate might be calculated per unit produced of a standard and homogeneous product, or it might be a rate per machine hour, per man hour, per process hour, etc. In order that goods produced shall be put into stock at a value including an allocation of overheads, the overhead rate must be calculated in advance for each financial year or part of a financial year. The rate so calculated is bound to be something in the nature of an estimate and, in general, the factors involved in the assessment of the rate will be:

(i) the budgeted volume of output for the period concerned;
(ii) the cost of the various items of overhead which are required to sustain that volume of output;
(iii) the efficiency with which the work is to be carried out, *i.e.* the number of units produced for a given expenditure of machine hours, man hours or some other measure of the key factor; and
(iv) the extent to which the capacity of the plant is to be used.

Thus, the extraction of overhead variances necessitates some form of budgeting. Furthermore, the broad picture shown by the variance calculations indicated below needs breaking down into considerable detail, so that expenditure can be controlled at its source. The source for this purpose might be the item or items of overheads which are causing an adverse variance, the operation which is inefficient and the workshop of which the capacity is not fully exploited.

For the maximum benefit to be obtained from this aspect of standard costing it is desirable that the overheads be grouped into those which are variable in relation to output and those which are fixed. Some items fall readily into these two groups, but others will need a fairly arbitrary allocation to the variable or fixed headings, and the variance figures must be interpreted accordingly.

It is also desirable, but not essential, that where production of a variety of dissimilar products or jobs is involved the output can be expressed in so many standard hours. The hours for this purpose can be man-hours, machine-hours or operating hours. The standard hour is the volume of work which ought to be produced in an hour, under the conditions on which the standard costing system is based, *i.e.* conditions of efficiency and utilisation of capacity. Once the output can be expressed in standard hours, two useful ratios can be obtained.

The first is the efficiency ratio which is:

$$\frac{\text{The actual output in standard hours}}{\text{Actual hours occupied by the work}}$$

The second is the activity ratio which is:

$$\frac{\text{The actual output in standard hours}}{\text{The budgeted output in standard hours}}$$

Both of these ratios can be multiplied by 100 to produce percentage measurements of efficiency and activity.

With these preliminary matters in mind a simplified example of the calculation of overhead variances may now be considered. The following are specimen figures relating to the activities of a workshop over a given period:

Budgets and standards

Output:		
Standard hours per unit	1,000 units	
	2	
Budgeted output in hours	2,000	
Variable overheads .	£2,000, *i.e.* £1 per hour or £2 per unit	
Fixed overheads .	£1,000, *i.e.* £0·50 per hour or £1 per unit	

Actual results

Output:	
Standard hours per unit .	1,200 units
	2
Output in standard hours .	2,400
Actual hours involved .	2,500
Variable overheads .	£2,600
Fixed overheads .	£1,050

In the first place it will be assumed that the overheads are applied to cost units as a rate per unit produced. This would not, in fact, be possible where the units of output were dissimilar, and would be unusual in any case, but the assumption is a useful one for demonstrating the variance calculations in a simple manner.

Variances calculated on units of output

(a) *Variable Overhead Variance*

In view of the fact that by definition variable overheads are those which move in direct relation to the volume of output, it is assumed that for this group of overheads there can be only one cause of variance between standard and actual, *i.e.* because the cost of the overheads is higher or lower than the standard. A usage variance or variance due to a change in the volume of output from that budgeted cannot exist in theory. Readers will note that this theory needs qualification in practice because there are few if any costs which move in direct relation to the volume of output. Nevertheless, the following calculation gives a useful guide to where further investigation is needed.

Expenditure Variance

The standard rate for the volume of output generated less the actual variable overhead incurred, or

$$£2 \times 1,200 \text{ units} - £2,600 = £200 \text{ adverse}$$

(b) *Fixed Overhead Variances*

(i) *Expenditure Variance.* The budget less the actual, or

$$£1,000 - £1,050 = £50 \text{ adverse}$$

(ii) *Volume Variance.* This variance reflects the usage of the fixed overheads, in much the same way that the variance due to the usage of material can be calculated. Some companies calculate only the expenditure and volume variances (price and usage), but it should be noted that, as shown below, the volume variance can be broken down into the element due to efficiency of the work (number of hours involved) and the element due to the extent to which the capacity of the workshop has been employed.

The budgeted volume of output at the standard rate less the actual volume at the standard rate, or

$$£1 \times 1,000 \text{ units} - £1 \times 1,200 \text{ units} = £200 \text{ favourable}$$

The variance is favourable because more output has been produced than was budgeted, and thus there has been an over-recovery of fixed overheads.

(iii) *Efficiency Variance.* This variance, which forms part of the volume variance, is intended to represent the value of the loss or gain due to the actual working times involved having produced more or less output than ought to have been produced according to the assessed standards.

The standard output which the hours involved should have produced less the actual output, multiplied by the standard rate, or

$$£1 (1,250 - 1,200) = £50 \text{ adverse}$$

The figure of 1,250 units represents the output which ought to have been produced in 2,500 actual hours at 2 hours per unit. The output was less than it should have been, so that there is to that extent an under-recovery of fixed overheads, and thus an adverse variance.

(iv) *Capacity Variance.* This variance represents the extent to which the overhead cost per unit is greater or less than it should be as a result of the usage of available capacity in the workshop.

The budgeted output less the standard output which the hours worked should have produced, all at the standard rate, or

$$£1(1,000 - 1,250) = £250 \text{ favourable}$$

In practice, the overheads might well be applied to unit costs as a rate per hour. If such a method were applied to the above example the variances would be the same but the calculations would be as follows:

(a) *Variable Overhead*
  (i) *Expenditure Variance*
  2,400 standard hours $\times$ £1 $-$ £2,600 = £200 adverse

(b) *Fixed Overhead*
  (i) *Expenditure Variance*
  £1,000 $-$ £1,050   = £50 adverse
  (ii) *Volume Variance*
  £0·5 $\times$ (2,400 hours $-$ 2,000 hours)   = £200 favourable
  (iii) *Efficiency Variance*
  £0·5 $\times$ (2,400 hours $-$ 2,500 hours)   = £50 adverse
  (iv) *Capacity Variance*
  £0·5 $\times$ (2,000 hours $-$ 2,500 hours)   = £250 favourable

When entered in the accounts the above figures would appear as shown below. In this connection it may be as well to point out that there are other methods of making the entries, although all methods should arrive at the same result, but the following example is designed to show how the double entry is completed. In this example it will be noted that the variances are accounted for before making the charges to the Work-in-progress Account, which is accordingly at standard. It will also be observed that the fixed overhead rate is applied not to the actual number of hours incurred but to the output expressed in standard hours.

VARIABLE OVERHEAD CONTROL ACCOUNT

	£		£
Various a/cs—actual overhead incurred	2,600	Work-in-progress . . .	2,400
		Variance—expenditure . .	200
	£2,600		£2,600

WORK IN PROGRESS

	£		£
Variable overhead control .	2,400		
Fixed overhead suspense .	1,200		

VARIANCES

	£		£
Variable overhead control—expenditure	200	Fixed overhead volume variance—capacity . . .	250
Fixed overhead control—expenditure	50		
Volume variance—fixed overhead—efficiency . .	50		

FIXED OVERHEAD SUSPENSE

	£		£
Fixed overhead control—budget	1,000	Work in progress . . .	1,200
Volume variance . . .	200		
	£1,200		£1,200

FIXED OVERHEAD CONTROL

	£		£
Various a/cs—actual . .	1,050	Fixed overhead suspense—budget	1,000
		Variance—expenditure . .	50
	£1,050		£1,050

VOLUME VARIANCE

	£		£
Variance—capacity . .	250	Fixed overhead suspense—	
		volume	200
		Variance—efficiency . .	50
	£250		£250

The inclusion of a separate account showing the volume variance is unorthodox, but its object is to show how the efficiency and capacity variances are derived from the volume variance.

F. Marginal Costing

1. The nature and purpose of marginal costing

The theory of marginal costing was probably derived from economic theory, in which the concept of the margin forms an important element. The marginal cost has been defined as: "The addition to total cost that results from increasing output by one more unit." * On the assumption that fixed costs remain unaffected by increasing output by one more unit, the marginal cost of a product will consist of the variable costs only.

It will be appreciated that many practical difficulties will arise in making use of this theory in connection with the control of business affairs, although it is now generally recognised that marginal costing is a useful additional technique for control and price-fixing. In practice, the marginal cost is likely to be required not for one additional unit of output but for a reasonable additional batch or additional production run; the marginal cost is also useful in connection with the costing of an additional contract. It is dangerous to assume that the costs of such additional output consist only of the variable costs, because after a certain point the additional output may be the direct cause of more administrative staff being engaged, more machinery purchased and more space and other so-called "fixed" costs being incurred. Such additional fixed overheads will certainly be incurred where capacity is already being fully utilised. Thus, in some circumstances the true marginal cost may exceed the average or "normal" cost.

In all circumstances where it is required to assess the marginal

* J. L. Hanson, *A Textbook of Economics* (Macdonald and Evans).

cost the accountant will have difficulty in deciding which are variable and which fixed costs. In fact, many accountants use a third category, semi-variable costs, which represent those costs which vary in relation to the volume of output, but not in direct proportion. Once again, the distinction must be rather arbitrary, for even the accepted variable costs of direct labour and direct material may be cheaper per unit of additional output, owing to economies of large-scale purchasing and longer runs resulting in the shortening of operating times. J. L. Hanson, in *A Textbook of Economics*, has said that "the distinction between fixed and variable costs is largely a short period distinction". There is considerable justification for saying that *in the long run* all costs are variable.

As a rough guide, however, and bearing in mind the qualifications indicated above, various useful calculations can be made using the simple assumption that marginal costs are the same as variable costs. The marginal costing approach is particularly useful in dealing with problems of the nature set out below.

(*a*) Finding the minimum price at which additional work can be accepted on a short-term basis, such as where it is desired to maintain productive capacity and employment during a temporary recession. It is the "contribution" to profits, *i.e.* the difference between marginal costs and the income from the additional work, which is the important factor.

(*b*) It is often said that, provided fixed overheads are recovered in the basic market, *e.g.* at home, sales can be made at a little above marginal cost in other markets, say, overseas, and thus help to increase the total profit. This approach is obviously dangerous, for if it amounts to "dumping" retaliatory action can be expected from other companies or overseas governments; there is a danger that the goods may be re-imported and undercut home sales; and finally, the additional market may become the staple market.

(*c*) Marginal costs are useful in assessing the relative merits of alternative investments, such as in different machines, different methods of manufacture, investments in branches and subsidiaries. Once again, the important question is the extent of the contribution to overall profits, not taking into account those fixed expenses which will be incurred in any event.

(*d*) The contribution derived from the marginal costs is an important factor in determining where effort is best directed in the short run, *i.e.* in comparing the profitability of different lines of sales. It is perhaps necessary to emphasise the short run in this connection, for, provided fixed overheads are properly apportioned to the products, it is reasonable to suggest that in the long run a proportion of the fixed facilities will be retained to keep in being a line of sales.

2. The arithmetic of marginal costing

A normal form of Profit and Loss Account for a business, product line or venture involves deducting works cost from sales to show gross profit and selling and administrative costs from gross profit to show operating profit, with a final stage of deducting from operating profit non-trading items to give net pre-tax profit. In such a layout works costs, or direct operating costs, will include overheads, both fixed and variable, applicable to the works, but otherwise there will be little distinction between the variable and fixed expenses.

Converting such an account for marginal-costing purposes involves separating the fixed from the variable expenses, irrespective of whether, under either category, the expenses belong to the works, selling or administrative headings. Such an account for the operations of a business for, say, the last three months, might appear as follows:

		£
SALES	. . . . . .	160,000
Less Variable costs	. . . . .	96,000
CONTRIBUTION	. . . . . .	64,000
Less Fixed costs	. . . . .	80,000
LOSS	. . . . . .	£(16,000)

On being presented with such an account management might well require the following information:

(*a*) What are the sales required to achieve a break-even position?

(*b*) What are the sales required to achieve profits of a given amount (perhaps a certain percentage of the capital invested in the venture).

(*c*) What will the profit be if sales of a given amount can be achieved?

Answers to these questions can be given as a result of a process of simple arithmetic, but always subject to the qualifications inherent in the marginal-costing approach.

From the above figures the following simple formula can be derived:

$$\text{Sales} - \text{Variable costs} = \text{Fixed costs plus profit}$$

Dealing first with the question of what sales are required to achieve a break-even position, it is apparent that, because with a break-even there will be no profit, the formula becomes:

$$\text{Sales} - \text{Variable costs} = \text{Fixed costs}$$

Variable costs in the above example are seen to be 60 per cent of sales and, on the assumption that variable costs will remain in the same relation to sales whatever the volume of activity, this percentage will remain constant. The other assumption is that the fixed costs of £80,000 will remain constant. Thus the equation now becomes:

Sales at break-even level — 60 per cent of those sales = £80,000
Then, 40 per cent of sales = £80,000
Sales at break-even = £80,000 × 100
                                                         ————————
                                                              40
                                                     = £200,000

The proof of this simple exercise can be demonstrated by reproducing the account as it will appear with sales at £200,000, as follows:

	£
SALES	200,000
Less Variable expenses at 60 per cent of sales .	120,000
CONTRIBUTION	80,000
Less Fixed expenses	80,000
PROFIT/LOSS	—

If the sales are required in units, such as, perhaps, standard hours of work, the same formula can be used, but variable expenses will have to be expressed as a rate per unit or standard hour. Adjustments may have to be made for changes in selling prices, variable cost rates and fixed overheads, which are brought about by the different level of activity.

Now assume that the business requires to make profits in the next three months of, say, £20,000, the latter figure representing a reasonable return on the capital employed. The equation now becomes:

$$40 \text{ per cent of sales} = £80,000 + £20,000$$
$$\text{Then, Sales} = £100,000 \times \frac{100}{40}$$
$$= £250,000$$

The projected account would appear as follows:

	£
SALES	250,000
Less Variable expenses at 60 per cent of sales .	150,000
CONTRIBUTION	100,000
Less Fixed costs	80,000
PROFIT	£20,000

Now consider the calculation if it is required to know what profit will be derived from sales of £300,000. The equation is:

$$£300,000 - 60 \text{ per cent of } £300,000 = \text{Profit} + £80,000$$
$$\text{Then, Profit} = £120,000 - £80,000 = £40,000$$

At this level of sales the account would appear thus:

	£
SALES	300,000
Less Variable costs at 60 per cent of sales .	180,000
CONTRIBUTION	120,000
Less Fixed expenses	80,000
PROFIT	£40,000

For further consideration of this subject the reader is referred to the following textbooks:

Cost Accounting and Costing Methods, by H. J. Weldon (Macdonald and Evans).

Management Accountancy, by J. Batty (Macdonald and Evans).

Marginal Costing, by Lawrence and Humphries (Macdonald and Evans).

A Report on Marginal Costing (The Institute of Cost and Works Accountants).

CHAPTER XI

BUDGETARY CONTROL

A. The Objectives of Budgetary Control

The preceding chapters of this book have described a variety of systems, techniques and methods, all aimed at presenting in monetary terms information of use to business managers. Whilst much of the information presented by the accountant is prepared with an eye on the future, the double-entry accounting system, which forms the basis of all accounting statements, is essentially a record of past events.

One of the primary functions of management, however—particularly the higher ranks of management—is to plan for the future and to ensure, so far as it is possible to do so, that its plans are put into effect. Whilst some business-men are able to maintain a somewhat precarious control over their affairs by carrying broad plans in their heads, the complexity and hazards of modern business are such that clearly defined objectives and an efficient system of control have become necessary for all sizes of enterprises. In a large company the necessity for a considerable degree of delegated responsibility makes it impossible for the managing director to co-ordinate the plans and the performance of the different functions without statistical aids. The very act of co-relating the functions of the operating, manufacturing, selling and financial departments requires that these functions shall be expressed in a common medium. With all its imperfections, money is the only medium which can express all activities in a common language.

Whilst the double-entry system has the advantage of providing a monetary record of events, its usefulness to management is limited because it is primarily concerned with the past. Budgetary control, working side by side with the accounting system, is primarily forward looking, and aims to provide all ranks of management with an instrument for recording plans and measuring performance in relation to those plans. It represents, therefore, an extension of the managerial function, and has been described as "the long arm of management".

B. An Outline of the Methods

1. The formulation of the budget

The precise methods used in fulfilling the objectives of budgetary control must, of course, vary widely according to the nature and size of the organisation. Certain broad principles for operating an effective budgetary system have been crystallised by experience of many years, and these principles will apply whether the system consists merely of notes made by the owner of a one-man business or whether it is operated by a separate department in a large company.

The first operation is to record future plans. For this purpose it is obviously desirable that top management shall set an overall objective for the business as a whole and that this objective shall be such as to influence the plans of each main function.

For most small one-man concerns or partnerships the overall objective is a profit target. Whilst the achievement of satisfactory profitability is always an important objective of private enterprise whatever the size of the business, undertakings with national or international ramifications are often more concerned with maintaining customer goodwill than achieving the utmost immediate profitability. Nationalised industries are required to meet due interest on capital and provide necessary reserves, but beyond that point may well divert further potential profits into the improvement of their service to the nation. The same is undoubtedly true of many large private enterprises.

Nevertheless, a profit target is a convenient starting point for forward planning. It may be combined with a more particular objective, such as the extension of the business overseas, the development of new products, the full utilisation of resources or the reduction of unit costs.

When the overall target has been communicated to the functional heads of the organisation the latter are required to prepare plans showing the contribution which their function can make towards producing the desired result.

It is often said that the sales programme should come first and that the production, buying, personnel and financial sides of business should then in turn consider the extent to which the sales programme can be met. Where, as is frequently the situation, potential demand cannot be met by the facilities available, the

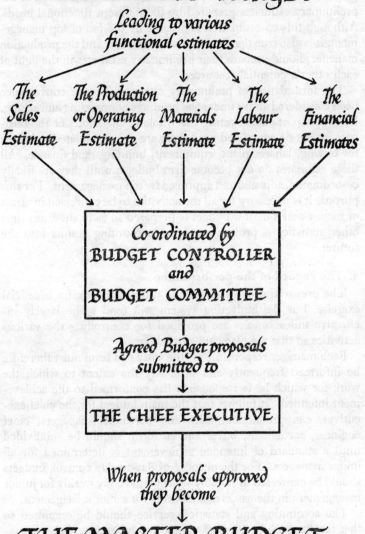

THE PROFIT TARGET

Leading to various
functional estimates

| The Sales Estimate | The Production or Operating Estimate | The Materials Estimate | The Labour Estimate | The Financial Estimates |

Co-ordinated by
BUDGET CONTROLLER
and
BUDGET COMMITTEE

Agreed Budget proposals
submitted to

THE CHIEF EXECUTIVE

When proposals approved
they become

THE MASTER BUDGET

production or operating capacity will dominate the budgetary system. In any event, one of the most important and difficult problems of budgeting is the adjustment and co-ordination of the preliminary estimates prepared by the different functional heads. Although this co-ordination is necessarily the job of top management, it is also true that both the sales manager and the production manager should prepare their preliminary estimates in the light of each other's potential resources.

The formulation of preliminary estimates has for convenience been considered above under the headings of operating and selling. But a coherent plan covering the whole of the affairs of the business cannot be completed until there are also formulated estimates for buying, labour, plant, equipment, buildings and finance. All these estimates do not become firm budgets until they are finally co-ordinated, adjusted and approved by top management. For this purpose it is necessary for all the activities to be expressed in terms of money and a master budget is prepared so as to show amongst other statistics a projection of the accounting results into the future.

2. The record of the performance

The preparation of plans for the future is in itself a beneficial exercise, but the budgeting system will tend to be largely ineffective unless means are provided for controlling the various activities so that the plans are carried out.

Each manager responsible for the work of a team must therefore be informed frequently and promptly the extent to which the work for which he is responsible has conformed to the achievement intended. It follows that the main budget for the chief executives, e.g. production, sales and personnel managers, chief engineer, accountant, buyer and so forth, should be subdivided until a standard of intended achievement is determined for all junior managers. For the purpose of day-to-day control, budgets should be expressed in suitably short periods, say weekly for junior management in the works and monthly for senior management.

The accounting and statistical service should be organised so that results, both in terms of money and other appropriate measurements, can be recorded under the budget headings or headings of responsibility. The information must be available within the shortest possible interval after the end of the period to which the data relates. The necessity for accounting under responsibility headings as well as under such conventional classifications as kind of expense and job may entail a reorganisation of the accounting and statistical service. The vital need for prompt accounting may, in addition, call from the accounting function a more efficient and imaginative approach to the work and a constant search for time-saving techniques.

The whole tapestry of interconnected budgets is expressed in money as constituting the universal medium, and whilst it is desirable that all concerned shall be informed at all stages of the monetary consequences of their actions, the more concrete measurements should not be omitted from the information supplied. If, for example, the budget for a foundry is the production of a certain number of castings at a certain cost, the results should be expressed in terms both of units and cost of production. Junior managers, such as foremen, often have limited control over the monetary aspect of their activities, e.g. the basic wages of employees, so that the statement of their budgeted and actual performance will have greater reality to them in terms of output, rather than money. In some cases, such as with the personnel budget, it may be expedient to express the budget as a quantitative measurement, i.e. numbers of employees, without reference to the monetary aspect.

One of the beneficial features of a budgetary system has been referred to as "control by exception". In other words, a manager's attention is directed merely to the instance where the performance for which he is responsible is significantly different from the budgeted performance. Other figures may be ignored, for elsewhere everything is conforming to plan. In order to achieve this economy in the time managers are required to spend in examining statistics rather than in getting on with their immediate task, the statements of results should be carefully compiled so as to bring into prominence variations from the budgeted intentions. The causes of significant variations require analysis on each statement. It is the analysis of variations from the plan which represent the pointers for action by management.

3. The organisation of the budget procedure

The responsibility of the officer controlling the administration of the budget scheme is therefore one of recording, advising and explaining. Depending on his skill, knowledge and personality, he may also have a considerable influence in formulating the budgets. But whether the person responsible for the administration of the system is the accountant or a budget officer independent of the accountant, at no point should responsibility for the formulation or control of the budgets be imposed on him; nor should he be allowed to arrogate to himself such responsibility. An essential pre-requisite to effective budgetary control is that the budgets shall represent the intentions of the top management and the responsibility of functional management. Even if an impracticable standard of performance has been imposed on a junior manager, his complaint is against his superior, not against the accountant or budget officer.

In a small business it is probably most convenient to delegate the administration of the budgetary system to the accountant, and in this respect (perhaps in every respect!) he will represent an extension—"the long arm"—of top management. But, it is suggested, the accountant responsible for the cost accounts only is hardly the proper person to administer a system of managerial planning and control which covers all aspects of the business.

A budget officer is appointed in many large organisations, and it seems desirable that such an executive shall be directly responsible to top management so as to ensure his complete independence from functions which the system he operates aims to control. In a growing number of cases a "Controller" responsible to the Board for all financial and commercial activities also assumes responsibility for budgetary control.

In order to provide a medium for the issue of top management's directives, for discussion on the results, for revision of the budgets and for the vital process of co-ordinating functions and pooling information, a budget committee is desirable. This committee should be presided over by the chief executive, e.g. the managing director; and should consist of the functional heads, such as sales manager, works manager, personnel manager, chief engineer and chief accountant or controller; and have as secretary the budget officer.

The minutes of this committee's meetings, which will probably take place at monthly intervals, will form a convenient record of decisions on overall planning and control and will constitute what is often referred to as "The Budget Manual".

The meetings of the main committee may well be preceded by subsidiary budget committees covering each of the main functions of the business.

4. The budget period and revision of budgets

(a) The long-term budget

One of the first duties of the committee is to decide upon the period which is to be covered by the budgets. There can be no set rules as to the most suitable period, which depends upon a variety of factors peculiar to the business concerned. Generally, however, it is found beneficial to prepare a long-term plan reflecting in figures the broad policy of the concern, and a short-term plan which forms the basis of day-to-day control.

The desirable period covered by the long-term plan can only be expressed as the furthest period for which it is possible to look ahead. For a business dependent on fashion or taste, such as one concerned in the marketing of a new garment or beverage, it may not be practicable to plan the scope of operations for longer than a year ahead with any great certainty. Since, however, budgeting is essentially a statement of intentions, rather than a system of forecasting, the management of even the most speculative enterprise can benefit by planning a number of alternative uses of the capital employed. By such means, if one field of operations fails an alternative plan will be available for putting into effect without delay.

In some cases it may be extremely difficult to budget far ahead for the precise nature and cost of production, or for the area and volume of particular lines of sales. Nevertheless, it is imperative that the chief executives should be continually informed as to certain minimum requirements, such as the desired turnover of costs and sales, the minimum profit required for the service of capital and cash requirements. Long-term budgets in these broad terms are of service whatever the nature or size of the enterprise.

Where the cycle of production or operations normally extends over a long period, or where demand is such that the order book indicates full usage of funds and facilities for some years, the long-term budget may be drawn up in reasonably precise figures. In such cases the provision of the necessary finance, the programme of equipment, the recruitment and training of personnel, and forward buying all depend upon the preparation of a coherent and comprehensive long-term budget. Budgets for at least five years ahead will be required in such industries as shipbuilding, bridge building and other heavy engineering, and where, as in the aircraft industries, either government contracts or the development of prototypes occupies many years of preparation and subsequent production.

Broadly speaking therefore it may be said that a five-year period is common for a long-term budget. It is desirable that the long-term plan be broken down into financial years so as to conform to the normal accounting system and form a basis for the short-term budgets.

For the long-term budget the following main headings will be required as a minimum:

I. CAPITAL BUDGET

    A. Capital funds, *e.g.* issued capital, including shares and debentures, other loans, reserve requirements.

    B. Capital assets, *e.g.* land and buildings, plant and machinery, fixed investments such as in subsidiaries.

    C. Current assets, including stocks.

II. REVENUE OR OPERATING BUDGETS

    A. Income, including trading sales and other income.

    B. Expenditure, direct labour, material and other direct expenses; overheads, classified broadly, as for instance under personnel, financial, depreciation, maintenance, etc.

The extent to which any further division of the long-term budget is desirable depends, of course, on the circumstances of each business, particularly on the position regarding forward contracts.

(b) The short-term budget

It is desirable that the short-term budgets be drawn up to coincide with the periods used by the accounts so that comparison with actual events may be facilitated. In the case of a stable business it is often possible to budget with some precision for a year ahead, and in such a case the budget period should conform to the financial year of the concern. Even where a short-term budget is prepared for a year ahead it will be necessary to break down the figures to lesser periods in order to give the various ranks of management opportunity to take corrective action when the intended results are not being obtained.

A monthly budget appears to be a desirable minimum for effective control, although in many factories junior managers, such as foremen, are supplied with weekly results compared with the budgets, and in some cases with daily results.

Where monthly figures are supplied it is desirable to avoid using calendar months with their varying numbers of working days. The division of the year into thirteen periods of four weeks has been used with success; alternatively, the quarters may be equalised by using successively periods of four, four and five weeks.

The short-term budget, as distinct from the long-term plan, should reach down to junior management, who, in their various capacities, are responsible for seeing that the work of the concern is carried out according to plan. Thus the short-term budget, which conforms to the broad lines laid down by the long-term plan, is in particular an instrument for departmental managers and must be so expressed. So that results may be promptly compared with intentions, a system of departmental accounting under headings of responsibility is required.

(c) *Revision procedure*

An essential factor in successful budgeting is the principle of flexibility. A budget once formulated and approved should be regarded as the one standard and objective whilst it is in operation. It is, however, the responsibility of the management, advised by the budget officer, to ensure that, as soon as changed circumstances make it impossible to fulfil the intentions, the budget is revised. The revision of a departmental budget because, say, the prices of material or the wage-rates of labour have risen, does not necessarily entail the amendment of the broader objectives, such as sales turnover or overall profitability of the company. A change in circumstances not envisaged when the original budget was prepared may mean that the pattern of the later budget requires revision in order that the main objectives may still be obtained. Thus a general rise in wage-rates may require improved methods or further mechanisation for the purpose of holding unit costs at a level sufficient to yield the desired profit. The failure of a particular market may entail the development of an alternative outlet for production in order to maintain the necessary level of turnover.

K

An important advantage of budgetary control is that it provides the necessary warning signals in time for management to plan anew.

C. The Profit Target

1. Minimum or maximum profit

Subject to the retention of customer goodwill and other considerations of policy, top management will be constantly endeavouring to increase profitability.

In deciding on the profit policy to be pursued, and for the purpose of giving some guide to the functional heads when calling for their plans, top management will need to know the minimum level of profits which must be achieved. Unless the capital employed in a business is going to earn at least as great a return as that obtainable elsewhere at the same risk, the continuance of the business may not be justified.

A question of first importance to be decided in any business is therefore: What is the minimum profit required? This question is, it is suggested, essentially an accounting problem and involves: (a) assessing the value of capital employed in a business, and (b) assessing the rate of earnings required on that capital if its present employment is justified. The assessment of capital employed and the interpretation of profit to be related to that figure were discussed in the chapter on financial accounting as an aid to management.

2. Assessment of the minimum rate of earnings on capital

The minimum rate of earnings on capital would depend on current rates of interest obtainable for invested money and on the nature of the risk involved. Thus an undertaking which is so well established as to constitute a virtual monopoly in an assured market might incur so little risk as to be satisfied with an earnings rate of as low as, say, 5 per cent, whilst the current return on a long-dated gilt-edged security was, say, 3 per cent. If, however, general interest rates rose, it might well be considered that the minimum desired profitability for that company should be raised likewise. The minimum rate applicable to a more speculative enterprise might be as high as 20 per cent or more.

Thus, the problem of assessing the minimum profit target involves not only the calculation of capital employed and a definition of profit for the purpose, but also a decision as to the rate of interest to be applied. The solution might be to apply in all cases the rate currently obtainable on a long-dated government security, such as $2\frac{1}{2}$ per cent Consols, as representing the basic return for the use of money. But such a computation would tend to have little reality in a speculative enterprise which was bound to pay high rates to investors and make substantial appropriations to reserve as an insurance against future hazards.

The solution, again, appears to lie in consistent treatment. So long as the rate chosen does broadly reflect the minimum earnings required on an investment bearing similar risks, the resultant calculation will provide a firm and consistent basis for profit-budgeting year by year. It will act as a standard against which to compare actual profitability, and for this purpose the absolute accuracy of the standard is of minor importance provided that it gives a firm basis for judging variations in the percentage profitability.

3. The use of the profit target

The establishment of a figure representing minimum earnings or "profit" in the manner suggested above will provide management with a starting point for the determination of their broad lines of policy for the ensuing period. The management will certainly aim to achieve at least the minimum, and may well propound a much higher profit target.

In addition to the establishment of a profit objective the budgetary system will be used for expressing top management's policy in other directions, and in controlling the execution of that policy. The budgets will, for example, be the medium for expressing management's intention to extend the size or nature of operations, to develop a new product or service, to enter a new market or to increase employees' benefits by means of pension funds or other welfare activities. In any event, it will be essential to calculate the effect such policy may have on profits, particularly on the relation between profits and capital. Thus, if a process of development involved obtaining fresh capital by means of long-term loans or an issue of shares, the calculation of the essential minimum profit target would have to be assessed on the basis of the intended rather than on the present capital.

It is unlikely that a profit target can be established until after the departmental estimates of potential activity have been prepared, considered by top management, adjusted and co-ordinated, except possibly in the case of a concern which is still struggling to attain the minimum. Nevertheless, some broad indication of policy with regard to profits will be helpful to departmental managers in framing their preliminary estimates. It is, in this connection, perhaps necessary to remark that whilst budgetary control has been defined as "replacing opportunism by considered intention", the fact remains that for many concerns the degree of profitability achieved depends to a large extent on the capacity of the various managers, senior and junior, to take advantage of the opportunities afforded by favourable markets, new processes, methods and machinery, and the availability of capital and labour.

4. The meaning of "profit" for the purpose

A profit target will represent an invaluable spur to the executives, but in order that the achievements may be compared from time to time with the intentions it will be necessary for there to be a clear and precise picture of what is meant by the term "profit" as used in this connection.

Taxation is conventionally regarded as an appropriation of profit and not as a cost to be charged against income before arriving at profits. The reality of this treatment, has, however, been questioned in the post-war years when the rates of tax have been exceptionally high, and in consequence there has been a tendency to allow for taxation liabilities when planning profits. When assessing whether the profits for the ensuing period are likely to be sufficient to pay reasonable dividends and "plough back" sufficient funds into reserves, taxation must be taken into account. For such purposes it will be necessary to estimate the tax attributable to the profits of the future period under consideration, although the actual liability to pay such tax will not normally arise until after the period concerned.

Another question to be decided before a profit target is established is whether or not that target includes probable allocations to specific reserves. For many large companies and some smaller bodies the annual allocation to certain reserves has, like taxation, assumed the nature of a charge against income rather than an appropriation of profits. Reserves of this nature would include those set up for the purpose of supplementing the fixed depreciation charge, where assets require replacement at values above the original cost; those for safeguarding the capital against losses on exchange or in stock values; reserves for essential research; and many other allocations which prudent business-men would feel bound to make before distributing profits.

Where a substantial part of the capital of a concern had been obtained in the form of long-term loans, such as debenture stock, a further question arises as to whether the profit target for budgetary purposes is intended to cover earnings derived from that capital. In other words, if the total capital of a company is worth, say, £1,000,000, of which £600,000 is attributable to shareholders (*i.e.* owners) and £400,000 is represented by debentures (*i.e.* loan capital) the question resolves itself into whether the profit target based on capital employed is to be calculated as a percentage on £1,000,000 or on merely £600,000. It has already been suggested that the most logical basis in such a case is the total capital of the concern, *i.e.* £1,000,000 in the case cited above. Where, however, the profit target is so assessed as to include earnings on loan capital, it will be necessary for the purpose of comparing actual with intended earnings to add back to the net profit as shown by the accounts debenture interest which has been charged against profits.

The remaining adjustment in assessing a profit target and comparing results with intentions, which it may be thought expedient to make, is to eliminate from net profit any exceptional income or charge. A profit made on the sale of a fixed asset due to inflation would fall within this category, and so would a loss caused by circumstances beyond the control of the enterprise, such as the sequestration of a company's assets by a foreign power.

If all the adjustments suggested above are adopted the periodic comparison between actual and budgeted net profit might take the form shown on page 259.

5. The profit target based on normal distributions

Another method of assessing the minimum profit target to be used as a basis for top management to establish the final profit plan is to assess the earnings necessary for the purpose of meeting contractual interest payable on loan capital plus normal dividends to owners. In making an assessment on this basis it would appear necessary to make the adjustments for essential reserves and for exceptional items as indicated in the preceding section. The calculation would, in theory at least, be simplified for nationalised undertakings, such as air- and rail-transport concerns, where the standard will be represented by the fixed interest payable on the undertaking's stock, plus interest on any long-term loans.

	£	£	£
Budgeted "free" profit for the period . .			100,000
Actual profit per the accounts			£250,000
Less: Estimated taxation on these profits . .		150,000	
Specific reserves:			
Research	20,000		
Fixed asset replacement	15,000		
Other specific reserves . . .	30,000		
		65,000	
Exceptional profits		15,000	
			230,000
			20,000
Add:			
Debenture interest		50,000	
Exceptional losses		20,000	
			70,000
Earnings comparable with budget . . .			£90,000
Adverse variance			£10,000

For private enterprise the variable and possibly debatable item will be the dividend payable to the owners, whether it is represented by division of profits due to a sole proprietor or to partners, or by a return on shares. In the case of many large and stable companies, where rates of dividend rarely alter, the recent rates of payment may form a convenient target for the future. The rate may possibly be amended if there is a substantial change in general rates of interest as reflected by the return on long-dated government securities or by the bank rate.

Where, however, the fortunes of the concern are continually fluctuating, and in the case of a new and developing business, it would seem that the minimum profit target can be assessed only on the basis of a return on capital employed as described above, irrespective of the rights of various classes of investors. In any event, it is desirable to check the amount of earnings calculated as a percentage on capital to ensure that the resultant sum will suffice to meet contractual interest, normal dividends, taxation and normal reserves.

The calculation of a profit target on these lines might take the following form:

Profit target based on normal appropriations.

		£
1.	Fixed interest on long-term loans	50,000
2.	Fixed interest on Preference Shares	100,000
3.	Normal dividend on Ordinary Shares . . .	150,000
4	Normal (or average) dividend on deferred shares . .	25,000
		325,000
5.	Normal reserve requirements	75,000
6.	Taxation	195,000
		£595,000

It should be noted that whilst dividends on shares are normally paid less tax, and the tax so recovered is not subject to reimbursement to the Inland Revenue, it would seem desirable for budgetary purposes to show the dividends gross, and to adjust the taxation requirements by the sum to be recovered from dividends. If this procedure is adopted for budgetary purposes, then the appropriate adjustment will be required to the dividends and tax allocation as shown by the accounts.

D. FUNCTIONAL BUDGETS

1. The sales estimate

Before the sales manager prepares his estimates for the future period he will require as much information as possible on: (a) the broad lines of top management's policy, and (b) the potential capacity of the producing or operating function.

Whilst budgeting should not place too great an emphasis on past circumstances or events which may not recur, it is obvious that records of sales achieved in the recent past will always be of vital assistance in the preparation of an estimate for the future. According to the size and nature of the organisation, therefore, the effectiveness of sales budgeting will depend to a considerable extent on the scope, pertinence and topicality of the statistical records of past performance.

Many companies maintain separate statistical departments for the purpose of recording the sales analysis and other detailed information. Since in the end these figures will have to be expressed in money and related to the results shown in money by the accounting system, it seems desirable that the statistical department should be under the control of the head of the financial division.

Sales statistics should be analysed as a minimum by: (a) product headings and; (b) areas.

Probably the most important basis for the sales estimate is market research. In this context the expression is used in a wide sense and is intended to apply to any method for assessing the extent of potential markets for the sales made or to be made by the business.

A great deal of market research is undertaken by specialist firms whose services may be engaged for a specific line of enquiry. Market research is also undertaken for a particular industry by or on behalf of a trade association. Information as to market possibilities may be obtained from government departments, and useful statistics bearing on the subject are available in government publications and trade and professional journals. In addition to these external sources of information, the reports of an undertaking's own salesmen and agents will form an invaluable aid to assessing potential sales.

Where it is possible to do so a statistical calculation of the market potential forms perhaps the best basis for sales planning. Thus, the potential sales of a motor-car accessory may be calculated on the basis of the number of car registrations as affected by the average life of the article for sale. In all cases, of course, such an assessment must in the end be reduced to the share of the market which the undertaking is setting out to obtain.

Generally, market research enables the sales manager: (a) to establish a sales policy, and (b) to fix quotas for areas, agents and individual salesmen, or counter staff. It may be desirable to communicate the results of the research to branch managers and even to individual salesmen, so that the latter may, on this basis, calculate their own estimates of probable sales. The sales manager's final estimate to be submitted to top management may, in this way, be built up from a number of individual assessments, amended where necessary.

When submitting his estimate the sales manager will probably wish to add notes as to alternative probabilities dependent on such matters as increases or changes in the pattern of output or operations; as to further expenditure on advertising, packing or staff or other services; reductions in price; improved quality or shorter delivery dates.

The sales manager's estimate will normally represent probable *orders* receivable during the period, and not deliveries, for the essential function of the selling organisation is to obtain orders. The point at which such orders become firm sales by virtue of delivery and acceptance of the goods or services will be largely the responsibility of the producing or operating departments. For these reasons the budget officer will usually have to convert the sales estimate of orders into probable sales (from the accounting point of view) to be achieved during the period of the budget. The proportion of the sales department's estimate of orders receivable which are to be treated as sales during the period concerned will depend upon: (a) the orders outstanding at the beginning of the period; (b) the stock in hand at the beginning of the period; (c) production during the period; and (d) stock levels required to be held at the end of the period. It is unlikely that the conversion of orders receivable into sales can be carried out until the producing or operating division has formed its own plans, probably after considering the sales estimate.

2. The output or operating estimate

For many organisations the volume of potential sales will dictate the nature and extent of the production or operations required. In such a case, obviously, the sales estimate must be made first. Frequently, however, producing or operating circumstances will dictate the pattern and volume of sales which are required. In farming, for example, the nature of the soil limits the variety of crops, and the acreage available limits the volume of output. The selling function in such a case should be directed to selling all the produce at the best possible prices. In any event, the closest liaison must be maintained between selling and operating divisions during the process of preparing preliminary estimates.

The works manager (or similar executive) should, therefore, prepare his estimate of output on the bases: (a) of potential capacity of the works or operating function, and (b) of the sales estimate. Often the works will not be best adapted in supplies of material, labour or machinery to satisfy the sales requirements in certain lines. Conversely, the work which can be most efficiently carried out may not be regarded as a profitable line by the sales department, or the potential market as assessed by the selling side may be less than the potential output. The works manager naturally tends to bias his estimates towards the articles which he can produce most efficiently. It is precisely in resolving these conflicting points of view that the routine of budgetary control takes so effective a part in the co-ordination of activities. The final decision as to the output and sales objectives in a particular line is made by the chief executive when finally adjusting the various estimates.

In assessing the potential capacity of the works, consideration should be given to available facilities of: (*a*) space; (*b*) labour; (*c*) material; and (*d*) machinery. The first objective of the works manager (and indeed of a business as a whole) is to make the utmost use of the fixed assets of space and machinery. This ideal may be limited by the availability of labour to work the machines and of material to supply them.

The manager of a machine shop, for example, should not be content until all the machine tools are in use for a normal working day and every day. In many cases it is found profitable to keep the fixed assets of factory space and machinery in use day and night, but careful consideration would then have to be given to the higher hourly cost of labour and other services when employed after normal working hours.

The potential output of an assembly shop will depend largely on the efficient usage of the labour force. In such circumstances the works management will plan to ensure that at least the present labour force is to be fully employed; or, perhaps, that sufficient work is obtained to justify the engagement of such additional labour as can be accommodated. In this connection it may be pointed out that the efficiency of a workshop or similar unit is thought by many managers to depend to a large degree on the conditions of employment which can be offered to employees. One of the most valuable attractions in the eyes of the employee is security of employment. From this point of view the maintenance of a body of contented employees, skilled in the work and systems of the concern, may be regarded as constituting a form of capital, something in the nature of a fixed asset which must be preserved.

A broad, but practical, means of expressing in simple terms the potential capacity of machines is so many machine-hours for a specific period, and labour potential may be expressed in man-hours. These figures will not be immutable. New and improved machines may reduce capacity machine-hours but increase output; machines may replace manual work and reduce capacity labour-hours. In air transport a potential expressed as capacity ton-miles may be increased not only by employing more aircraft but also by using aircraft of greater speed, endurance and carrying capacity.

Other factors limiting the assessment of works or operating capacity may, for convenience, be summarised under the heading of works services. In some circumstances the availability of material may be included under this heading. An asbestos-manufacturing unit dependent on its own mine would have a potential output of finished products dependent on the mine output. Normally, however, the supply of material is a matter for a separate budget and does not initially affect the works manager's estimates unless he knows that increases in supplies are impossible.

Works services, such as supplies of power, water, heating and storage space, will, however, normally fall within the works manager's responsibilities and might limit extensions further of output.

In planning to meet the sales estimate the works manager should also give some consideration to costs, at least direct costs. He should be in a position to give some guidance as to the effect on unit costs of an estimated reduction in orders for a particular product or service, and should insist on the production of economic quantities. If increased sales entail considerable overtime or, say, the acquisition of costly plant, the works manager should record the fact when presenting his estimates.

3. Ancillary estimates

The functions of making and selling dominate industrial activity, and the operation of providing materials, finance and the administrative organisation may be considered as ancillary to these two main functions. It seems, therefore, necessary as a first stage in budgeting to effect a workable compromise between any conflicting requirements of the sales and works divisions before consideration is given to the demands which will be made on the ancillary services.

In particular organisations or in a special set of circumstances certain of the functions which are here treated as ancillary assume such a level of importance that they must be considered at the same time as the selling and working functions. The buying potential may well limit sales in the retail trades, particularly those dependent on fashion. The research and experimental activities in developing a new product may also overshadow for a time the normal business of producing and selling.

Subject to the above qualifications, it is usually found expedient for a preliminary reconciliation to be made between the sales and works or operating estimates through the medium of the budgetary committee, as a first stage in the procedure. The potential sales and potential output are then examined by the buyer, the personnel manager, the head of the financial division and other chief executives so that the buying, labour, and finance activities may be integrated with the main objectives of the concern. This represents the second stage of budgeting.

In drawing up a preliminary buying programme, information will be required as to present and required stock levels in addition to the rate of internal consumption expected to occur in the future. The buyer will take into account the present volume of orders outstanding on suppliers, and for this purpose requires the aid of the statistical service. When reporting to the budget committee on the ability of the buying function to meet the production programme envisaged, the buyer should note the probable effect on unit prices of changes in demand. The relative economy obtained by bulk purchases will need examination in relation to storage space and the freezing of capital involved in maintaining large stores of materials. It may well be that a revision of the output and sales estimates is required owing to the impossibility of supplying the necessary material or because material costs become uneconomic.

The personnel manager likewise prepares a programme indicating the extent to which he is able to supply the estimated labour requirements of the business as they are affected by the estimates so far examined. The personnel budget takes into account not only the needs of the operating division in respect of hourly labour but also indirect workers, weekly and monthly paid, for all departments. This entails enquiries being made of all departments as to their probable personnel requirements in the ensuing period. Notes will be attached to his preliminary programme by the personnel manager indicating the probable future trend of wage-rates and his requirements in advertising and welfare facilities. Again, the personnel estimate may well necessitate a further revision of the other main estimates.

The financial implications of the programmes so far prepared fall within the responsibility of the head of the financial department, whether that position is occupied by a Director, a Controller, the Chief Accountant or the Company Secretary. The financial estimates are discussed in the next section.

4. Financial estimates

The first operation in connection with the finance of the programme is to prepare a broad estimate of the probable cost of carrying out work envisaged so far. This broad estimate of costs should be divided into: (a) capital items, and (b) revenue items.

The capital expenditure estimate will be composed of: (a) expenditure on fixed assets, and (b) other capital items, such as, for example, the financing of subsidiaries. Many large companies appoint an executive, possibly a director, responsible for ensuring that fixed assets are maintained, or replaced and expanded as and when necessary. If such is the case that officer is responsible for preparing the fixed assets estimate, but otherwise the duty falls to the budget officer or accountant. Requirements in fixed assets have then to be obtained from individual departments, prices discussed with the buyer and any major extension of, say, factory space agreed with the chief executive. It is probable that the fixed-asset budget will require final approval by the board of directors in the case of a company.

In order that a cash budget may be prepared it is desirable to record the fixed-asset estimate in terms of the payments likely to be made at stated periods, preferably monthly.

The preliminary revenue expenditure budget may be compiled in two ways, depending on the kind and precision of the information available. In either case it will be found expedient to prepare the estimate under at least the three broad headings of variable, semi-variable and fixed costs. Where a standard costing system is in operation and the standards of unit variable costs are unlikely to be significantly affected by the future programme, it is possible to draw up an estimate of variable costs under product headings. An alternative method is to assess, on the basis of the estimates so far prepared, the probable cost of the direct labour and material requirements plus other direct expenses, such as work sub-contracted. The total cost of these elements may, if they are in fact strictly variable with output, be calculated by applying a factor to the output envisaged. Thus, if the planned output represents, say, 1,000,000 direct man-hours and the average cost of labour is 4s. per hour, the direct labour cost may be estimated at £200,000.

Semi-variable expenses need more detailed consideration, and probable requirements should be discussed with the executives concerned. Indirect hourly labour requirements should be obtainable from the departmental estimates, and indirect material may be assessed in relation to indirect labour.

Fixed expenses should, in theory, involve no problem, but in fact few expenses are found to be unvarying. For the expenditure estimate it is probable that fixed expenses may need individual consideration.

Reference has already been made to the desirability of budgeting for tax, and the remuneration of capital whether in the form of dividends, fixed interest or specific reserves.

The above headings, subdivided where necessary, constitute the expenditure side of the capital and revenue financial estimate. The expenditure should be expressed in stages, say, monthly, for the purpose of showing the extent to which receipts are available to meet payments period by period.

The second operation in financial estimating is to convert the sales estimate from orders receivable into deliveries and to express such firm sales in monetary value. The income from sales should be amalgamated with the income expected from other sources, such as investment income, royalties and commission receivable, and expressed by stages corresponding to the expenditure estimates.

When receipts and payments are set against each other month by month, the difference indicates the cash surplus or deficiency. If a substantial surplus results at any stage, general management will need to consider whether such surplus is to remain on current account at the bank or is to be invested either on deposit account or in some other profitable direction. If a deficiency results from the comparison of probable receipts and payments, arrangements must be made to meet that deficiency by overdraft, bank loan, the realisation of investments or (where the deficiency would otherwise be permanent) by a fresh issue of capital. At all times it is assumed that the accounting function is taking the necessary action to obtain prompt payment from creditors and to report to management on the relation between funds and current liabilities.

E. Comparing the Performance with the Budget

The assessment of the budget is only one phase of a comprehensive system of budgetary control. However carefully they are compiled, the budgets will be largely ineffective unless an efficient routine is in operation for comparing results with the budgets and explaining the causes of variations. It is wrong to assume that there are standard forms and methods which may be applied to any business; it is, on the other hand, most important that the routine shall be adapted to conform to the organisation of the business concerned and to the personalities of the managers to whom the statements are directed. The essential principles are: (a) that the results compared with the budget shall be presented promptly after the events to which they relate have occurred; (b) that the statements shall be drawn up in such a manner as to be readily understood by the persons to whom they are addressed; and (c) that variances shall be explained and those which are controllable shall be distinguished from those which are due to circumstances beyond the control of the manager concerned.

The attention of superior management need be directed only to the significant variances, and the relative importance of a list of variances may be effectively high-lighted by showing the percentage variance compared with the budget.

It is always desirable to show the monetary consequence of a failure to reach the budgeted performance, but greater reality is often given to budget statements by also relating monetary figures of cost or income to an appropriate measurement of the work from which the monetary figures are derived. Thus a budget statement for a works department or shop should so far as possible compare the performance with the budget in terms of output for the period, the cost of the output and the unit costs.

The growth of mechanisation in works and offices and the increasing complexity of modern business has caused a movement towards a higher proportion of overheads or indirect costs. For many operations direct costs are controlled to a large extent by bonus schemes and material control. It is therefore the overheads which are often the particular target of budgetary control. In the long run it is desirable to control overheads by relating them to the volume of operations, the size of output or, in some cases, the sales.

Difficult questions arise in attempting to show managers of indirect or service departments the relation between costs or income and the direct work of the concern. Whilst it is theoretically possible to relate the cost of each department to the work which that department carries out, the connection between a departmental cost and the output or operations of a concern are often too remote to form a useful basis for comparison, except, possibly, over a very long period. Advertising and other selling expenses are often high when output is low, and vice versa; the effort and cost of a buying department and of a works planning department may well be at their highest *before* a new project or selling line is put into production.

Nevertheless, a number of factors can be established with a view to relating the cost of overhead departments to activity. Some examples are given below.

So far as the monetary budgets are concerned, the factors of activity, of which suggested examples are given below, are useful in the separation of controllable from non-controllable variances, and generally in explaining divergences from budgeted figures. Thus an increased direct labour force may explain an overspending in the Inspection Department; a movement towards more customers with smaller accounts may explain an adverse variance in the receiving and despatch and in the accounts departments.

Department	Control factor
Buying . . .	Number of orders placed.
Salaries and wages . .	Number of employees.
Counter sales . . .	Number of sales, and/or value of sales.
Employment . . .	Number of interviews.
Inspection	Direct labour, and/or bought-out parts cost.
Receiving and despatch .	Number of packages handled.
Financial and cost accounts .	Total revenue expenditure.
Sales accounts . . .	Number of customers' accounts.

Variances may be due to errors in budgeting. If such is the case it must be acknowledged and the budget submitted to the appropriate authority for revision. In too many cases it is assumed that a budget once approved is infallible, and thus the faith of junior management in the budget system is undermined. In fact, the most carefully assessed budget is bound to contain some element of opinion and approximation. Work study and rate-fixing have to be adjusted to the characteristics of a mythical employee of average ability. Sales budgeting, in particular, is often a hazardous exercise in assessing the trend of fashion and even of the possible developments of science and technology.

The principal justification of budgetary control is in its use to management as a means of co-ordinating diverse activities, and because it distinguishes those variances from the plan which are subject to control from those which are not.

The continuous appraisal of efficiency, so as to provide a means either of correcting budgeting errors or remedying inefficiencies, is being increasingly assigned to a highly specialised internal audit department.

The function of the modern internal audit department has developed from a routine checking of accounting entries to the audit of methods and organisation in all departments. Whilst it is desirable for an internal audit department to include accountants amongst its personnel, other members will be experts in the production, operating, service or sales departments. The internal audit manager, like the budget officer, can be regarded as an off-shoot of top management, where his responsibilities lie. The appearance in large organisations of departments dealing with budgets, internal audit and organisation and methods appears to raise some problems as to the division of duties between these groups.

F. Practical Budgeting

1. General

The following outline of a system of budgeting in operation is of necessity confined to a reasonably simple system of accounts, but it may be used as the framework on which to construct a more complicated pattern according to the circumstances of a particular business.

It is assumed, in the following example, that a manufacturing business is involved and that the budgetary periods selected are (a) long-term budgets on broad lines covering the next five years, and (b) short-term budgets covering the next twelve months, the short-term budgets to be broken down further into calendar monthly periods or periods of thirteen weeks each.

The first operation is to compile broad Profit and Loss statements and Balance Sheets for the next five years. These statements will be based on the sales manager's estimate of the probable turnover required to meet the profit target and the policy of development established by the Board. In considering these forecasts regard will be had to the practicability of producing sufficient output, with the existing facilities, to meet the sales targets. In addition, the selling, administrative and other services involved will be examined from this point of view, as well as the requirements of space, equipment and cash. The preparation of the broad five-year plan will undoubtedly entail several processes of amendment until it is considered to represent a practical objective from all points of view.

Once the long-term budgets have been established they will dictate the form of the more detailed assessments required for short-term purposes. In all exercises in forecasting, management will be aware of the need for frequent revision in relation to changing circumstances. Long-term budgets should be reviewed at least annually, and at that time projected forward for a further year so that the business is always looking five years ahead, or for such other long-term period as the management decide to be feasible.

The method of compiling long-term budgets does not differ in principle from that applicable to shorter periods, and the following exposition will set out the broad accounting mechanics of compiling budgets for a year ahead.

2. The profit target

At the time of budgeting the capital employed in the business is £150,000

At a basic rate of 5 per cent this capital would require a *minimum* return of £7,500

After having regard to the risks and possibilities inherent in the business the Board lays down a profit target before taxation, of 20 per cent, *i.e.*   .   .   £30,000

3. Factory capacity available

The factory capacity which is or can be made available will clearly limit the scope of the short-term budgets for a manufacturing business. It should be noted in this connection that there are always one or more factors in the operation of any kind of business which restrict the extent of the forward plans and, according to the nature of the business, these factors include man-hours, machine hours, floor space, counter space in a stores, number of vehicles in a transport undertaking, number of rooms in a hotel and so forth. In a purely financial concern the controlling factor may be simply the availability of cash, and this element will naturally influence the forward plans of any business.

In the present example it is assumed that the basic controlling factor is the floor space available to accommodate the employees. Thirty thousand square feet are in fact available, and it is calculated that this space can accommodate some 300 employees working an effective 40-hour week. Thus, for 50 working weeks in a year the capacity of the factory may be expressed as 600,000 man-hours a year. At an average hourly rate of £0·20 full utilisation of the factory will entail a direct labour cost of £120,000 a year.

4. The sales potential

Meanwhile the Sales Manager will be preparing his forecast of sales. The initial stage of preparing a sales forecast consists of a careful evaluation of the market for the type of product concerned. With the aid of market research techniques, reports from salesmen in the field and statistics published by trade associations and government departments, it should be possible to assess how many units of a particular product could be sold by all suppliers in a given period, *i.e.* the value of the potential market. Let it be assumed that such an assessment had been made in the present case in respect of three distinct types of product and that the figures are as follows:

	Product A units	Product B units	Product C units
Potential market . .	50,000	120,000	80,000

The next step is to assess what share of the potential market the business in question can obtain in the year. The share so assessed will represent the volume of orders which can be obtained and, since all the orders are unlikely to be delivered in the period in which they are obtained, a further calculation must be made of what the orders represent in deliveries or invoiced sales for the period. Further information which is now required is the average price obtainable per unit. With these facts the following statement can be prepared:

	Product A units	Product B units	Product C units	TOTAL units
Share of the market (orders receivable)	12,000	72,000	24,000	—
Share of the market (deliveries) .	10,000	60,000	20,000	
	£	£	£	
Average price per unit . .	7	5	3	
Provisional sales forecast . .	£70,000	£300,000	£60,000	£430,000

5. Relating the sales forecast to capacity

It is now necessary to ascertain whether the sales forecast can be met out of available capacity. For this purpose a calculation is required of the number of man-hours which will be involved in making one unit. The figures are calculated as follows:

	Product A man-hours	Product B man-hours	Product C man-hours	TOTAL man-hours
Man-hours per unit . .	10	8	8	
Total man-hours required .	100,000	480,000	160,000	740,000

It is now clear that the forecasted sales, which involve working 740,000 man-hours in a year, cannot be met out of existing capacity of 600,000 man-hours as originally assessed. After a further review the factory manager reports that, as a result of reorganising the factory and some overtime working, he is able to increase capacity to 660,000 man-hours in a year. This still falls short of the total required by the sales forecast, which it is, therefore, decided to adjust. An adjustment is also made to allow for a necessary increase in stockholding, and the direct standard cost of each unit, in materials and labour, is assessed. The situation is then as follows:

	Product A man-hours	Product B man-hours	Product C man-hours	TOTAL man-hours
Man-hours available . .	110,000	370,000	180,000	660,000
Less: Man-hours required to meet growth in stocks . . .	5,000	10,000	20,000	35,000
Forecasted sales in man-hours	105,000	360,000	160,000	625,000
	Units	Units	Units	Units
Units of sales represented by the above man-hours .	10,500	45,000	20,000	—
	£	£	£	£
Therefore, Sales Turnover	73,500	225,000	60,000	358,500
Standard Cost per unit .	£4·00	£3·50	£2·00	
Standard Cost of sales .	42,000	157,000	40,000	239,500
Gross margin . .	£31,500	£67,500	£20,000	£119,000

6. Overhead estimates

Overhead estimates are now compiled by the managers of the various departments in respect of the costs for which they are responsible. These estimates are considered by the Budget Committee, presided over by the chief executive and assisted by the Budget Officer, in relation to the expected volume of business indicated by the foregoing forecasts. A summarised statement of these estimates is prepared in the following form:

OVERHEAD ESTIMATES

	Factory £	Sales £	Admin. £	TOTAL £
A. Fixed Expenses				
Space costs	9,000	2,500	2,250	13,750
Depreciation	2,000	450	550	3,000
Insurance	300	100	900	1,300
Communications	700	700	800	2,200
Employee benefits	5,500	250	500	6,250
Total Fixed Expense	17,500	4,000	5,000	26,500
B. Variable Expenses				
Salaries, wages and commissions	26,000	5,000	11,000	42,000
Indirect materials	7,000	2,250	500	9,750
Communications, variable	500	750	1,000	2,250
Travel and entertainment	300	2,000	1,500	3,800
Publicity	—	7,000	—	7,000
Distribution	—	1,500	—	1,500
Professional fees	—	—	2,500	2,500
Subscriptions and donations	100	500	500	1,100
Miscellaneous	1,100	1,000	500	2,600
Total Variable Expenses	35,000	20,000	17,500	72,500
Total Overheads	£52,500	£24,000	£22,500	£99,000

7. Finalising the revenue budgets

The potential sales have, at this stage of the budgeting procedure, been reconciled with the potential output, and the overhead expenses of the business have been assessed. The projected profit resulting from these forecasts is as follows:

	£
Sales	358,500
Less: Direct cost of Sales	239,500
Gross margin	119,000
Less: Overhead expenses	99,000
Net margin, subject to tax and interest	£20,000

The projected net margin is, however, £10,000 short of the profit target set out in paragraph 2 above, so that the estimates must be once more reviewed with the object of meeting the profit target if it is at all possible to do so.

After reviewing the situation the Budget Committee agree that the following adjustments can be made to the figures:

(a) As a result of the Purchasing Manager finding an alternative source of certain materials the standard cost of Product A can be reduced £0·25 to £3·75 a unit. The cost of sales of Product A thus become:

10,500 units at £3·75	£39,375

(b) By reducing stock requirements the sales turnover of Product C can be increased by 2,000 units to 22,000 units. Thus the profitability of this product becomes:

	£
Sales—22,000 units at £3	66,000
Less: Standard costs at £2 a unit	44,000
Gross Margin	£22,000

(c) Administrative salaries can be reduced by £500.

The Profit and Loss Account for the year now appears as follows:

	Product A £	Product B £	Product C £	TOTAL £
SALES	73,500	225,000	66,000	364,500
Direct cost of sales .	39,375	157,500	44,000	240,875
GROSS MARGIN .	£34,125	£67,500	£22,000	£123,625
Overhead Expenses:				
Factory				52,500
Selling				24,000
Administration				22,000
Total Overheads				98,500
PROFIT before tax and interest				25,125
Estimated tax provision				12,000
PROFIT after tax but before interest on capital . . .				£13,125

8. Cash forecast

An important tool in management accounting to control the use of cash is the Cash Forecast. Its purpose is to estimate the actual cash requirements at future points in time to ensure that:

(a) sufficient cash is in the bank, in hand or immediately available to meet expenditure; and

(b) cash surplus to requirements is put to good use, perhaps in temporary investments.

The Cash Forecast should take into account receipts from customers, payments to suppliers, payments for operating expenses, capital investment payments, periodic items such as interest and dividends and any exceptional items.

Cash Forecasts are prepared in tabular form, and the following is a typical example. In this example it is assumed that a minimum balance of £10,000 is required.

CASH FORECAST FOR THE PERIOD ....

Details	Months			
	June	July	August	etc.
	£	£	£	£
Balance at beginning of period	20,000	5,000		
Net receipts from debtors	52,000	59,000		
Other receipts (per schedule or listed)	8,000	6,000		
TOTAL RECEIPTS	£60,000	65,000		
Net payments to suppliers	58,000	40,000		
Payment for expenses (per schedule or as listed)	14,000	5,000		
Dividends	3,000			
Capital items	—	—		
TOTAL PAYMENTS	£75,000	45,000		
Summary				
Balance to begin	20,000	5,000		
Total receipts	60,000	65,000		
	80,000	70,000		
Less Total payments	75,000	45,000		
Balance at end	5,000	25,000		
Minimum balance required	10,000	10,000		
SURPLUS OR DEFICIENCY	£(5,000)	15,000		

Although such a monthly forecast will be useful to give a general overall picture, it will usually be necessary to break this down into shorter periods, weekly or perhaps even daily, in cases where large lump-sum payments have to be made or are received on special days.

9. Balance Sheet projection

For the purpose of preparing the projected Balance Sheet at the end of the period it will be necessary for a schedule of the proposed purchases of raw material to be prepared, analysed by the different categories of material required and by delivery dates. Such a buying programme must be closely reconciled with the production programme so as to ensure that adequate stocks of raw material are available when they are required by the workshops. This aspect of budgeting is directly related to the function of production control, progressing and scheduling, and a failure to carry out this reconciliation may jeopardise the whole company forward plan. If it so transpires that the material cannot be supplied at the appropriate dates, a further review of the budgets may become necessary.

For present purposes material requirements may be assessed in accordance with the statement below:

	Product	Product	Product	TOTAL
Man-hours required to produce the budgeted output . .	110,000	370,000	180,000	660,000
Man-hours per unit . .	10	8	8	
Units of output . . .	11,000	46,250	22,500	79,750
Standard Cost per unit . .	£3·75	£3·50	£2·00	
Standard Cost of output . .	£41,250	£161,875	£45,000	£248,125
Labour Cost at £0·20 per hour.	22,000	74,000	36,000	132,000
Material Cost . .	£19,250	£87,875	£9,000	£116,125

Estimates are required of the likely payments which will be made to the creditors and of the receipts from the debtors during the period. The estimated payments to creditors will have regard to the present indebtedness of the business and to the purchases as assessed above. Receipts from debtors will, likewise, be considered in relation to the amounts now owing to the business and the budgeted sales for the year ahead. In both cases the figures will, in addition, be influenced by the terms of credit received and given.

Let it be assumed that £324,500 is received from debtors and £150,000 paid to creditors in respect of material purchases.

Capital budgets will be required from departments and will, subject to the necessary approvals, indicate the additions to and sales of fixed assets envisaged. The accountant will assess the depreciation charges required on such assets.

Further somewhat minor complications in compiling the Balance Sheet projection are the prepayments and deferred charges which occur with respect to such items as rent, rates and insurance, but, for simplicity, these items have been ignored in the statement set out below.

BALANCE SHEET PROJECTION

	Beginning of year	Additions		Deductions		End of year
FIXED ASSETS	£	£		£		£
At cost	65,000	5,000		—		70,000
Depreciation	15,000	3,000		—		18,000
Net	50,000	2,000	—	—		52,000
CURRENT ASSETS						
Debtors	40,000	364,500	Sales	324,500	Receipts	80,000
Stocks	50,000	143,000	Creditors	116,125	Issues	76,875
Work in progress	20,000	132,000	Labour	240,875	Cost of sales	27,250
		116,125	Material			
Total Current Assets	110,000	755,625		681,500		184,125
TOTAL ASSETS	160,000	757,625		681,500		236,125
CURRENT LIABILITIES						
Overdraft	1,000	95,500	Overheads	324,500	Receipts	54,000
		132,000	Labour			
		150,000	Creditors			
Creditors	9,000	12,000	Tax	150,000	Payments	19,000
		143,000	Stock			
		5,000	Fixed assets			
Total Current Liabilities	10,000	537,500		474,500		73,000
CAPITAL EMPLOYED	£150,000	£220,125		£207,000		£163,125

It will be observed that the above Balance Sheet Projection incorporates a cash forecast, which would, in practice, be set out in more detail, and probably at monthly intervals, in a separate statement.

The increase in capital employed over the year is £13,125, as indicated by the Profit and Loss Account set out in Section 7 above. The projection may now be extended by setting out changes in the sources of funds, in the manner indicated below:

	Beginning of year £	Additions £	Deductions £	At end of year £
Issued capital . . .	108,000	—	—	100,000
Revenue reserves:				
General Reserve . . .	40,000	—	—	40,000
Profit and Loss Account .	10,000	13,125	—	23,125
	£150,000	£13,125	—	£163,125

10. Subsequent control procedure

The foregoing projections of the Profit and Loss Account will be broken down into monthly or at least quarterly periods for control purposes, and estimated Balance Sheets will be prepared as at the end of each future month or quarter. Comparisons between the budgeted and actual results will be made not only so far as each month's figures are concerned but also on a cumulative basis so that management can review the extent to which inevitable variances occurring in a particular month are made up in subsequent months. Management's attention need only be directed to the areas where actual performance is not in conformity with the plan, but it is desirable that the statements presented to managers should contain appropriate comments indicating the causes of variances.

The Profit and Loss Account and Balance Sheet comparisons between budget and actual will constitute the overall medium of control available to top management, but subordinate managers will require more detailed and probably more frequent statements covering the functions for which they are responsible. Thus statements of workshop costs compared with budgets and standards will be required weekly and possibly daily; sales managers will need to check, probably at weekly intervals, the extent to which both incoming orders and invoiced sales are meeting the budgets; and financial management may need figures relating to the cash position more frequently than monthly. Whatever may be the frequency with which a statement is submitted a most important feature for control purposes is that the statement shall be made available as quickly as possible after the events to which it relates.

THE PROVISION OF CAPITAL

The growth of the large-scale organisation in this country can, to a large extent, be attributed to the existence of the limited-liability company. The principle of limited liability enables promoters of companies to collect the capital they require from a variety of sources. The consideration of the sources available will be divided into the following aspects:

(1) the provision of initial capital to finance a new concern;

(2) the provision of additional capital for an established firm which requires further finance to expand its productive facilities or to improve its existing ones;

(3) the provision of additional permanent capital.

1. Provision of initial capital

The two main forms of limited company are the private company and the public company. The private company is prohibited under the provisions of the Companies Act, 1948, from making any invitation to the public to subscribe for any of its shares or debentures. Consequently, the capital of a private company must be obtained from sources known to the promoters. The public company may, as its name implies, invite subscriptions for its capital from any source.

The London Stock Exchange and the provincial stock exchanges provide the traditional mechanism for the raising of capital funds. The function of the stock exchanges is to provide a market for the purchase and sale of securities. The initial capital of a new company will usually take the form of an issue of share capital, and arrangements must be made with a finance house or member of the Stock Exchange to arrange the issue. The firms which specialise in this kind of work are called "issuing houses". They may arrange the issue in the following ways:

(a) *A public issue.* Invitations will be made to the investing public to apply for shares or debentures. The invitation may be through advertisements in the Press, or through banks or other agencies which have access to investors, such as stockbrokers, accountants and solicitors.

(b) *An offer for sale.* Under this method of finance an issuing house will purchase the shares in the first instance, and then make its own invitation to the public to buy the shares from them. The issuing house will either offer the shares for sale to the public at a stated price or will invite tenders. If the shares are offered at a stated price the issuing house will make a profit representing the difference between what it paid for the shares and what it eventually receives for them. In some cases the offer for sale will be at the same price as the issuing house paid for the shares, and it will rely for its profit on receiving a fee or commission for its services. If the shares are offered for tender the issuing house will again expect to receive tenders at a price above that which it paid for the shares. The advantage to the Company of these methods of financing is that the risk of under-subscription is normally borne by the issuing house, which may, of course, protect itself by means of an underwriting contract.

(c) *The placing of shares.* The issuing house will arrange with a number of private investment sources to take up the issue.

During the last two decades a change has occurred in investment sources. No longer is the private investor the main source from which capital may be sought. To-day there exists what are known as the "institutional investors". These consist of two main classes. First, the investment trusts; these are companies formed for the purposes of holding shares and debentures in other companies, and their revenue is derived from the dividends and interest they receive. The second class of institutional investors are the insurance companies, building societies, pension funds and the like who may have surplus funds which they wish to invest. It is the existence of institutional investors which make important Offers for Sale and Placings of Shares.

2. Provision of additional capital for expansion

(a) *Working capital*

The traditional method of providing additional working capital is the appropriation of profits to reserve, the "ploughing-back" of profits. The present incidence of taxation makes it difficult for a business to make sufficient reserves for working capital, since such appropriations attract taxation.

For increased working capital most companies must seek outside sources, and the most important of these are bank loans and overdrafts. A bank loan means that a bank has placed a fixed sum to the credit of the customer's account, and interest is charged on this fixed amount. An overdraft indicates that arrangements have been made with a bank to allow the customer to overdraw his account up to an agreed limit, interest being payable when the account is "in the red". Usually the bank will require some security to be deposited with them.

(b) *Capital for expansion*

Where a business requires additional short-term capital for expansion or improvement of existing productive facilities, there are a number of special finance corporations which are sponsored by the Government and which have funds provided by banks and other finance institutions.

The two important corporations for general purposes are:

(i) The Industrial & Commercial Finance Corporation Ltd. This corporation provides finance for new buildings, new plant and general expansion of industry. The finance is usually provided in the form of long-term loans on fixed terms. Amounts range normally from between £5,000 and £200,000.

(ii) The Finance Corporation for Industry. This corporation provides finance for the re-equipment of industry, and its loans are subject to a minimum of £200,000.

In addition, there are corporations which have funds available for special purposes or industries. Examples are the Estate Duties Investment Trust, the Agricultural Mortgage Corporation and the National Film Finance Corporation.

(c) *Additional permanent capital*

The methods here are similar to the provision of initial capital by an issue of share capital or debentures. An offer is often made to existing shareholders to invest additional money in the company on advantageous terms. After the shareholders have had their opportunity the balance of the issue will then be offered to the general investing public.

TAXATION

1. Taxation and management

Taxation of various kinds has so great an influence on profits available for dividend or reserves, and, indeed, on management decisions in general, that no study of accounting is complete without consideration being given to this important subject.

The connection between taxation accounting and accounting applied as an aid to management may not be obvious. Profit is a broad gauge of the efficiency of management, and available profit may be considerably limited by taxation dues. The amount which has to be provided for taxation in respect of a particular period of account will depend to some extent on the capital structure of the company, dividend policy and the nature of the transactions in the accounts. Taxation aspects may be decisive where consideration is being given to the investment of capital in a new selling line, an additional factory, further plant and machinery and in expansion overseas.

It is important to bear in mind that the figure of profit on which tax becomes payable by a business is not identical with the profit shown in the accounts. Some business expenses customarily considered as properly chargeable against income in the accounts, *e.g.* entertainment, certain charitable subscriptions and depreciation, will not be chargeable for tax purposes. On the other hand, the taxation law and practice may permit the charging of items, *e.g.* capital allowances, which do not appear in the business accounts. Taxation liabilities may be affected by the time when transactions are carried out; thus, it may be expedient to defer capital expenditure where there is an expectation of an increase in taxation rates. It is one of the functions of the accounting service to give advice on these matters, but at the same time the avoidance of unnecessary taxation must depend to some extent at least on a broad understanding of the subject by the managers who are responsible for the decisions.

2. The scope of taxation

Taxation, so far as it affects industrial and commercial organisations, includes: (*a*) customs dues on certain imported goods;

(b) excise duties on certain goods produced in this country, *e.g.* alcoholic beverages, tobacco, etc.; (c) miscellaneous direct taxes such as motor vehicle licences and stamp duties; (d) local taxation in the form of rates; and (e) taxes on income, including income tax, surtax, profits tax (now cancelled), capital gains tax and corporation tax.

This appendix concentrates on the last category as being the most complex and of which the effect is most frequently misunderstood.

Income tax is chargeable on the income receivable by individuals, including persons in partnership with others, and such income may comprise not only salaries but also profits from businesses, interest and dividends, royalties, capital profits and miscellaneous income. Basically, each individual is liable to pay income tax on his total taxable income at the standard rate, 8s. 3d. (£0·413). In calculating an individual's taxable income, however, he may deduct from his actual income for tax purposes certain personal and other reliefs and allowances, so that few individuals pay income tax at the standard rate in relation to their total income.

In addition to income tax, individuals, whose income exceeds £2,000 p.a., may be liable to pay surtax, of which the rates are progressive, beginning at 2s. (£0·1) in the £ and ending at 10s. (£0·5) in the £, where the taxable income exceeds £15,000 p.a. (1965/66). Thus it is possible for an individual to be liable to income tax and surtax at a combined rate of 18s. 3d. (£0·913) on the last portion of his income. Allowances for earned income (*i.e.* from salaries and profits, but not from dividends or interest) mean that a taxpayer whose income is entirely earned does not pay surtax until his income exceeds £4,000 p.a.

The allowances and reliefs applicable to individuals are frequently changed by the annual, or sometimes biennial Finance Acts, and details of the current rates may be obtained from any tax office.

Corporate bodies, with some exceptions, have been liable, since 5th April 1965, for corporation tax on their profits. Before that date they paid income tax at the standard rate and profits tax, of which the last rate was 15 per cent. Corporation tax is dealt with in more detail below.

3. The administration of tax

The statutory rules which govern the rates and adminstration of tax are contained in the Income Tax Act of 1952 and subsequent

Finance Acts. The interpretation of these rules may vitally affect a taxpayer's liability and has been the subject of a vast body of case law, non-statutory "concessions" published from time to time by the Inland Revenue and a code of practice established over the years between the tax offices and tax advisers. Thus, for any complicated tax problem expert advice should be obtained.

The central administration of taxation is in the hands of the Board of Inland Revenue, who operate under the direction of the Treasury and advise the Chancellor of the Exchequer on tax matters. Responsible to the Board of Inland Revenue are the local Inspectors of Taxes and Collectors of Taxes. The latter are, in effect, the cashiers of the tax system; they collect the sums due under assessments and take action against taxpayers who are in default. The local Inspectors have power to make assessments for income tax and are generally the officials with whom the taxpayer deals so far as the computation of tax liability is concerned.

If a taxpayer (including a corporate body) cannot reach agreement with the local Inspector as to his liability an appeal may be made either to the General Commissioners or to the Special Commissioners. The General Commissioners are appointed by the Lord Chancellor, so that they are independent of the Inland Revenue officials. They are usually local persons of prominence, akin to magistrates, are unpaid and in general have the duty of protecting the interests of the taxpayer, subject to the law. The Special Commissioners are appointed by the Treasury, so that they are paid civil servants, but they have expert knowledge of tax law and practice.

The duties and powers of the Commissioners, Inspectors and Collectors are set out in the Income Tax Act, 1952, as amended by various Finance Acts and by the Income Tax Management Act, 1964.

Tax is leviable in respect of the fiscal year, which runs from 5th April to the following 5th April, and this is the period which is covered by the current standard rate and other rates of tax and allowances. Alterations to current taxation are set out by the Chancellor of the Exchequer, usually at the beginning of April in each year, and the amendments he then proposes generally take immediate effect, although they may be revised in Parliament before the Finance Act is finally passed, usually in the following autumn. Although a person or corporate body is assessed for tax in respect of the fiscal year, the income or profits which form the basis of the assessment are not necessarily those actually received in that period. Except in the opening and closing years businesses are assessed for *income tax* on the basis of the profits earned in the accounts year which falls in the preceding income-tax year; corporation tax is, however, assessed on the chargeable accounting period which is the accounts year falling within the current fiscal year.

Assessments to income tax are issued by the local Inspector of Taxes, usually in November, and assessments to surtax are issued by the Board of Inland Revenue. The assessments are based on returns of income and allowances which every taxpayer is obliged to make, except that this requirement is usually dispensed with where a taxpayer's income consists largely of salaries or wages subject to collection through the P.A.Y.E. system. It should be observed that Inspectors of Taxes receive information from various sources, *e.g.* companies, building societies, banks, the Post Office, etc., against which a taxpayer's return can be checked.

Tax payable on the profits of individuals or partnerships is payable by two instalments, on 1st January in the year of assessment and on the following 1st July. In the case of corporations paying corporation tax and for income from property, tax is payable on 1st January in the year of assessment in one amount. Surtax is payable on 1st January following the year of assessment.

For certain types of income, tax is not payable by the taxpayer direct to the Inland Revenue, but is deducted by the payer, who is obliged to account to the Inland Revenue for the total amount so deducted. This does not necessarily mean that the payer actually pays the total sum concerned to the Inland Revenue, but, as is the case with annual payments, he bears tax in effect on the sum concerned by failing to charge the payment against his own income. Thus, when a company pays interest on its debentures it will deduct tax at the standard rate from the interest so that the debenture holders receive the net amount. A company will also deduct income tax at the standard rate from dividends to shareholders, but since a dividend is an appropriation of profits and not in any event allowable in the company's computation for corporation tax, the tax so deducted has to be refunded to the Inland Revenue by the company. Before the advent of corporation tax no such refund was made, as the company was only recouping from the shareholder a portion of the income tax which it had suffered on its profits.

L

Tax on employees' salaries and wages is deducted by the employer under the P.A.Y.E. system, and the employer pays over to the Inland Revenue the total amount so deducted, usually at monthly intervals.

4. Income tax—the five schedules

Assessments for income tax fall within one or more of the five schedules to the Income Tax Act, 1952; some of these schedules contain further subdivisions called "cases." The rules applicable to each schedule and case determine how the income is to be measured and assessed. A person's income from all sources may necessitate a number of assessments, depending on the schedules involved, but that individual will pay income tax only on the total assessments, subject to personal and other allowances. The schedules and cases are briefly summarised as follows:

Schedule A related to income from the ownership of landed property, but this schedule was cancelled by the Finance Act, 1963, actual income (rents) from property being transferred to Case VIII of Schedule D.

Schedule B. The application of this Schedule was severely attenuated by the Finance Act, 1963, and it now relates only to income derived from woodlands where an election to be assessed under Schedule D has not been made.

Schedule C. Income under this schedule consists of interest and dividends payable out of public revenue of the United Kingdom or of a foreign country. The assessment is made on the paying agent, usually a bank, and covers the tax which the paying agent deducts from the several payments of interest which he makes. It should be pointed out that interest on certain government securities, *e.g.* $3\frac{1}{2}$ per cent War Loan, is normally payable gross (*i.e.* without deduction of tax), so that such interest is taxable in the hands of the recipients and not under Schedule C.

Schedule D. This is the schedule under which the major part of the income earned by businesses is assessable, and it is subdivided into eight "cases" as follows:

Case I. This covers any trade carried on by a person, partnership or corporate body, and refers therefore to the normal trading income of most commercial and industrial undertakings.

Case II. Profits earned by a profession or vocation are assessed under this case, and it would therefore apply to the earnings of such professional people as medical practitioners, solicitors and accountants, whether in partnership or sole practice.

Case III. This case covers tax on annual payments, such as interest on loans, discounts, bank interest on deposit accounts and interest on government securities paid gross.

Case IV. Tax on foreign securities paid gross falls under this case.

Case V. Tax on foreign possessions, including foreign investments, trades, professions and employments abroad.

Case VI. This is the miscellaneous case which covers tax in respect of profits and gains not falling under other schedules or cases, in particular furnished lettings.

Case VII. This was the case originally introduced by the Finance Act, 1962, to deal with the taxation of short-term gains (or capital profits). It applied to assets, including landed property and shares and securities, but not tangible moveable property, owner-occupied property or business machinery. The assets must have been in existence on 10th April 1962. Although the provisions of the Finance Act, 1962 in respect of short-term gains have been largely supplanted by the extension of the capital gains tax introduced in the Finance Bill of 1965, the former provisions still apply to assets in existence on 6th April 1965. The Finance Act, 1962, charged to tax capital gains on land and buildings sold within three years of acquisition and on shares and securities sold within six months of acquisition. The provisions of the Finance Bill, 1965, are dealt with below.

Case VIII. This case was introduced by the Finance Act, 1963, to cover the taxation of income from property (largely rents) following the cancellation by that Act of Schedule A.

Schedule E. This is the schedule which applies to salaries, wages, fees and other income from employment. Tax under this heading is normally collected by means of the Pay As You Earn system (P.A.Y.E.), which was introduced in 1944. Under the P.A.Y.E. system the employer has the obligation of deducting tax from the employees' pay in amounts obtained by applying a code number issued by the local Inspector in respect of each employee. This code number is applied to tax tables which give the necessary weight to the employee's personal and other allowances. The tax so deducted is normally paid by the employer to the local Collector of Taxes at monthly intervals, and the paper work involved entails considerable clerical effort and time. There are exceptions to the operation of P.A.Y.E., for instance, employees earning less than £22 15s. od. a month (in 1964/65), and full details may be obtained from pamphlets available from tax offices. The assessment of tax under this Schedule falls into the following cases:

Case I. Persons resident in the United Kingdom who are mainly or wholly employed in the United Kingdom. In this case the whole remuneration is taxed, for the majority under the P.A.Y.E. system, in the year in which it arises.

Case II. Persons not ordinarily resident in the United Kingdom, but part of whose employment is in the United Kingdom. In this case it is the United Kingdom employment only which is assessable.

Case III. Persons resident in the United Kingdom but not falling within Cases I and II, *i.e.* where they earn remuneration abroad. In this case the taxpayer pays tax on the remittances he makes to this country, and it applies, in particular, to employees of a United Kingdom business who work abroad on long-term assignments.

It will be observed that residence is important in connection with assessments under Case E. The question as to whether a person is resident or ordinarily resident in this country has not been clearly defined, but, in general, a person is resident if he maintains a permanent abode in this country and if he is in this country for six months or more in any tax year. The question whether an employee who is assigned to a position abroad is liable to pay United Kingdom tax as well as local tax is obviously of considerable importance to businesses trading abroad and needs expert guidance.

Schedule F. This schedule was introduced in the Finance Bill, 1965, to cover income tax on dividends and other distributions, following the inception of the corporation tax. The assessment under this schedule is thus on the company paying the dividend and deducting income tax from the gross amount paid.

5. Taxation of business profits

As indicated above, the major part of the net income or profits of industrial and commercial undertakings is assessed under the pro-

visions of Schedule D, Case I. It is important to appreciate that
the profit shown in the accounts, as drawn up in accordance with
normal accounting practice, is rarely the same as the profit on
which tax is chargeable. The reason is that certain items, customarily shown as income or expenditure in business accounts, are
not so treated for income-tax purposes. Generally, income in the
form of trading sales is assessable, but, except to the extent that the
capital gains provisions apply (see below), income of a capital
nature, *e.g.* a payment for the termination of an agreement, will not
be assessable.

The principal adjustments which have to be made for tax purposes to the business accounts refer to expense items. A large body
of case law and practice has accumulated on this subject, and the
general principle is that expenditure must be wholly and necessarily laid out for the purposes of the business. Capital expenditure is chargeable only in accordance with the provisions applicable
to capital gains. Among the major items of expense which are dis-
allowed for tax purposes, the following are worthy of specific
mention: general provisions, such as a percentage of debtors to
allow for doubtful debts (but specific provisions are allowable);
depreciation, which is replaced by certain capital allowances (see
below); items of a capital nature such as improvements to property
and legal charges on the acquisition of property; entertainment
expenses except for foreign buyers; payments made subject to
deduction of tax, *e.g.* loan interest; expenses of a personal nature,
such as the private usage of cars; appropriations of profit, such as
dividends; charitable subscriptions, except those connected with
the trade; and taxation.

After the accounts profit has been adjusted in respect of such
items as those indicated above, and the resulting taxable profit
reduced by capital allowances, the final figure would be subject to
income tax and profits tax up to the fiscal year 1965/66 and thereafter to corporation tax, in the case of a business run by a limited
company or other corporate body (with some special exceptions).
So far as concerns businesses run by one person, or partnerships,
the resulting figure is still subject to income tax, profits tax having
been cancelled by the Finance Bill, 1965.

Where a business was subject to income tax, and where in the
case of the sole owner and the partnership it is still so subject, the
assessment for the current fiscal year (6th April to the following

L 2

5th April) would normally be based on the taxable profits derived from the accounting year ending within the preceding fiscal year. Payment was due, in the case of corporate bodies, in one instalment on 1st January in the fiscal year of assessment; and in the case of other businesses by two instalments, one on 1st January in the fiscal year of assessment and the other on the following 1st July. Thus, income tax on the profits made by a business in its current accounting period would not be payable to the Inland Revenue until many months after the end of its accounting year. In order to ensure that the tax on those profits would not be distributed, it became the practice of most companies to reserve for the tax likely to be due on current profits, and to show the reserve in the Balance Sheet under some such title as "Future Taxation". Subject to any adjustments which might become necessary, "Future Taxation" would become "Current Taxation", and shown under current liabilities, in the accounts of the following year.

Corporate bodies will, in general, cease to be liable for income tax on profits after the accounting year which falls in the fiscal year 1964/65, *i.e.* the basis period for the 1965/66 assessment. After that date the taxable profit will be subject to corporation tax, chargeable on the actual profits made in the fiscal year, at rates to be settled by Parliament, probably annually. The Chancellor of the Exchequer indicated in his Budget speech of April 1965 that the rate for 1965/66 was likely to be between 35 per cent and 40 per cent. Corporation tax is payable on 1st January each year.

Both before and after the advent of corporation tax a limited company is bound to deduct income tax from dividends. When income tax was payable on profits the amount deducted from dividends did not have to be accounted for to the Inland Revenue, because the deduction merely represented a portion of the tax which would be payable by the company. Since the shareholder had suffered tax on the dividend at the standard rate, he was not liable to pay tax again on that dividend in his personal assessment, but he could make a claim to the Inland Revenue for repayment if he was not liable to pay income tax at the standard rate.

When a company suffers corporation tax on its profits the income tax which it is still bound to deduct from dividends must be repaid to the Inland Revenue. Thus, before corporation tax the cost of a dividend to a company was the gross dividend less income tax; after corporation tax the cost of the dividend to the company was the gross cost. Corporation tax is therefore expressed to have the object of encouraging retentions of profit.

In this connection it may be pointed out that a company has been obliged, both before and after corporation tax, to deduct income tax from debenture interest paid, and to account for such tax deducted to the Inland Revenue.

6. Capital allowances

Although, as mentioned above, the depreciation of fixed assets charged in the accounts is not an allowable deduction from income for tax purposes, a business is entitled to deduct from its assessment to tax certain capital allowances, or allowances for capital expenditure. These allowances are based on the cost of (a) industrial buildings, and (b) plant and machinery, the latter expression having a wide meaning and referring also to instruments, vehicles and industrial equipment generally. Essentially three kinds of allowances may be claimed: an investment allowance, an initial allowance and an annual allowance (formerly known as a "wear and tear allowance"). The rates of allowances and the conditions under which they may be claimed have altered from time to time in relation to government taxation policy, but in 1965/66 the principal rates and conditions were as set out below.*

Investment allowance. The rate for industrial and agricultural buildings is 15 per cent of the cost; for industrial plant and machinery 30 per cent of the cost; and for new ships 40 per cent of the cost. The investment allowance is not applicable to second-hand plant and machinery (except that for second-hand ships an investment allowance of 30 per cent of cost may be obtained), nor to private cars. This allowance may be claimed in respect of the accounting period in which the expenditure on the asset was made, and is not deductible from the cost of the asset for the purpose of calculating initial or annual allowances. Because the whole cost of an asset will be covered eventually by the initial and annual allowances, the investment allowance provides, in effect, tax relief on a sum in excess of the cost of the asset, *i.e.* on new plant capital allowances will, in total, accumulate to 130 per cent of the cost of the asset.

Initial allowance. The rate for industrial and agricultural buildings is 5 per cent and for machinery and plant 10 per cent. This

* Readers are advised to refer to later legislation for the latest scale of allowances and to Command Paper 2874, issued by H.M. Stationery Office in January 1966 and entitled "Investment Incentives."

allowance is given in the year when the asset is acquired and paid for and is additional to the investment allowance, where that allowance is applicable. Where an investment allowance is not applicable, such as on second-hand plant and machinery, the initial allowance is increased to 30 per cent. The initial allowance must be deducted from the cost of the asset at the end of the first year for the purpose of calculating subsequent annual allowances.

Annual allowances. The rate for industrial buildings is 4 per cent, and for plant and machinery, according to the type of asset concerned, 15 per cent, 20 per cent or 25 per cent. This allowance is given for each year in which the asset is held. For the first year it is calculated on cost, so that in the first year in which a new item of plant is acquired it is possible to obtain tax relief covering the investment allowance, 30 per cent, the initial allowance, 10 per cent, and an annual allowance of, say, 25 per cent, totalling a possible 65 per cent of the cost of the asset.

In addition to the foregoing, balancing allowances and balancing charges will arise on the disposal by sale or otherwise of assets subject to capital allowances. The effect of these allowances and charges is to ensure that the total initial, annual allowances and balancing allowances or balancing changes, given in respect of an asset exactly agree with the net cost, after deducting the proceeds on sale from the cost.

An example of the application of capital allowances is set out below:

		£
A machine was bought in year 1 for		£5,000.
The capital allowances which could be set against the taxable profit for that year were:		
		£
Investment allowance—30 per cent .	.	1,500
Initial allowance—10 per cent .	.	500
Annual allowance, say 20 per cent .	.	1,000
Deduct from cost of asset . . .		1,500
(*Note:* The total allowances for year 1 were £3,000.)		
Written-down value at beginning of year 2 .		£3,500
Year 2		3,500
Annual allowance—20 per cent .	.	700
Written-down value at beginning of year 3 .		£2,800

Assume that at the beginning of year 3 the machine was sold for £2,500. The net cost of the machine was £5,000 − £2,500 = £2,500. Total initial and annual allowances amount, however, to £2,200, so that in the third year the taxable profit of the business will obtain a balancing allowance of £300.

7. Business losses

Tax losses, which may be increased by capital allowances, may be carried forward from year to year until there is sufficient profit to absorb them, but a loss so carried forward cannot be set off against the profits of another business operated by the taxpayer. So far as taxpayers liable to income tax are concerned, an actual loss as shown by the adjusted accounts in a particular year can be set off against the statutory income of that year. This situation would apply, for example, where a partnership made a taxable profit of £10,000 for its year ending 31st December 1964 and this profit was assessed for income tax for the fiscal year 1965/66. The adjusted accounts for the year ended 31st December 1965 showed, however, a tax loss of £6,000. The £6,000 can be set off against the assessment of £10,000, leaving the partnership liable to pay tax on £4,000 in 1965/66. Where corporate bodies have income-tax losses brought forward in 1965/66 those losses can be set off against subsequent profits chargeable to corporation tax.

8. Capital gains

The taxation of capital profits, *i.e.* profits on the sale of certain fixed assets, was first introduced by the Finance Act, 1962, and applied to assets acquired after 10th April 1962. The provisions of this Act excluded "tangible moveable property", so that its scope largely covered profits on the sale of landed property (but not the private residence of the taxpayer) and shares and securities. A profit on the sale of land and buildings was taxable if the sale took place within three years of acquisition, and on shares and securities if the sale occurred within six months of acquisition. There were numerous exceptions.

The provisions of the 1962 legislation continue to apply to the relative assets which were still held on 6th April 1965, but the Finance Bill published in that month considerably widened the scope of the capital-gains taxation. The 1965 legislation provided for the taxation of both short-term and long-term gains and extended the range of chargeable assets to include tangible moveable property, so that, subject to the exceptions indicated below, the general scope of the capital-gains tax now covers all forms of property, whenever acquired and wherever situated. The principal exceptions are: the private residence of the taxpayer; Savings Certificates, Premium Bonds, Defence Bonds and National Development Bonds; the liquidation of life policies; chattels sold for no more than £1,000; objects of national interest sold to a national institution; the first £5,000 of net gains accrued at death; gifts up to £100; and private cars.

The provisions of the 1962 legislation will eventually cease to apply. The budget proposals of 1965, however, apply a short-term gains tax to the wider class of assets acquired after 6th April 1965 and disposed of within twelve months of acquisition. The profit made on the sale of assets falling within the scope of the 1965 short-term gains tax provisions will be treated as income in the hands of individuals and corporate bodies; thus, individuals may be liable to pay income tax and surtax on these gains, and corporate bodies will be liable to pay corporation tax (at a fixed rate of 35 per cent in 1965/66).

The long-term gains taxation introduced by the Finance Bill of 1965 taxes capital profits made by individuals or corporate bodies where the assets are disposed of twelve months or longer after acquisition. These provisions apply to chargeable assets acquired at any time, e.g., before and after 6th April 1965. It is, however, only that proportion of the gain which accrued after 6th April 1965 which needs to be taken into account. The rate of tax chargeable on long-term gains is 30 per cent in the case of individuals and the current rate of corporation tax in the case of corporate bodies. Individuals may elect to be charged at their highest rate of income tax and surtax on two-thirds of the gain. In assessing the value of the asset concerned at 6th April 1965 quoted shares and securities are valued at the quotation; development land needs actual valuation; and the value of other assets may be arrived at by apportioning the profit on a time basis. In all cases the actual valuation can be used, if the taxpayer so elects.

Where assets are replaced the gain is applied to reducing the price of the new assets, so that no tax on the gain is payable until there is no replacement. The cost of plant, machinery and leases of up to fifty years is taken as the written-down value, so that a taxable gain will arise if the price on disposal exceeds the written-down value.

Losses under the short-term gains provisions can be set off

against profits chargeable under the same provisions; and likewise losses under the long-term gains provisions can be set off against profits under those provisions; but in neither case can capital losses be set off against trading profits.

9. A specimen computation

The following simplified computation is intended to illustrate the method of computing the taxable profit of a business, and the difference between the profit for normal accounting purposes and for tax purposes.

The Trading and Profit and Loss Account of a manufacturing company showed the following figures for its accounting year:

	£	£
SALES		112,000
Less Direct cost of sales (including depreciation of £10,000)		40,000
GROSS MARGIN		72,000
Less Administrative and selling expenses, including the following:		
Legal expenses on the purchase of property	5,000	
Loss on sale of plant	1,000	
Provision for doubtful debts, at 5 per cent of debtors	1,250	
Charitable subscriptions not connected with the trade	250	
	£7,500	
		20,000
OPERATING PROFIT		52,000
Less Debenture interest, gross	4,000	
Preliminary expenses written off . . .	6,000	
Loss on sale of investments. . . .	500	
	£ 10,500	
Deduct Defence Bond interest . . . 300		
Bank deposit interest . . . 200		
	500	
		10,000
PRETAX PROFIT		42,000
Tax provision		20,000
NET PROFIT FOR THE PERIOD . . .		22,000
Balance of profit brought forward . . .		2,000
AVAILABLE PROFIT		24,000
Less Recommended ordinary dividend at 10 per cent on £80,000	8,000	
To general reserve	15,000	
		23,000
BALANCE OF PROFIT CARRIED FORWARD . .		£1,000

Note that when a corporate body was subject to income tax on its profits the ordinary dividend would have been shown at the net figure after deducting income tax.

The tax computation based on this account will then take the following form:

	£	£
Profit per accounts (pretax)		42,000
Add back:		
Depreciation	10,000	
Legal expenses of a capital nature . .	5,000	
General provision	1,250	
Charitable subscriptions	250	
Capital loss on plant	1,000	
Capital loss on investments	500	
Preliminary expenses, being of a capital nature	6,000	
		24,000
		£66,000
Deduct:		
Defence Bond interest, taxable under Case III	300	
Bank deposit interest, taxable under Case III	200	
		500
Assessable profit		65,500
Deduct Capital allowances, say		15,500
		£50,000

The company would bear tax under Case I of Schedule D on the £50,000, under Case III on the Defence Bond and bank-deposit interest (which would have been received gross) and may be liable for capital-gains tax on the capital profits on the sale of the plant and the investments. In addition, the company would be obliged to repay to the Inland Revenue the income tax which it would deduct from the debenture interest and the dividends.

Authors' Note. Since writing the above the Selective Employment Tax has been introduced. For details of this important new form of taxation readers are recommended to refer to Command Paper 2986 entitled "Selective Employment Tax" and issued by H.M. Stationery Office in May 1966 and to the Finance Acts 1966 and onwards.

QUESTIONS

CHAPTER II

1. Explain concisely why in your opinion it is necessary for (*a*) a Marketing Manager and (*b*) a Works Manager to be familiar with the principles of accounting.

2. Explain (*a*) the distinction between Capital and Revenue for accounting purposes and (*b*) the meaning of "double entry".

3. As the Manager of a small business, draft a short memorandum to your accountant setting out the principles which you wish him to follow in dealing with cash transactions, with the particular objects of preventing losses and achieving administrative economy.

4. Distinguish between:

   (i) Issued Capital;
   (ii) Called-up Capital;
   (iii) Paid-up Capital.

5. List three categories of fixed assets and three categories of current assets for any type of business you select, stating the nature of the business concerned.

6. What is the purpose of the trial balance and what type of error will it *not* disclose?

7. Rule a Petty Cash Book with columns for Postage and Telegrams, Cleaning, Stationery, Travelling and Sundries. Enter therein the following:

				£
Jan.	1	Balance in hand	. . . . . .	10·00
„	1	Bought postage stamps	. . . .	2·50
„	2	Paid travelling expenses	. . . .	2·10
„	3	Bought string and envelopes	. . . .	0·50
„	3	Paid for staff teas	. . . .	0·25
„	5	Paid cleaners	. . . .	1·00
„	5	Sent telegram costing	. . . .	0·23
„	5	Paid for window cleaning	. . . .	0·65
„	6	Received imprest balance from cashier.		

8. W. Caxton started in business as a printer on 1st March with a capital of £1,000 cash in the bank, and his transactions for the first month were as follows:

£

Mar. 2 Drew out of bank for petty cash 100
  „ 3 Paid one month's rent in advance by cheque . . . 30
  „ 4 Purchased stock of paper and printing supplies on credit from
        Pulp Co. Ltd. 200
  „ 5 Bought from Printing Equipment Co. Ltd., furniture and fit-
        tings on credit but subject to a deposit of 10% paid by cheque 500
  „ 7 Paid wages in cash 40
  „ 8 Drew a cheque for self 50
  „ 9 Sales on credit to Stationery Supplies Co. 60
  „ 10 Paid sundry expenses in cash 20
  „ 11 Made up petty cash to original amount by cashing a cheque at
        the bank
  „ 12 Sales on credit to Sales Circulars Co. Ltd. 150
  „ 13 Paid Pulp Co. Ltd. by cheque on account 100
  „ 14 Paid wages in cash 40
  „ 18 Sales Circulars paid their account by cheque which was paid
        into the bank
  „ 20 Stationery Supplies Co. paid in cash 30
  „ 21 Paid wages in cash 40
  „ 22 Obtained a loan of £200 from Printers' Credit Co., their
        cheque being paid into the bank
  „ 24 Purchased further equipment from Printing Equipment Co.
        Ltd. for £400 and paid them by cheque £500 on account
  „ 26 Sales for cash to various customers 50
  „ 28 Drew out of cash for self 20
  „ 30 Made up cash to original £100 by drawing from bank

You are required to write up W. Caxton's accounts for the month, distinguishing between "capital" and "revenue" accounts, and to prepare a Trial Balance as at the end of the month. No Profit and Loss Account or Balance Sheet is required.

9. Give an example of one transaction in each of the following cases:

(*a*) increase one asset and decrease another;
(*b*) increase an asset and increase a liability;
(*c*) increase an asset and increase proprietors' capital;
(*d*) decrease an asset and decrease a liability;
(*e*) decrease an asset and decrease proprietors' capital;
(*f*) increase a liability and decrease capital.

10. Your Company assigns you the task of opening a branch for the purpose of buying and selling second-hand motor cars and places £6,000 in a local bank for you to draw on in the course of business.

(*a*) During the first year of operations all your transactions are in cash drawn from or paid into the bank. You buy cars for £12,000 and pay expenses of £1,500. Sales amounted to £11,000. At the end of the year you have a stock of unsold cars for which you paid £6,000. All equipment is provided by your head office, so that no depreciation is involved.

What was the profit or loss during the first year?

(b) In the second year sales amounted to £15,000, but the customers actually paid in cash only £10,000, leaving the balance (which you expected to obtain in due course) owing on a month's credit. Purchases of cars cost £8,000, and were all paid for in cash, and overhead expenses, also paid in cash, were £1,700. You bought a van for business use at a cost of £500, and you estimated that this van would last for five years and then have no residual value. You obtain a loan from the bank of £1,000, but by the end of the year you had repaid £200 of this loan, the interest being included in the overhead expenses of £1,700. The stock of unsold cars at the end of the year was valued at the original cost of £2,000.

What was the profit or loss in the second year and what was the capital employed at the end of that year?

(c) If, during the second year, Head Office had been paid the profit made in the first year, how would this have altered the answers to (b) above?

CHAPTER III

1. From the following Trial Balance prepare a Trading and Profit and Loss Account and a Balance Sheet:

The following Trial Balance was extracted from the books of A. Donaldson on 31st December 1961:

	£	£
Capital 1st January 1961		16,124
Premises	5,000	
Advertising	127	
Motor vans	927	
Purchases	68,485	
Postage	138	
Lighting and heating	91	
Salaries	2,837	
Rates and water	101	
Telephone	34	
Furniture	1,104	
Sales		73,498
Returns	56	392
Bad debts	26	
Insurance	192	
Commissions received		1,750
Debtors	4,882	
Creditors		8,405
Cash in hand	352	
Balance with bank	3,792	
Stock 1st January 1961	12,025	
	£100,169	£100,169

Prepare Trading and Profit and Loss Accounts for the year ending 31st December 1961 and a Balance Sheet at that date, taking into account the following:

(i) The Stock at 31st December 1961 was £10,787.

(ii) Depreciation to be written off as follows—

Premises at 5 per cent;
£200 off value of motor vans;
10 per cent off furniture (to nearest £).

(iii) Provide £300 against possible future bad debts.

(iv) Telephone Account owing, £22.

(v) Rates paid in advance, £15.

2. An investor, who has no knowledge of business, receives a number of annual accounts from the companies in which he has investments. He asks you to advise him in simple but practical language how he can assess the financial position of the companies from the accounts he receives. Draft your reply.

3. Give a short account of stages necessary in an accounting system, making clear the circumstances in which you would introduce subsidiary books of original entry.

4. Explain the objects of the following accounts and indicate the principal entries you would expect to see in such accounts:

(a) Manufacturing Account;
(b) Operating Account;
(c) Trading Account;
(d) Profit and Loss Account;
(e) Appropriation Account.

5. Simplicity Vehicles Ltd. values its work in progress on the basis of direct labour and direct materials, including sub-contracted work and bought-out parts, but excludes all overheads from the valuation. Examine the merits and demerits of this method of valuation.

6. From the following Trial Balance and other information draw up statements showing cost of production, gross profit, net profit, appropriations and a statement of the financial position at the end of the year.

Manufacturing Enterprises Ltd.
Trial Balance at 31st March 1961

	£	£
Authorised and issued capital:		
20,000 Ordinary Shares of £1 each . . .		20,000
Stock of raw materials	2,000	
Stock of finished goods	2,600	
Work in progress	3,000	
Depreciation reserve—plant		8,000
Depreciation reserve—other fixed assets . . .		6,000
Sales		15,000
Purchases of raw materials	1,000	
Sales of scrap.		500
Plant at cost	20,000	
Other fixed assets at cost	12,000	
Direct labour.	800	
Selling expenses	2,100	
Returns inwards	100	
Share premium account		5,000
General reserve		4,000
Bought out parts	600	
Production overheads	800	
Debtors	2,800	
Creditors		1,800
Administrative expenses	800	
Distribution expenses	400	
Cash in hand	1,600	
Provision for bad debts		100
Bills payable		300
Financial expenses	700	
Goodwill	11,400	
Tax reserve		500
Profit and Loss Account		1,500
	£62,700	£62,700

The following adjustments were made in the accounts after the above Trial Balance was extracted:

 (*a*) Stocks at the end of the year:

	£
raw materials	1,500
work in progress	2,200
finished goods	1,700

 (*b*) Addition to tax reserve 2,700

 (*c*) Recommended dividend (ignore taxation) . 3,800

CHAPTER IV

1. Enter the following transactions in the appropriate accounts, charging depreciation on the reducing balance method at the rate of 5 per cent per annum:

1st January 1959. Balance on plant and machinery account, at cost, £5,000.

1st January, 1959. Balance on depreciation reserve account, £800.

1st July, 1959. Purchased additional machinery for £2,000.

1st January, 1960. Sold surplus plant originally purchased for £1,000 and depreciated to the extent of £900 for £120.

Accounts are made up to the 31st December in each year and depreciation should be charged for the two years 1959 and 1960.

2. The owner of a small business who has not had a commercial training asks you why it is necessary to charge depreciation in the accounts. Draft a clear and concise reply.

3. A manufacturing business is contemplating the purchase of new machinery at a cost of £2,000 and asks you to show the comparative effect of (a) writing off the machine on the straight line basis over 5 years, and (b) charging depreciation on the reducing balance method at 25 per cent per annum. Set out the comparative figures for 5 years and comment on the respective merits and demerits of the two methods.

4. Owing to rapid developments in the electronics industry a manufacturer of test equipment finds that plant and instruments are rapidly becoming obsolescent and replacements tend to cost more than the original assets. The manufacturer wishes, therefore, to provide for the estimated higher cost of replacing the plant concerned. Explain fully what accounting arrangements you would recommend to satisfy the manufacturer's wishes.

5. A business purchased a machine for £1,000 on 1st January and estimated its useful life at 3 years, at the end of which the scrap value was expected to be £100. In fact, the machine was sold exactly two years after purchase for £75. Using the straight-line method of depreciation, show the ledger accounts recording these transactions.

6. Describe the operation and purpose of three methods of depreciating fixed assets.

7. Discuss the following statement: "Despite a declining gross profit margin we have been able to maintain net profits by charging less depreciation than in former years."

8. Cosmic Engineers intend to acquire on 1st January next a set of transfer machines at a cost of £55,000, and the estimated life of the machines will be five years, with no residual value. With a view to retaining sufficient funds in the business to replace the installation at the end of the five years, and having regard to inflation of machinery prices at the rate of 5 per cent per annum, the directors express the wish to provide for depreciation on the basis of the estimated cost of replacing the machines.

You are required to state how you would deal with the directors' requirements in the annual accounts and to set out a statement for the five years comparing: (a) depreciation on the basis of original cost, and (b) provision for replacement cost in accordance with the directors' wishes.

CHAPTER V

1. What do you understand by the slip system of posting records?

2. Design a ledger card suitable for customers' accounts kept on manual posting equipment.

3. What are the advantages of using book-keeping machines?

4. What is the main cycle of operations in punched-card accounting?

5. Explain the operation and use of a posting board in connection with the Sales Ledger of a small firm.

6. Discuss the extent to which electronic computers can improve efficiency in the accounting department.

7. Set out in brief your suggestions for effecting clerical cost reduction in the offices of a manufacturing company.

CHAPTER VI

1. What is a partnership?

2. For what reasons might a sole trader decide to enter into partnership?

3. Draw up a form of Partnership Agreement to cover a small business with which you are familiar.

4. What are the legal limitations on the number of partners in a firm?

5. What do you understand by goodwill?

6. What are the defects of the partnership form of business unit?

7. Jones and Robinson are in partnership with capitals of £6,000 and £3,000 respectively. The credit balances in their current accounts at the beginning of the year were Jones, £500, and Robinson, £500. Net profit for the year is £1,200 divided in proportion to capital.

Interest on capital is allowed at 5 per cent per annum, and Jones is entitled to be credited with a salary of £750. During the year Jones has drawn £1,800 in cash and £90 in goods, and Robinson has drawn £500 in cash.

Draw up their Current Accounts at the end of the year.

(*Solution*: Balances—Jones, £460; Robinson, £550.)

8. J. Masters and B. Burton are in partnership under the name of Masters & Company, their capitals are Masters, £3,000, and Burton, £1,000. Credit with interest at 5 per cent.

They share profits equally, and Masters is entitled to be credited with a salary of £400 per annum. During the year they have drawn in cash: Masters, £1,600; Burton, £1,000. In addition, car expenses chargeable personally to Masters to the amount of £150 have been charged to the Repairs Account in the firm's books, and Burton has taken goods value £50, which have been credited to sales.

Write up their Capital and Current Accounts, taking into account that at the beginning of the year there were credit balances on current accounts of Masters, £550, and Burton, £150. Also show the Balance Sheet entries. Profit remaining after above, £1,900.

9. What are the important provisions of the Partnership Act, 1890, with regard to partners and their entitlements at the end of a financial year? In what circumstances do these provisions of the Act apply?

10. The following is the Balance Sheet of Alpha and Beta, who are in partnership:

Balance Sheet as at 31st December 1961

Capitals:	£		£
Alpha	5,000	Fixed Assets . . .	6,000
Beta	3,000	Current Assets . . .	4,000
Creditors	2,000		
	£10,000		£10,000

The Profits for the recent years are as follows:

		£
1958	. . . . .	2,000
1959	. . . . .	2,600
1960	. . . . .	1,800
1961	. . . . .	2,400

Calculate the value of the goodwill of the business by the "super-profits" method, and assuming a normal rate of 12 per cent per annum and 5 years purchase.

11. Higgins and Mallard are in partnership sharing profits $\frac{2}{3}$ and $\frac{1}{3}$ respectively. They decide to dissolve partnership and realise the assets. The firm's Balance Sheet at date of dissolution was:

Balance Sheet as at 31st December 1961

Capitals:	£		£
Higgins . . .	3,000	Assets	1,800
Mallard . . .	500	Stock	2,450
Creditors . . .	1,200	Cash	450
	£4,700		£4,700

The assets realised £1,400 and the stock £1,450. Expenses amounted to £190. Prepare the necessary accounts, assuming the partners settled in cash.

CHAPTER VII

1. What do you understand by the term "Limited Liability"?

2. Why are the shares of companies divided into such classifications as "Ordinary", "Preference" and "Deferred"?

3. Distinguish between a "Memorandum of Association" and "Articles of Association". What is "Table A"?

4. How does a company deal in its accounts with:

(*a*) an oversubscription of shares;

(*b*) calls in arrear;

(*c*) calls in advance.

5. What is a Share Premium Account?

6. Enumerate the statutory and other books which a company must keep.

7. Assuming the total revenue of a company is £100,000, prepare an Appropriation Account from the percentages shown in Fig. 4, page 143.

8. Prepare a Balance Sheet to illustrate the diagrams shown in Fig. 5, on page 143.

9. What is a holding company?

10. What would be the functions of a Financial Controller in a large company?

11. What is a "private company"? What are the advantages of registering as a private company?

12. X.Y.Z. Co. Ltd. commenced business on 1st January 1968. Its Authorised Capital was 50,000 Ordinary Shares of £1 each and 100,000 5 per cent Preference Shares of £1 each. It had issued 50,000 of each class of share and they were fully paid.

On the 31st December 1968 the following balances were extracted from its books:

Share Capital:	£	£
Ordinary Shares		50,000
Preference Shares		50,000
6 per cent Debentures		20,000
Share Premium Account		10,000
Purchases	132,000	
Sales		147,000
Directors' Fees	2,500	
Debenture Interest	1,200	
Other Expenses	7,000	
Interest Received		200
Preliminary Expenses	4,000	
Trade Creditors		1,000
Debtors	6,000	
Bank	5,500	
Premises	60,000	
Machinery	30,000	
Goodwill	30,000	
	£278,200	£278,200

You are required to prepare Trading and Profit and Loss Accounts for the year, and a Balance Sheet at 31st December 1968, after taking into account the following:

(1) Provide for a dividend on Ordinary and Preference Shares at 5 per cent per annum.

(2) Transfer £4,000 to General Reserve.
(3) Write off the Preliminary Expenses.
(4) Depreciate Machinery at 10 per cent per annum.
(5) Stock at 31st December 1968, £12,000.

13. (*a*) What is the object of preparing a Consolidated Balance Sheet?

(*v*) Prepare a Consolidated Balance Sheet of Major Ltd. and Minor Ltd. From the following:

BALANCE SHEET OF MAJOR LTD.

	£		£
Capital in shares of £1 each	15,000	Fixed assets . . .	7,000
Creditors . . .	5,250	Current assets . . .	6,250
		Loan to Minor Ltd. . .	2,000
		Investment in Minor Ltd., 4,000 Shares at cost .	5,000
	£20,250		£20,250

BALANCE SHEET OF MINOR LTD.

	£		£
Capital in shares of £1 each	6,000	Fixed assets . . .	6,500
Creditors	1,525	Current assets . . .	3,025
Loan from Major Ltd. .	2,000		
	£9,525		£9,525

14. Explain briefly what you understand by the following terms:

(*a*) debentures;
(*b*) share premiums and discounts;
(*c*) Table A;
(*d*) circle graphs;
(*e*) minority interests.

15. A motor haulage company plans to enlarge its activities by covering a wider area of the United Kingdom and for this purpose needs an additional £500,000 to buy vehicles and to erect further depots. The funds will be required in three stages spread over the next two years, but at the end of seven years it is calculated that a surplus of working capital above normal requirements will result.

Discuss the type of capital which should be raised and the sources from which it might be obtained.

16. With a view to diversification your Company is considering the acquisition of a controlling interest in a smaller company operating in a related field. You are asked to examine the published accounts of the company to be taken over and to report on its financial position. State the principal matters to which you would direct your attention and indicate what, if any, further information not normally disclosed in published accounts you might require for the purpose.

CHAPTER VIII

1. A limited company with a capital employed of about £750,000 and some 2,000 employees produces and sells direct to farms in the United Kingdom, various fertilisers. The managing director receives from the accountant regular statements of sales, unit costs, orders and cash holdings, but detailed accounts are prepared half yearly only. The managing director requests your advice in general terms as to whether monthly accounts would assist him in controlling the business and increasing profits. Draft a brief reply.

2. The rateable value of the property owned by a business is £600 per annum and the current rate in the pound is 18s. 6d. (£0·925). Rates are payable on 1st April and 1st October in each year covering the ensuing six months, and the business makes the payments on the due dates. Monthly accounts are prepared. Show the relevant ledger accounts and indicate the entries to be made in the balance sheets for the months of April, May and June.

3. Indicate the ratios or other factors of measurement which would assist management in appraising the following: (a) stocks; (b) debtors; (c) profit in relation to capital; and (d) liquid resources.

4. What statistics can the financial department provide for the personnel manager?

5. What is a Gantt Chart?

6. Prepare a Z Chart from the following information. The sales of the Acme Co. Ltd. were as follows:

	1967 £	1968 £
January	2,500	2,600
February	2,800	2,200
March	3,000	2,200
April	2,500	2,400
May	2,500	2,500
June	3,000	2,700
July	3,100	2,300
August	3,000	2,600
September	2,500	2,500
October	2,700	2,000
November	2,500	2,100
December	2,900	2,900

(Submit tabular working statement.)

7. Write an essay of about 400 words on the subject of "How Accounting Can Aid Management".

8. From the following information prepare the Manufacturing and Trading Accounts of the X.Y. Manufacturing Co. Ltd. for the year ended 31st December 1968:

	£
Sales	90,239
Purchases of raw materials . . .	24,520
Factory wages	22,750
Depreciation of machinery . . .	1,750
Fuel and power	10,650
Factory rent	5,700
Factory expenses	2,200
Carriage inwards	2,000
Returns to suppliers	450
Returns from customers . . .	740
Warehouse expenses charged to Trading account	2,000
Stocks:	
1.1.68	
Raw Material	6,500
Finished Goods	5,200
31.12.68	
Raw Material	5,020
Finished Goods	5,800
Work in progress	
31.12.68	1,620
31.12.67	1,400

9. What is meant by "capital employed"? Give a specimen computation of capital employed for a public limited company with loan capital, a bank overdraft and preliminary expenses not yet written off.

M

10. InterUniversal Printers Ltd is the holding company of a group and has an authorised capital of 6,000,000 ordinary shares of 5s. (£0·25) each and 1,000,000 6½ per cent Preference shares of £1 each. After drawing up the consolidated Profit and Loss Account the group balances stand on the books were as set out below. You are required to prepare a statement of the financial position of the group in a form which a shareholder without an accountancy training can understand, noting what additional information may be required to conform with the requirements of the Companies Act.

	£ million
Preference shares	0·6
Land and buildings at cost	16·5
Proposed dividends	0·5
Cash in hand	0·2
Ordinary shares	4·6
Plant and machinery, at cost	8·4
Overdraft	5·2
Bills receivable	0·6
Share Premium Account	1·5
Depreciation provision—land and buildings	6·0
Debtors	4·2
Current taxation	0·6
General reserve	5·0
Depreciation provision—plant and machinery	2·0
Prepaid expenses and deposits	0·5
Bills payable	0·6
Balance on Profit and Loss Account	1·1
Trade investments	0·8
Creditors	5·0
Accrued expenses	0·5
Minority interests	5·1
Quoted investments	1·0
5½ per cent Debenture stock	4·0
Stocks and work in progress	7·5
Goodwill	2·6

11. A successful private limited company retails groceries through twelve shops in various districts in and around Manchester. The new Managing Director has drawn up a ten-year plan for opening large self-service stores in Manchester and the principal northern industrial towns. Each store is expected to involve a capital investment of around £30,000–£40,000, and only the first of these projects can be financed out of the company's resources. The Board of Directors request your advice as to the basis on which they should gauge the financial merits of the plan. State what information you would require for this purpose and draft your advice to the Directors.

12. Male Toiletries Ltd. have a machine which produces the

caps for a certain type of container. Owing to a rapid rise in demand they are having to buy out additional caps at a price of 1s. each. The existing machine cost £5,000 when it was bought two years ago, and it is being depreciated at £500 a year. It is capable of producing 20,000 caps a year at a variable cost of 1d. a cap. Fixed costs are £100 a year. The Production Manager submits a proposal for purchasing a new machine at a cost of £7,500 less the saleable value of the old machine, which is £3,000. The new machine will produce 40,000 units a year, which is approximately the output required; its variable costs will be only ½d. per cap, and fixed costs will remain at £100 a year. The Production Manager urges immediate action, as he expects the resale price of the old machine to fall to £2,600 by the end of the year.

You are required to report to the Managing Director whether, on the basis of the information available, the Production Manager's proposal should be adopted.

13. On the basis of the following Balance Sheet and notes you are asked to draw up proposals for reorganising the finances of Spendthrift Textiles Ltd., and to draw up a statement of the financial position of the Company as it would appear after your proposals had been carried out.

Spendthrift Textiles Ltd.
Balance Sheet as at 31st March, 19...

Left hand side

	£	£
Authorised capital		
3,000,000 7½ per cent Cumulative Preference Shares of £1		3,000,000
4,000,000 Ordinary Shares of £1		4,000,000
		£7,000,000
Issued Capital		
2,500,000 7½ per cent Cumulative Preference Shares of £1, fully paid		2,500,000
3,400,000 Ordinary Shares of £1, fully paid.		3,400,000
		£5,900,000
5½ *per cent Debenture Stock* secured by a Trust Deed on the land and buildings		2,700,000
Current Liabilities		
Creditors, including accrued debenture interest and and other accruals	2,600,000	
Overdraft	400,000	
		3,000,000
		£11,600,000

Right-hand side

	£	£
Fixed Assets		
Land and buildings, at cost		2,900,000
Plant and equipment, at cost	6,400,000	
Less Depreciation	3,700,000	
		2,700,000
Net total fixed assets		£5,600,000
Goodwill, patents and trade marks, at cost . .		500,000
Investments, quoted (market value £1,000,000). .		1,500,000
Current Assets		
Stock and work in progress	1,600,000	
Debtors and prepayments	1,100,000	
Bills receivable	790,000	
Cash in hand	10,000	
		3,500,000
Profit and Loss Account		500,000
		£11,600,000

Spendthrift Ltd.
Notes on the Financial and Trading Position

1. Turnover has fallen over the last five years from around £10,000,000 to £6,000,000 p.a., due to a decline in the market for natural fibres.

2. Net profits and losses over the last five years have been as follows:

		£
5 years ago		700,000 profit
4 years ago		(350,000) loss
3 years ago		(10,000) loss
2 years ago		(500,000) loss
Last year		(650,000) loss

3. The fixed assets have recently been revalued on a going-concern basis at the following figures:

	£
Land and buildings	3,400,000
Plant and equipment	2,200,000
Stock and work in progress . . .	1,100,000
Goodwill	Nil

4. The Directors are convinced that, subject to a sound reorganisation of the Company's finances and the acquisition of further plant at a cost of £1,465,000, future net profits will be at least as follows:

	£
Next year	10,000
2nd year	500,000
3rd year	700,000
4th year	1,000,000

These profits are before taxation (but there are accumulated tax losses of £1,500,000) and before payment of interest on any permanent capital.

5. The bank are pressing for repayment of the overdraft; the Debenture-holders' interest is one year in arrear, and the trustees have given the directors a month to produce proposals for correcting the situation before taking action to protect the Debenture-holders' interests. The dividends of the Preference Shareholders are two years in arrear, and these shareholders now have full voting rights.

14. The following Balance Sheet is for the Waxman Co. Ltd., as at 31st December 1968. From this Balance Sheet you are required to prepare a Funds-flow Statement.

The Waxman Co. Ltd.
Balance Sheet as at 31st December 1968
000s omitted

1967 £		1968 £	1967 £		1968 £
	Issued capital:			*Fixed assets:*	
8,703	Ordinary Shares	8,703	777	Land and buildings . .	774
3,603	7% Preference Shares . .	3,603		Plant, *less* depreciation . .	14,293
9,773	Revenue reserves	10,175	11,787	Vehicles, *less* depreciation .	3,449
549	5% Debentures.	610	3,149	Investments:	
	Current Liabilities:		197	Government securities . .	210
3,397	Creditors . .	3,753		Other investments—	
24	Bank loan . .	31	3,267	Quoted .	1,064
	Proposed dividends . .		2,620	Unquoted .	280
259	dends . .	259		Current assets:	
5,097	Taxation . .	2,750	2,334	Cash . .	2,149
			2,528	Debtors . .	2,637
			3,998	Stocks . .	4,247
			748	Prepaid expenses	781
£31,405		£29,884	£31,405		£29,884

CHAPTER IX

1. The manufacturers of vehicle accessories find that costs are rising and employees becoming redundant owing to a recession in the industry. Subject to a limited expenditure on re-tooling, additional sales can be made in the Continent of Europe, but the best prices that can be obtained in that market are below total costs, including normal allocations of all overhead expenses. Summarise the matters which you would wish to take into consideration when examining the proposal to enter the European market in these circumstances.

2. A company assembling components for the electronics industry "recovers" its factory and administrative overheads by applying a rate of 150 per cent on direct labour, this rate having been calculated from last year's figures. Owing to a sudden increase in demand from one of the principal customers, who has received a large government contract, considerable overtime is being worked and the whole cost of the overtime is treated as

direct labour. The accountant now finds that the actual overhead rate has fallen to 110 per cent. Discuss whether, in your view, the percentage to be applied to direct labour as a "recovery" of overheads should be amended to 110 per cent.

3. Suggest cost units appropriate to the following organisations: (a) an assembly shop; (b) a foundry; (c) an arable farm; (d) a self-service store; (e) a passenger aircraft line.

4. Explain clearly the difference between job costing, process costing and contract costing.

5. A rapidly developing business manufactures and sells to the wholesale trade a very successful and simple ball-point pen. No unit costing is carried out as the owner/manager maintains that all operations are under his personal control. Draft a brief report to the owner stating the objects of a costing system and indicating the extent to which the installation of such a system in his business might be desirable.

CHAPTER X

1. To what extent, in your opinion, should prices be based on recorded costs?

2. What are the objectives of premium-bonus schemes? Illustrate your answer by comparing the Halsey and Rowan systems in the following case: The time allowed for a job is 20 hours, and the basic rate is $17\frac{1}{2}$p an hour, a workman completes the job in 12 hours.

3. Describe the organisation of a stores routine for a medium-sized factory. Illustrate your answer with diagrams of any forms or records which you consider essential.

4. Draw up a suitable form to be used for price fixing in any business with which you are familiar.

5. Explain fully the meaning of the expression "cost centre" as used in costing.

6. Examine the comparative effect on profits of using the F.I.F.O. and L.I.F.O. methods of valuing material issues.

7. Explain the principles and methods used for applying overheads to cost units in any business with which you are familiar.

8. The general manager of a jobbing engineering works employing 1,000 personnel asks your advice as to the advantages to be derived from installing a standard costing system. Draft your reply.

9. Prepare a standard costing statement for any manufacturing operation with which you are familiar, and show the variances analysed as appropriate.

10. Discuss whether and to what extent overheads should be included in the valuation of work in progress.

11. Why is it important to segregate fixed, variable and semi-variable costs?

12. Explain the process by means of which standard labour times are assessed for standard costing purposes.

13. You have been asked to consider a proposed change in the method used by your company in valuing its stocks and work in progress and in the pricing of material requisitions. In the past the business has been using the "First in First Out" method and the proposal is that the "Last In First Out" method should be used instead. The following is a statement of the purchases and issues from stores during the first six months of the year. No stock was held at 1st January.

					Purchases	Issues
January	.	.	.	.	1,000 units at £5·00	
February	.	.	.	.	2,000 units at £5·50	
March .	.	.	.	.	1,000 units at £6·00	1,000 units
April	.	.	.	.	2,000 units at £6·50	3,000 units
May	.	.	.	.		1,000 units
June	.	.	.	.	1,500 units at £7·50	

Prepare a statement showing (a) the value at which the issues will be charged, and (b) the value of the closing stock, under both F.I.F.O. and L.I.F.O. methods.

Prepare also a policy recommendation containing a comparison of the two methods.

14. A manufacturer of household equipment finds that during recurrent slumps unit costs tend to rise, thus resulting in an over-valuation of stocks, which therefore need heavy depreciation at the end of a year in which a slump in the market occurs. Costing is on an "historical" basis and includes various machine-hour rates designed to recover the cost of the machines, their operatives, power, space, etc., over the anticipated hours of usage. Labour costs are calculated at an hourly rate which includes an allocation of current overheads applicable to labour. Material is costed on average cost basis.

Submit your recommendations for avoiding the difficulties inherent in the present system of costing.

15. The standard cost of a certain article, based on the production of 15,000 units a month, was as follows:

		£
Labour—3 man-hours at 25p an hour	=	0·75
Material—5 lb at 50p per pound	=	2·50
Overheads—at £1 per man-hour	=	3·00
Total unit cost	=	£6·25

During a certain month the following actual figures were recorded: when output was 12,000 units:

	£
Direct Labour—48,000 man-hours—cost . .	9,600
Material—66,000 lb used—cost . . .	36,300
Overheads	44,000

Draw up a statement showing the variances which occurred during the month.

16. An engineering works is asked to quote for a machining job which it is estimated will occupy one operative earning 25p an hour on one machine for 12 hours. In estimating it is the practice of the business to add to direct costs 40p per hour to cover factory overheads, to add 10 per cent to factory costs to cover general administration and selling and 12½ per cent on total costs for profit.

Information applicable to the machine is as follows:

Cost, £5,000.
Estimated life, 10 years.
Estimated scrap value, £200.
Area occupied, 500 sq. ft.
Normal operating hours, 8 per day.
Assume 250 working days in a year, but allow 10 per cent for idle time for maintenance.
Insurance is at 12½p per cent p.a.
Rent and rates costs 50p per sq. foot.
Electric power costs 5p per hour.
Electric light costs 2½p per hour.
Maintenance costs £500 p.a.
Consumable stores cost £44 p.a.

You are required to set out the estimate for the job.

17. A British company manufacturing tape recorders and hitherto selling exclusively in the United Kingdom has spare capacity sufficient to add 25 per cent to its output. Owing to market conditions, it is considered that no substantial expansion of

sales can be made in the United Kingdom, and the company is contemplating absorbing the excess capacity by selling on the continent.

	£
The present annual rate of sales is	800,000
Variable costs are	200,000
Fixed costs are	560,000

The General Sales manager estimates that prices for continental sales must be 50 per cent lower than United Kingdom prices, the continental buyer paying for export packing, freight and insurance and that, to prevent the re-export to the United Kingdom of products sold on the Continent, prices in the home market must be reduced by 10 per cent.

Briefly advise the Company whether their proposals for absorbing excess capacity are financially worth while.

18. Last year's results for a division of a manufacturing company are summarised as follows:

	£
Sales	570,000
Variable costs	380,000
Contribution	190,000
Fixed costs	180,000
Profit	£10,000

Assuming no change is made in the sales price or in the ratio of variable costs to sales or in the amount of the fixed costs, you are required to answer the following questions:

(a) What is the break-even level of sales?
(b) What sales are required to produce a profit of £25,000?
(c) What profit should be achieved if sales were £720,000?

19. For a particular month in the year the budgets for a workshop included fixed overheads at £12,000 for an output of 4,000 units, for each of which the standard time was 2 man-hours. The actual figures recorded at the end of the month were:

	£
Fixed overhead cost	14,000
Output	5,000
Man-hours	11,000

You are required to calculate the following fixed overhead variances:

(*a*) Expenditure;
(*b*) Volume;
(*c*) Efficiency; and
(*d*) Capacity.

CHAPTER XI

1. What is Budgetary Control? Describe the methods to be adopted in the formation of a Master Budget.

2. Describe briefly the various stages in the compilation of a sales budget for a manufacturing company marketing consumer products.

3. How would you assess a profit target for a large public limited company? What adjustments would be required to the periodical profit and loss statements before they could be used for comparison with the assessed profit target?

4. Set out clearly, with specimen figures, how you would compile monthly cash budgets.

5. Prepare a month's programme of work for an internal audit section, indicating the nature of the business concerned.

6. Comment on the statement that "budgetary control replaces opportunism by considered intention".

7. What considerations affect the choice of the budgetary period?

8. Discuss the meaning of the expression "control by exception".

9. To what extent are budgetary control and standard costing inter-dependent?

10. The Balance Sheet of St. Mary Products Ltd., at 31st March 1968 was as follows:

Issued Capital:	£	*Fixed Assets:*	£	£
550,000 £1 shares .	550,000	Cost . . .	500,000	
General Reserve . .	200,000	*Less* Depreciation .	200,000	
Profit and Loss Account	25,000			300,000
Current liabilities:		Current assets:		
Creditors . . .	175,000	Cash . .	20,000	
		Debtors . .	150,000	
		Raw materials .	50,000	
		Work in progress	160,000	
		Finished goods .	270,000	
				650,000
	£950,000			£950,000

Budgets for the ensuing year contain the following figures:

	£
Sales, all on credit terms	1,200,000
Cost of sales, including total overheads . . .	1,070,000
Net additions to fixed assets, paid in cash . .	40,000
Net additions to depreciation provision . . .	30,000
Purchases of raw material	200,000
Raw material transferred to production shops . .	190,000
Direct labour and overheads (excluding depreciation)	845,000
Cost of completed output	850,000
Payments to creditors	185,000
Receipts from debtors	1,100,000

You are required to prepare the Balance Sheet Projection as at 31st March 1969.

11. Office Economics Ltd. is a private company with a capital employed of around £800,000, according to the last balance sheet drawn up as at 30th September 1968. The business has been established for ten years, in which period considerable success has been achieved in the manufacture and marketing of an improved design of typewriter. Direct selling methods are used for sales in Great Britain, and about 15 per cent of these sales are on hire-purchase terms, carried out without using a finance company. Of hire-purchase accounts, 30 per cent are in arrear. Other sales are on monthly terms, and 25 per cent of total sales are in the export field, all carried out on open account. Sales turnover was about £1,000,000 in the year to 30th September 1968; debtors at that date totalled £200,000; material and work in progress was £200,000 and finished goods £250,000.

The Directors propose to increase output in the current financial year by 25 per cent, in view of what they consider to be a considerable unsatisfied demand for the product, but they are concerned about the rapidly diminishing cash balance. They ask you to make specific recommendations as to the action they should take for conserving cash so that they can proceed with their plans for profitable expansion without recourse to a large overdraft or the necessity for obtaining further fixed capital.

Draft your detailed recommendations.

12. A workshop with a capacity of 200,000 man-hours a year was set up to carry out assembly work on three dissimilar products. The results for the first year's operations were summarised as follows:

				A	B	C
Units sold	.	.	.	25,000	30,000	40,000
Man-hours used	.	.		25,000	45,000	80,000
				£	£	£
Sales value	.	.	.	50,000	30,000	20,000
Variable costs	.	.		45,000	24,000	5,000
Contribution	.	.		5,000	6,000	15,000
Fixed costs	.	.		15,000	9,000	6,000
Profit/(Loss)	.	.		£(10,000)	£(3,000)	£9,000

The fixed costs shown above £30,000 in total, were for the work-shop as a whole and had been arbitrarily allocated to products on the basis of turnover, that being the only practical basis.

In the process of budgeting for the second year the Sales Manager said that the utmost he could sell of each product were as follows, prices to remain unchanged:

A	B	C
£100,000	£40,000	£30,000

Assuming that fixed costs will remain unchanged and variable costs will remain at the same rate per unit, what is the sales mix that will produce the greatest profit?

THE COMPANIES ACT, 1967, AND THE ACCOUNTS

The Companies Act, 1948 (later called the "1948 Act") is still the main Act which governs the activities of limited companies. The Companies Act, 1967 (later called the "1967 Act") contains amendments to the law regarding companies generally. Some items of the 1948 Act have been superseded, in some cases the wording has been altered, and some entirely new provisions have been enacted. Although the 1967 Act is relatively short, nevertheless all its provisions and schedules are important because they have to be read in conjunction with the 1948 Act.

This Appendix does not attempt to describe all the changes in detail, but only those which have relevance to the book as a whole. The principal changes which will be described are:

> Abolition of status of exempt private company;
> Particulars of directors' emoluments;
> Particulars of salaries of employees over £10,000;
> The Directors' Report;
> Directors' interests;
> Obligation to notify changes in voting shares;
> Disclosure of turnover.

Abolition of Status of exempt private company

The 1948 Act designated certain companies as "exempt private companies," the principal advantage of which was that they did not have to file with their Annual Returns a copy of their accounts. Section 2 of the 1967 Act abolishes this status together with the privileges it had.

Directors' emoluments

In the 1967 Act there are a number of detailed provisions regarding the publication of directors' emoluments in the accounts. The principal changes refer to emoluments paid to individual directors. First, the company must publish in the accounts, or in a statement annexed thereto, the emoluments of the chairman and the emoluments of the highest paid director if they were greater than those of the chairman. There must also be published the number of directors whose emoluments amounted to not more than £2,500, and the number who received between £2,501 and £5,000, then on a scale rising by £2,500 at each step (this excludes directors who discharge their duties outside the United Kingdom). No particular form of statement is specified, and the following example would comply with the Act:

EMOLUMENTS OF DIRECTORS

£ p.a.	Number
0– 2,500	2
2,501– 5,000	—
5,001– 7,500	2
7,501–10,000	2
10,001–12,500	3
12,501–15,000	1

The Chairman's remuneration amounted to £6,500, and that of the highest paid director to £15,000.

Employees' salaries

The company must publish details of the number of employees whose salaries are between £10,000 and £12,500 and thence on a rising scale in multiples of £2,500.

In addition, there must be disclosed the average number of persons employed and their aggregate remuneration. This information is not required where the number of employees is less than 100, or where the company is a wholly owned subsidiary of another United Kingdom company.

Directors' Report

Under the 1948 Act the Directors' Report tended to be a short formal document. The 1967 Act specifies a number of matters which must appear in the Report. These include:

(i) the names of the persons who at any time during the year were directors of the company;

(ii) the principal activities of the company and any significant changes in the activities;

(iii) any significant changes in the fixed assets of the company, and the market value of interests in land, if the directors consider that such value is significantly different from the book value;

(iv) details of interests by directors in contracts entered into by the company;

(v) details of arrangements whereby directors obtain benefits by means of the acquisition of shares or debentures in the company; also details of their interests in shares and debentures at the beginning and end of the financial year;

(vi) where a company has carried on two or more classes of business which in the opinion of the directors differ substantially from each other, the turnover and profit of each class of business;

(vii) the average number of employees and their aggregate wages (see also under *Employees' salaries* above);

(viii) particulars of contributions for political and charitable purposes, and in the case of political contributions the identity of the political party;

(ix) details of exports, except where the company's turnover is below £50,000.

The 1967 Act contains a number of detailed sections dealing with directors' interests in a company. The schedules to the Act also provide for changes in the information to be shown in the Balance Sheet and Profit and Loss Account. Two particularly significant changes are as follows:

(i) The 1948 Act requires fixed and current assets to be shown separately. In the 1967 Act there is the requirement that "Fixed assets, current assets and assets that are neither fixed nor current shall be separately identified."

(ii) The turnover of the financial year, and the method by which the turnover is arrived at, shall be stated by way of note, if not otherwise shown in the accounts and statements.

Certain classes of business, *e.g.* banking and discounting, are exempted from many of the provisions, such as those relating to the disclosure of turnover.

As stated in the beginning of this Appendix, the foregoing outlines some of the main changes introduced by the Companies Act, 1967; for full details reference should be made to the Act itself.

SUGGESTIONS FOR FURTHER READING

BOND, George Dennis. *Financial Aspects of Industrial Management*. Butterworth. 1954.

SOLOMONS, David, editor. *Studies in Costing*. Sweet & Maxwell. 1953.

DOBSON, Warwick R. *An Introduction to Cost Accountancy*, Vols. I, II and III. Gee. 1954.

WHELDON, H. J. *Cost Accounting and Costing Methods*. Macdonald and Evans. 1952.

BLOCKER, J. G. and WELTMER, W. K. *Cost Accounting*, 3rd ed. McGraw-Hill. 1954.

PARKINSON, Bradbury B. *Accounting Ratios in Theory and Practice*. Gee. 1952.

INSTITUTE OF PUBLIC ADMINISTRATION. *Financial Control; its Place in Management*. Macdonald and Evans. 1951.

ASSOCIATION OF CERTIFIED AND CORPORATE ACCOUNTANTS. *Management Accounting; a Concise Appraisal*. A.C.C.A. 1954.

SMITH, BEDFORD, D. R. *The Break-even Chart*. Incorporated Accountants Research Committee. 1954.

INSTITUTE OF CHARTERED ACCOUNTANTS IN ENGLAND AND WALES. *Developments in Cost Accounting*. Gee. 1947.

BRITISH INSTITUTE OF MANAGEMENT. *Accounts for Management*. B.I.M. 1954. *The Flexible Budget*. B.I.M. 1951.

MANAGEMENT ACCOUNTING TEAM. *Management Accounting*. Anglo-American Council on Productivity. 1950.

ORGANISATION FOR EUROPEAN ECONOMIC CO-OPERATION. *Cost Accounts and Productivity*. O.E.E.C. 1952.

J. SANFORD SMITH. *The Practical Application of Electronic Computers*. Macdonald and Evans. 1956.

T. G. ROSE. *The Internal Finance of Industrial Undertakings*. Pitman.

E. F. L. BRECH. *The Principles and Practice of Management*. Longmans.

ASSOCIATION OF CERTIFIED AND CORPORATE ACCOUNTANTS. *The Modern Approach to Internal Auditing.* A.C.C.A. 1955.

WALLACE CLARK. *The Gantt Chart.* Pitmans.

INSTITUTE OF COST AND WORKS ACCOUNTANTS. *The Accountancy of Changing Price Levels.* I.C.W.A. 1952.

OFFICE MANAGEMENT ASSOCIATION. *Form Design.* O.M.A. 1955.

ASSOCIATION OF CERTIFIED AND CORPORATE ACCOUNTANTS. *The Planning and Measurement of Profit.* A.C.C.A. 1957.

INSTITUTE OF CHARTERED ACCOUNTANTS. *Standard Costing: An Introduction to the Accounting Processes.* Gee. 1956.

BRITISH INSTITUTE OF MANAGEMENT. *Interfirm Comparisons for Management.* B.I.M. 1958.

ASSOCIATION OF CERTIFIED AND CORPORATE ACCOUNTANTS. *Electronic Data Processing I to V.* A.C.C.A. 1959 to 1964.

D. R. C. HALFORD. *Differential Costs and Management Decisions.* Sir Isaac Pitman and Sons Ltd. 1960.

DE PAULA, F. C. *Management Accounting in Practice.* Gee. 1957.

INSTITUTE OF COST AND WORKS ACCOUNTANTS. *A Report on Marginal Costing.* I.C.W.A. 1961.

H. W. BROAD AND K. S. CARMICHAEL. *A Guide to Management Accounting.* H.F.L. (Publishers) Ltd. 1960.

BRITISH INSTITUTE OF MANAGEMENT. *Increasing Profits in the Smaller Business.* B.I.M. 1960.

J. BATTY. *Management Accountancy.* Macdonald and Evans. 1963.

PERIODICALS AND PAMPHLETS. The most up-to-date source of information on matters of current importance are the journals of the various professional bodies, and the pamphlets and occasional papers published from time to time.

INDEX